Compilation of Escorts and Clients

True Crime

D.E.Z. Butler

Book five in the Madam Series: A compilation of two books in the series ... the Madam's Escorts and the Madam's Clients. Now revised: 2013

First Edition
Revision 2013 by D.E.Z. Butler

ISBN-13:978-1461010425
ISBN-10:146101042X

Published in the United States

In Memory of Jim and Richard

Other books in the *Madam Series* are:

Bellflower Boulevard
The Madam's Escorts
The Making of a Madam, a 20th Century Woman
The Madam's Clients
The Marin Madam
The Madam's Cookbook

For continuing information go to the following web site where the author may also be contacted: http://www.freewebs.com/dbutler33

D.E.Z. Butler

Forward

This book is about the clients and escorts who once were part of *Professional Escorts and Fingers Outcall Massage* service, which were both located in Marin County, California. The timeframe was 1974 until 1990. The escort service was first an outcall massage service called *Fingers that* saw clients all over the northern counties of California. *Fingers* lasted from 1974 until 1976. The owner pulled the plug on the service due to a car accident and her inability to manage the service at that time. Then, with the same management, it re-surfaced as *Professional Escorts* in the year 1977, again, at a Marin County headquarters. The month the phone went "live" was October of that year.

The escort service began with just one dedicated business telephone line. This phone line was in the home of the owner's mother. The service expanded exponentially in a very short time, and then the owner moved to a rented home in Novato, California where she continued the escort business. The owner's days were filled with answering the three-line telephone extension setup and; dishing out calls to the various escorts and, she even went out on some assignments.

The phone lines were the most critical function for the business. Secondly, the owner was the primary public relations person and, the first escort the business had. The owner quickly hired many other women and men to work for her after the first, small three-line-ad in the *San Francisco Chronicle* "news-papery" mushroomed into a huge business. Along with several media interviews, which the owner subjected her to was for the purpose of having free publicity for the business. Dian, the owner, never turning down an interview because the publicity that came with the interview, both positive and negative, worked out well for the business to obtain new clients and more escorts. Those public interviews drew lots of attention to the business.

More people were applying to become escorts; and clients kept phoning to see all the new escorts. Once a new escort began, I would telephone the waiting clients, so those clients were able to see the new person. ("I" being the former owner of *Professional Escorts* and person writing this book and all books in the Madam Series of books.) Allowing each client to feel special. This small business effort worked well for the continuing flow of business. On a flow chart, the business increased revenue each time a new escort began. This was a "win-win" for not only the new escort but the rest of the escorts. The rotation of clients kept up with the pace. Each client calling, was usually asking for a person who was seen a month or two prior or the new escort. If the new escort was busy, the client may wait or would see someone he saw before. Because of this "rotation" by the clients, it allowed for all the escorts to be busy making money. Money, being the core purpose for the escort's incentive to work. Other reasons existed, but money was at the top of the list for the "why" each escort was working at the service. I justified that reason by saying, "No matter what business you work for, it is for the pay." This statement was the logical reason that many escorts left other jobs to work for *Professional Escorts*. "Right?" Was one word always thrown in at the end of the first sentence during an interview; and, few, potential escorts disagreed. The business just kept flourishing from the "word of mouth" publicity, given out to the community from the clients and escorts.

The escort telephone was answered 24 hours each and every day of the year. There were catnaps in between answering the telephone, for the owner, me. This went on for many years. The clients knew my voice and the familiarity of the tones I projected, over the telephone receiver, encouraged each client to keep phoning the service. I spoke in an earthy and sexy voice that helped ease the man's conscience, inhibitions, and possible reluctance to ask for an escort.

Those "inhibitions" were over-emphasized, by him, because he was phoning an escort service, and, in his mind, the assumption was that his every need would be met by the escort when she arrived at his home. But, sometimes, he had some hesitancy in his voice when giving me his idea of the perfect escort. Just because my voice, the voice on the other end of the receiver, hinted that his every need would be met, did not mean he was going to get what he was paying for. Sometimes the client told me, truthfully, what he wanted and expected when the escort arrived, but for the most part, the person phoning did not speak his mind, truthfully, about what he wanted. It was up to the person answering the phone to guess what his need was and then relay that information to the escort.

What happened at his home?

Well, the truth was held as a "top-priority" secret by the escort, and the client had no fears she (the escort) would reveal his needs, desires, or wants.

How he knew his life was a priority?

The escort let him know and told him, "I am not in the business of exposing why you called the escort service and your actions with me would not be divulged."

The secrets were kept, because the escort service wanted to stay in business. As the owner of the service; I made it perfectly clear to each escort that telling secrets would not get the escort any more "calls". The escort's prime motivation in working was her wanting more "action", so she kept her mouth shut. Telling, would not serve her purpose to have clients call back for her, or the owner giving her anymore "calls".

The male or female client provided the location and the escort service made available the entertainment for an hour or two and sometimes all night. Of course money was exchanged. The elements of what went on for the hour or two or all night resided within the inner-soul of each person making the connection and went beyond money. All or most "hookups" were not for entertainment or even enjoyment. For some clients, a psychiatrist, in the form of an escort, was now in front of the person paying. No doctor's credentials and a much cheaper alternative to hear his problems. His past was at the forefront of his mind and, he had to tell someone. The escort was now a cheap form of counseling. Not a doctor or priest, but someone to expose his deepest secrets too.

The client knew the escort was only half-listening and could care less what he had to say. She would be there for an hour, usually, and then gone. His secrets, he felt, were safe. For the escort, this was just another person with "issues" and listening was what she was there for or other "things", if that was what he wanted. Many great escorts were exceptional listeners.

Big boys, and, actually, in some cases big girls needing a different confident who was promiscuously trusted. It was because the escort was promiscuous that the client felt comfortable with whatever he had a need to talk about. The client did not ask for any background checks or even insistence that the person's health was intact; just someone to confess to; and the client held the belief his secrets were safe. For the most part, those secrets were safe. The owner picked escorts that could keep the confidence of the clients. Occasionally there was an escort with a loose tongue, but those escorts were rare.

Writing about my clients has been exceptionally rewarding for me, a person who was once the owner of the escort service. Recalling the good and bad times helped me to understand the life I found so enjoyable. First I had to look over my many diaries for the years I was in business, and, in those pages, I found memories. Some great, some okay, and some --- well forgettable. All the clients contributed to *Professional Escorts* service being well-known and a must do for many men living in the San Francisco Bay Area, during those years.

Clients, who could afford the escorts, were happy to pay and in some cases the man just emptied his bank account or accounts, as the case may be. If dying, the money never mattered to the client.

The men, who needed to scrounge around for the various fees, always or near always, wanted to complain over the littlest, nonsensical moment/s or person/s that came to see them. They were a pain in the ass when they tried to haggle over price. I did not wish to barter with the clients. I had set the pricing and if they did not like the price, well, they could look elsewhere for companionship.

In writing the previous books in the madam series, some clients may have been mentioned but not fully spoken about ... within the following pages they are truthfully portrayed for their likes and dislikes and a few conversations as to how I felt about them. The beginning, of this madam's book, starts with the money guys that loved throwing the cash around for awhile ... until they either were caught or died. Then conversations into the white collar and blue collar men --- because there were so many clients, I have tried to limit the remarks to men who called more frequently or stood out for some odd reason.

Although, times did exist, when just one day or one night with people phoning the escort service, developed and ended, with an interesting set of circumstances; many of those instances are related in this book. Not because a great deal of money was made, but because it holds some interest for the reader.

If I disparage someone, that person deserved the grumbling with him or her. The comments are not made just to hurt any person's feelings. These comments are made, to allow readers, to understand what the escorts had to put up with, and, as the owner of the escort service, how I had to deal with certain aspects of the business; the internal workings of the escort service is what this book circumvents through the escorts and clients.

The female clients are touched upon. It would have been nice if there had been more female clients because they added a different layer to the escort business. One layer which featured a woman's chance to pay for what she needed or wanted from a man.

This is a truthful and original work about *Professional Escorts*. For most of the years in operation, the business was run out of many homes … at one point there was an office on the peninsula which is down from San Francisco, going south toward Menlo Park. The peninsula office had been given to a trusted escort to run. Trust was not easy, to come by, for me, with most of the escorts. The fear I had was real, that the escort would operate my service, and then take all the money earned from that second office or any office opened. Many male owned escort services had that type of problem with the people whom were trusted to answer phones owned by them.

In this case, hardly was my fear realized. The office was too far for any trips down there. So I had a trusted friend, Cheryl, who drove there. Just about on a daily basis because I could not devote my time to a second location. The peninsula office was too far from my home base. After a short six months, the office had to be closed; which happened when the initial lease was up on the office. With hindsight playing a prominent role, I believe, I should have had more than one office in many counties; using different names for each office. This may have worked out well. Regrettably, I was too 'hands on' with the service and had the ever-present fear of losing control. Through my own qualms and distrust, I kept the business from reaching its full potential. I micro-managed the business and knew this held down any police interactions with the escorts. But it also limited the possible huge revenue increase that was possible if there were more offices. The intense way in which I managed, did have a positive benefit for the escort service, because this micro-managing helped keep the women safe. Money was just not my entire reason for operating the escort service. I, truly, liked the interactions with the clients and the escorts. The business was fun and entertaining. Please enjoy this book, which is a compilation of two books, The Madam's Clients and The Madam's Escorts that are newly revised with this edition of the Compilation of Escorts and Clients, in 2013.

I felt compelled to put this book together, along with some added information, which attempts to give a more complete picture of the escort business. I continue to have fond memories of the many men and lovely women who once used and worked for my escort service. As a "compilation" the reader has a more cohesive sense to the happenings in the escort service and a better idea how the escort service "worked".

Everything, included in this book, is taken from many diaries.

D.E.Z. Butler

Prologue

There comes a time, in every person's life, when the party ends. The drinking and taking of drugs just loses any mystic those vices once had and, reality sets in. That is about how it all happened with this escort service owner. When the party was going it was great, but then the vomiting, bitching, losses, hack-lovers, bad sex, and continually, ringing, phone calls are just another annoyance which had to end. And not to forget the awful relationships that ended badly as a result of owning an escort service. The time had come. The business was over. I was done! Totally deep-fried!

Some people getting into the escort business now, think the glamour of meeting new people will satisfy some "hunger" inside of them. And possibly the "hunger" felt, will be satisfied, but you do have to wakeup someday and, know the consequences of your narcissistic life. A coming face-to-face with what you now have changed into; and slowly crept away from. The family and friends you had before becoming an escort. As an escort and owner of such a business you do decide, one day, that you did not change the game of relationships or sexual encounters, but just the opposite. The game played you and your brain DNA, until you were not the person you once were. The time, a long time ago, when you may have playfully begun the service, was no longer fun. Sinicism was now part of your personality. A yawn when people began to tell you about some party or friend of theirs. The feeling that you had heard it "all" was now present and part of your persona, your very being. There was no going back to what you once thought you were, and the ideas of purity mixed with innocence, you had held close to your bosom. You were now officially "jaded" to the point of there never being a chance to return to a "lollipop" mentality. The business was no longer "candy"; it was a royal pain in your ass. You had grown up.

The "sex-escapades" were many in the 20th century. The men and women were exploring their inner desires and respective g-spots. Men learned to please women, and, what a wife would not do, the men wanted an escort to do, and, do it often. The really weird clients wanted an escort to pee or shit on them. Even bondage games came of age during these times, and those types of services had special locations, or other businesses, to please the people wanting such, in some cases, violent episodes to play out the client's retarded aggression toward women. The prices then and now were and are astronomical for such services. All sexual ideas came alive and people made bad and good choices. The difficulty was felt, and a cry was heard as to when to stop chasing sexual encounters and desires. Just like any addiction it was difficult for the men and the women to stop; then and now, because going back to what they once did for a living or how they handled their relationships, well, it did not exist anymore. Their age of innocence was over.

The new exhibitionists love putting their photos on the Internet in the 21st century, so all can see what they are selling. Maybe the escort business has generated a new life; a life which has its' center from a computer screen. What I would tell the idiots placing their bodies and faces on the web, loudly, I would say, "You are so damn dumb, it is like getting the milk from the cow and drinking it and then asking for payment. Men will use your photos like they do the porno magazine photos of women and, then rethink phoning or seeing you in person. Not a great way to make money. Men do not sleep with your body. I mean some do, but primarily they look at your face. It is your face they make love too. There are men who would be happy having sex with you, with a sack over your head, and, feel just as satisfied when you leave. Thus, with your face online, well, figure it out what the men are doing with your face in their imaginations.

The men phoning my escort service depended upon my judgment about what escort should be seen; which one to spend his cash on. Men like variety. You can sell them or have them see anyone. A few exceptions to the rule, will not want every woman, but that is rare.

The older guys are just happy, someone would take the time to drive and see them. The younger men want the experience of paying for a woman.

This is where the "hook" comes in to play.

The young man becomes "hooked" when he sees a woman for his first sexual experience and if she is great looking, and all he has to do is pay her, to have her, well the "hook" has just been accomplished, for all his ensuing years to come. The "rush" the man has, can be felt in his chest when the escort holds him or lies on top of him. His heart beats a little faster with anticipation and his adrenaline moves through his body quickly. A feeling that he just does not have with his wife or girlfriend and, that is why the men pay. The clients are "hooked" on the experience. Not necessarily the sex. I will say it again, it is the experience. Very similar to those people who like to jump out of airplanes, or people involved with risky behaviors and sports. Adrenaline flies through the man's system hooking him to sex, as any drug addict is hooked on a drug. Sex is a drug. For some people it is "the" drug. The following chapters speak about the men and women who have used escort services and enjoyed them. They all or most all had the pleasure of giving money to someone who was there to meet their physical needs. Possibly take the escort to events, where the person wanted others to see the escort. Not always was "ego" involved with a date to the prom or wedding. This was, most times, a necessity.

The escort service provided the needed companion. Arm candy for a man and the *Knight in Shining Armor* the woman has been telling her friends about all year. The guy she now has to produce at some annual event. He is her lie come true. (Yes, we did have a client such as this one.) "Hopefully he will still be working for the service the next year when she has to produce him again"; thinks the escort owner, me. The lies and how they catch up with people, kept the stories round the fireplace interesting, as each escort reminisced how the "lie" was a focus of their appearance, and the neat, and tidy story told to all her friends or his friends, as the case may be.

We were the escorts they phoned and had fun with and allowed their lives to experience another side of life, and, we collectively thought this was a brighter side of life; bringing sunshine into a dark life or a life without happiness.

This was profoundly a "lie" in the person's life, which really needed us to share a part in his or her life, to make the "lie", real. The client was on some fantasy tour among his or her friends. The client believed the "lie". Yes, eventually all good things come to an end. The escort service had ended, but the memories were still there in journals and diaries kept by the owner, me. Enjoy the following chapters. This is not a sex book. But it is about men who want to pay for sex or companionship and women who wanted to be played with for a fee. All the situations are the truth. What you need to do now, is put yourself in an escort's place. Then ask the question which begs to be asked: "Could you be an escort?" The first part of the book is about the clients and the last part concerns the escorts.

Diary Comment 1992

The days of the drug dealers and money they were willing to spend are over. The stop came gradually and was possibly similar to the prohibition days of the 1920s. The days of prohibition and, now recent times of drug dealing in America are incredibly similar. The fight to stop the problem will need another Elliot Ness.

Unfortunately, today in the United States, finding an Elliot Ness would take an Act of Congress. (Provided Congress could do anything.) Just as it was tricky for J. Edgar Hoover to find Ness in the 1920s; and with corruption, so wide-spread, as how it was in the Roaring 20s; the country needs another J. Edgar Hoover to help us through and into the next century. If "we" as a country are ever to be rid of drugs.

Diary Comment, late 1992

After a few years of escort services in communities, the District Attorneys, from various cities, found that many drug dealers were using the escort services to have beautiful women close their illegal business transactions. Within the Marin County area of California, the Chief Investigator in the District Attorney's Office, R.R. had my phone bugged. He ultimately made many arrests from the fact he listened to my conversations.

There is no way that I could have complained, after I found out. The way I found out was through a friend and sometimes boyfriend. We would play talk on the telephone and more than a few times he said on the phone, "I want to be your slave. I will do anything for you." This and more of the same, plus lots of sex talks, and, he happened to be a black man. One black officer listening knew him from the same gym they attended, and told him that it was disgusting that he wanted to be a white women's slave.

This detective must have been outraged over our conversations. We knew there was a possibility the phone was tapped, but this guy confirmed there was a tap, by what he said to my friend. And, as memory serves me well, the cop told him the phones were bugged. Every conversation was listened too. So of course I gave them lots of sex talk. It was my duty to help keep the days and nights of these officers interesting.

The trap had been set between the Chief Investigator and the District Attorney … I was merely a pawn. They (through R.R.) had promised me I would be the first female investigator in the DA's office --- never --- intended to full-fill the promise. What they wanted was pawn to play when the elections were in sight. I would be a possible "bust" with headlines to show the DA was doing something to stop crime, while he was in office. An easy bust, but I did not make anything easy for these rats.

The incidents were soaring, all over the country by police using escort and massage services to acquire their own lists of known drug dealers; and, other people doing criminal acts. It was not unusual for them to listen to the conversations and even easier to have a judge sign the necessary papers for a search and seizure or better yet, a warrant to arrest the drug dealers. All the judge had to do was listen to the tapes from the bugged phones.

Sometimes the authorities even opened their own escort or massage services, with the intention of accumulating lists and ultimately arresting as many people that they were able to entrap. It did not take long for the drug dealers to catch on to what was happening.

They stopped using services.

This hurt all the services finances. But some services were branching out into sex phone lines. Sex talk lines, where the customer could call in and speak to a woman and never see the person. A new flowering business to compete with the escort services had been turned into a multimillion dollar venture. Most phone lines then charged by the minute. This was taking money from all services because disease had also stepped in … people were panicked about catching something that brought death to their homes.

Diary Comment 1979

Falling in love, in love with the green made a black day doable. An idea of how much money could be made at the end of the '70s with drug clients. One night I was training a girl to answer my phones and it was close to 4 a.m. in the morning. We were ready to call it quits for the night and go to sleep. Then three other girls came over to my house, all wanting to wait for calls. At approximately 4:10 a.m. a man phoned who sounded nice to me. He told me he wanted a young girl. I then asked him if he wanted two girls. He said, "Yes." Immediately my phone girl put her hand up to go to the call. I was surprised by her doing this, because she had never wanted to do calls and was a confirmed lesbian. So then I asked him, "How about four girls?" "Yes." Came back quickly through the phone wires and, then I gave the phone to one of the girls to write down directions to his home. We giggled a lot about the call and, then I sent them on their way to Kentfield in Marin County. Also went with them were instructions to phone me immediately upon arriving. This was to let me know they were okay and this guy could pay for all of them. I waited close to half an hour or so and the phone finally rang. The girls were still in a good mood.

The man they were going to stay with had just paid each one of them $1,000 dollars and wanted them to all stay until noon. I was shocked. What really shocked me was how loose this guy was with them. In one of the rooms of the house was a full-load of cocaine. The girls and he did drugs for hours. Needless to say, I lost my phone girl. What a call to go out to her first time. The phone girl never wanted to answer phones again. It was calls for her after that first encounter. At the time there were so many drug dealers calling, it was difficult to keep the women off of the drugs. I had to fire and hire a lot of women. This hiring and firing did not make many friends for me. I could not risk drugged out women working for me. These women also would see the "straight" (not using drugs) clients. I found it very difficult to keep up with the problem. I was happy and sad when the guys stopped calling. The money was great but the health of the women was more important to me at the time.

Diary Comment 1980s

The early 1980s --- typically the phone rang without a set pattern. This was the worst part about operating *Professional Escorts*. The never knowing when the calls would come in --- because when the calls came in the clients wanted a person to phone them immediately. This was a real pain. Every now and then I heard coming from the receiver of the phone, a person who was polite, respectful, and not in a hurry; the perfect client, a man who could wait for just the right escort. In today's world of the 21st century having a cell would have made this escort service even larger and more efficient than it was; although the control factor would be diminished.

Chapter One
Drug Dealers and Users
"Chase the devil and he chases you" D.E.Z. Butler

Wow!

How can anyone forget these "masters" of the money? "Just throw the damn 'stuff' at the women and try your best to turn them into customers and someday 'Freebees' ... for your pleasure."

Yes, all the escorts had many of you (drug dealers) and a few of you (drug dealers) were friends of the escort service. I was your confidant, in some cases, and in many ways kept your lifestyles secret. Occasionally someone would ask about the drug dealers and with my ever cautious self, I declined speaking about the many dealers using the escort service. And, there were times I only was using generalities to say some fact; never pinpointing a dealer and maybe an escort or two listening to the conversation would chime in with a more exacting or direct remark, which told who you were. They could pinpoint the person or location. I was found smiling in the background but never validating the escorts' comments.

There were times when the phone calls coming into the service were only from drug dealers, depending upon the economy, and if there was an upturn or downturn with the financial markets. You could say these men supported our services.

The businesses that always flourished seemed to be those that gave pleasure to people when the economy was stagnant. Sex and drugs always went together in those days and both acts gave pleasure; each and every lust-filled desire to use drugs or become a slave to sexual desires. Don't forget alcohol beverages playing a huge part into why many men phoned the escort service. Not too much has changed in the 21st century, just the faces.

Vices of the men and women kept the minds of those calling in a state of perpetual evasiveness concerning their own private state of financial circumstance; and may also be the reason that there seemed to be fewer instances of violence. Because people took in all the vices they liked and could live with. More bars and pool halls kept the business of escorting booming.

Drugs and sexual pleasures were present when the economy was bad, to allow people to forget about their problems. The sins provided by the escort services were what the churches preached against on Sunday.

Those escort services were always present to give solace to the users not "feeling" church. Definitely filling a void that the churches were not able to, and, without being able to condone or qualm the souls of malcontent with the dwindling finances of the parishioners.

The churches wanted the extra money each member had and the competition was strong to shore-up those measly bank accounts. You could almost visualize the church man with one hand filled for the escort service and the other hand almost empty of money because the escort service was reeling in all the man had to give; leaving little or no money for the churches. It benefited the churches to preach against sexual pleasures. The churches had the laws to throw around in court, which would put the sinners into jail. The escort services had tried and true entertainment on their side giving the people moments to forget about the world problems and especially local economic downturns.

Sometimes the churches won and other times the escort services had their win in court. The clients kept coming back often and for more and more escorts. You might think the people charging were winning. Now, in the 21st century, I do not see the cycle of instant gratification seekers slowing down. By all reports on the Internet and in the dwindling hardcopy newspapers, where sex and drugs are alive and well with people selling some form of sexual gratification. This can include the lusting after pictures of women on the Internet (moving or still). The satisfaction may be free except for the cost of the ISP service. But intense sexual satisfaction needs are aroused and the possibility of more than a few demented people wanting perverse pleasures rises. Women, also, do their own lusting on the websites and plenty locations are available for women to get an eyeful. The increase in male web sites has women looking along with all or many of the gays. The gays are joining in and finding new 'closets' to hide out in for those men and women unable to deal with their true identities.

The Drug Dealers

Somehow all the drug dealers merged into this one man. He was not the best looking client, but in his arms you felt secure. Security for most women in the escort business is important. When I speak of him, remember, he was a client; and, security for a woman charging is money. Make no mistake it is money first and any love second. This was a client who acted as though he owned the business I was running. A person, who used the business to cement drug deals. He made money, and, so did I, because the escort service, as he, both were in the business of keeping peoples wants and desires satisfied. He had a twinkle in his eye and could have sold absolutely anything. If he was talking you knew he was going to sell you something. I admired the way he ran his business. What level of "play" he was at in the drug business; I never found out and never wanted to know. He was good at what he did; he had to be.

I begin with him and call him…

Drug Man #1

Here was a guy that when he phoned the service the first time, I thought maybe he was a cop because he lived too close to me in Novato. He was living --- well --- I actually can't tell you that location. But it was close to where I was at the time. Let's call him Big Daddy. His rented home over-looked a nice valley and the view was spectacular from his living room and kitchen areas. The road up to the place was winding. Halfway up that road I wished that there were more girls working that night, so I didn't have to make the drive. Lost in the back of my mind were many thoughts and one major thought was how I dressed too quickly. "Maybe my clothes wouldn't look good enough" and then I began second-guessing my makeup and hair. Cussing out the girls that wanted off that night was trumping through my head. I could hear them now, tomorrow, yelling and laughing at me that I take all the good calls. Ugh! Just plain ugh! I would have rather been in bed all nice and toasty. But the women would never believe me, no matter how much I told them it was better to send them, so I could stay at home and answer the phone for more clients.

Somehow he had talked me into coming up to see him and his friend. The entire time letting me know that it did not matter what I looked like; they just wanted some company. This was a con many of the men used, to see who was at the end of the phone. And many times it was because the person calling knew I was the boss. He was a boss and wanted a boss. That's what I was there for…when the boss needed me. "Yeah!" I said, as he was talking me into seeing him and his friend. "Never believe a client," was my motto.

The time was here.

"Showtime!"

A time when I just wanted to walk or run away and phone someone else, but not this night and here I was driving. No one was available, so I was stuck doing the call. Instinct was setting in place. I had to park the car, and, I always parked the car facing the "out" direction. If you have to leave in a hurry you don't want to take time backing out. This driveway was long and I did not want to get stuck. Not wanting to get trapped in some terrible situation and the car is stopping me from leaving, just because I am faced the wrong way. "Yes, yes, and yes again." I had to face the car outward, so it was ready to leave. I even thought of leaving the keys in the ignition.

Damn, the moment

I always dreaded, the first time you meet the man. His eyes tell the story if he is happy with you or not. Most men were happy with me, but there were a few that just went through the motions of giving me the money and asking what they wanted.

God, how I dreaded the opening of the door and if it squeaked the more my nerves set in. A blind date, sort of, and he was going to have to pay me whether he liked me or not. No turning back for either one of us now. This unwritten rule that the client had to pay, no matter what, if he ever wanted to phone the service again because there was always one or two escorts he really liked and those women were usually the loyal ones; the escorts who did not give out their phone numbers to clients.

"Damn it", I was almost there walking up the driveway; and I knew by the neighborhood that he either had money or thought he had money. No matter to me, as long as he was going to pay the price and he had cash. No checks, because this was the first time we had ever been to this address. The outside lights to the house were on and I saw someone looking through the glass on the side of the entrance doors.

Now, it was "Showtime." Not just parking, it was really here. The actual applause or disgust that "you" had come to "his" home. "Not good enough? No, don't go there." Self-doubt can creep into your mind before he opens the door. The tingle in your stomach is always there. This is the escort's stage and she better be good. Always the 'one' to like grand entrances I moved slowly as a cat so he knew this woman was cautious. I had already gotten past the parking of the car. My usual saying, "Just get out of the car slowly so he doesn't think this one is in a hurry and will cheat him out of his time." What I was usually thinking. Now I am at the damn door. Damn I hate this.

Time, was always a factor.

Many of the men would phone me after the escort left and complain, repeatedly, how the escort was looking at her watch the entire time. It didn't happen often, but it did happen. Some girls just wanted the money and no matter how much I told them to stay the entire hour, the girl looking at her watch, would push the man to let her leave early, and, then I had to deal with the objections. The men always phoned as soon as the woman left. As I approached the door he opened the door as if magically knowing I was ready to ring the buzzer. "Damn, forgot he was looking out the side window by the door".

Every now and then I had a nice surprise. Big Daddy was average in height and size. Size meaning man-hood (peeking out from his robe) and his hair looked brown with many highlights. He was groomed well. I think I remember Big Daddy having blue eyes. Nice guy.

"Come on in."

"What would you like to drink? We have just about anything here." The other guy chimed in.

"Diet Coke." Trying to not to appear as if I needed a drink.

"Anything else to put in it?"

"Sure, some Vodka." Resigning myself, I did need the drink.

After the drink was handed to me, he just laid out the money in front of me, and, also some lines of cocaine. Not asking if I wanted any; he just expected I would want some "blow." Smiling at him I took a "hit" on the drink and then the "blow." Damn that was good "stuff" and I asked him, "Where will we be?" He said, "The bedroom is more comfortable."

If I didn't use the "coke" there would have been be this tension in the air. After doing a line he was satisfied that I was not there to do some "cop" harm to him. His friend was nice to and he was average in size and height, looks were not his best feature. This guy had more hardness or harshness to his features; and his body screamed "hard work" at one time in his life. Very average in looks and could have robbed a bank and no one would give the correct description for him. He was very run of the mill. Both had hands that were soft to the touch. You would never have pegged them for drug dealers. Maybe office workers of some kind, but not drug dealers.

The two of them were anxious and just wanted me to get inside the house and then off to the bedroom. But the drink and the "blow" had to come first with the money taken care of, to have me comfortable. These men, (drug dealers) are always about the money. Now done with the preliminary stuff; the walk to the bedroom felt comfortable. I was ready to party with them. My look or my eyes told it all, as I got up to "escort" them to the bedroom, after picking up the money. I could count the money in the bathroom, where I changed. Now it was time for me to lead. No more nerves. Just a happy face; for that is what they just purchased. Everything else we were about to do was consenting. Something we all wanted. Even possibly peace of mind and body.

The snorting of the "blow" (this is done up a person's nose) had put them at ease, and, it helped them to forget to think, that I had some police following me and the cops would rush in as soon as we were in a compromising position. That is the usual, "panicky", thoughts of drug dealers. Always, paranoid the police are watching their every move. Yes, it was easier to have, or, that is take the drugs with them to the bedroom, so they did not bother themselves with thinking police would be coming after me or even worse, some bodyguard that they did not want to deal with before molesting my body. Their hands were eager and so were their "dicks." Life was now to be a joyous time for fun. We all settled down and enjoyed what seemed like a short time in the bed. Which meant to me the time in bed was good, that is why I thought it was "short".

All drug dealers are paranoid and think everyone is out to "get" them. They were no different. Paranoia is at its highest strength in the late-of-night. Big Daddy had phoned the service after 1 a.m., just like many drug dealers. The drug deals were over and now it was time to have some fun with their ill-gotten spoils. (Often, the dealers had money counters, so there was no problem in counting out the money for the escorts.)

I knew he and his friend were expecting to have someone younger over to see them; because I was still great to look at they were happy to keep me. Older, but attractive helps, even if you are not in your early twenties. We decided to make it a threesome for a couple of hours and then I was just with the 'main' man, my Big Daddy. This was his place and he let me know it. Although the other man kept coming into the room just to make sure his friend was okay. The bed antics were simple and easy. For them you could tell it was what they needed, but just to help them go to sleep. It was late.

There was coldness about his face (Big Daddy) and this was typical of all drug dealers. No matter how high up the ladder they were, consistently all had a cold exterior to people they had just met. But after you knew them awhile, they would be there for you if you needed anything, and only a few dealers were exceptions to this rule.

Right now, the two men wanted sexual pleasure and stroking their egos about how much tasty pleasure I was having with their surprisingly well-endowed bodies. The "coke" was working its magic on their libidos and both were very ready. On top of one and then the other and giving them the night they phoned the service for and lucky them, they got me. Bragging that I was the best escort in my stable is superfluous, because it was the truth. After we finished our two hour marathon it was time to leave and their eyes told me they had a colossal time, as did I. But just a little more time with Big Daddy. He had to let the other guy know of his dominance, not just in the bedroom but as a business partner.

This is definitely a "man thing." So I had to give him some special treatment. Together we didn't need food; all we wanted and needed was cocaine between our bodies for one more hour.

Surprisingly, a fine time!

He and I spoke a great deal about life and all the finer things in the world. In between the great sex sessions, my job was to cement the deal for my service. The "business" wanted him to phone back and the girls would be kept happy if he felt comfortable.

Drug dealers always called back if they were happy with the female merchandise sent to them. While leaving I just did a pat on the wallet which was full. I was content and he was happy, and, I knew, would be calling back.

I arrived back home … jumped into bed. The next thing I know … the phone is ringing long and hard because he won't hang up; he is calling back and all weekend that first time. Definitely his "Mojo" was working and ready for much more. This was a big weekend for business; he needed entertainment.

The first phone call had him requesting four or five escorts and they were to be at his place the entire night, at the fee requested; that is the fee stated by me. Not the price they wanted to pay, but the price the women were told to have or receive and this was $1,000.00 per night for each woman and no exceptions. That was the price, and, I would not budge on the price. If each escort had worked all night doing other "calls" she may have made just as much money, so there could be no negotiation on the fee.

Big Daddy agreed to the fee.

This was great for the service, and, so the four women were set to go there. I had to make sure the women liked drugs. This was important because sending an uptight girl would not be good for the other three women going to see him and his friends. The guys wanted to "party", and that meant with drugs, booze, and loose women. The four women, I called, came to my place first. This was going to be a big money call for all four of them and I had to go over the ground rules. If someone was not up to being there all night … I had to know.

The girls chosen were familiar with the type of men they would see (drug dealers) and did not hesitate to say they were up for the "party". This was the second confirmation on their part that they all four wanted to go there. A little last minute primping and out the door. All four escorts piled into one car and I drove my car to show them where the place was and pick up the payment. When we arrived the door was open and the guys inside were ready to party. The men had their eyes on the women, looking them up and down, their smiles getting broader by the minute; they were introduced.

Big Daddy walked me to his bedroom, and, where we had been the night before. He was happy with the women. There was no problem with the fee being paid. "Happy" was my favorite word; and the next best word was "money." Both words went together and the women that worked with me liked those two words too. This getting the money up-front made me comfortable and it was my time to exit; I told everyone to have a nice time. The women knew they would pick up their money, from me, the next morning and I gave them my "eyes", which said the unspoken words that all was "Great,"

"See ya tomorrow." Saying, "Great" as I walked out the door, just to make sure they knew what my "eyes" had said. The meaning was clear; I had their respective fees in my purse and was off to my house to sleep. All the players were in place and I was able to rest. This evening would take care of itself.

The next morning came as fast as the evening left. All four women were looking a little tired when they arrived at my place. I handed them their money and they were more than pleased with what they had made for the night. If they had made any more money, such as tips, they did not tell. My holding of the money meant that each one of the escorts was guaranteed not to lose the money while entertaining her host. Sometimes an escort would get to "high" drinking or doing drugs and her money was "lifted" out of her purse. Just another reason to hold the money, so there were no problems.

The guys did whatever business they had to do and phoned again the next evening to have the escort service send over another four women. There seemed to be no end in sight for these "dealers". One or two of the girls were asked back.
(Same scenario --- three days in a row and then Big Daddy stopped phoning until the next time; the next time being, when another drug deal would be going down and he would want and need women.)

Yet, another memorable time he phoned; there were no escorts available at the exact hour he phoned. His statement from the bar phone was; "Don't make us have to ask a freebie waitress home or some of these "bar flies"." The dilemma for me, was I had to phone every escort, who might be up for the assignment of seeing him and his friends, for some good money. He was very happy the service was able to come through for them that night. But this was a hustle and a hassle to find some women.

It was terrible when the guys would call late and expect there to be many women just sitting around waiting for their call. The object of the "game" is to have the women available, but there were other customers and the business was a popular one and women were working or at another client's home, just about the time when many a "drug call" would come in.

Would have been nice to have had some notice, but drug dealers were never big on notice. I doubt if that has changed. Big Daddy and his business interests were secure and content with the women sent and they all had fun. He ended up being a customer for a long time. Phoning the service, for him, was proved a safe bet and he did not take chances. He never was thought to be a dangerous person to send women too. But maybe he was dangerous, because he stayed in the business longer than most drug dealers did. Of course, he eventually did get busted and phoned me and he was in tears on the other end of the phone. He only had a couple hundred thousand left and was going to jail. My heart went out to him, but there was nothing more I could do for him except be a good listener. (Can't --- send women to a prison as escorts.)

The next time I saw him was a couple years later and he phoned while I was married. I wanted to see him. He was with a guy I did not know. I took another stellar girl to see them. They both liked her. For him, we were friends and talked for a few hours. (Did nothing! The girl the next day was taken on a shopping spree for leather goods.) While sitting there baring my soul to him about what was going on with my life; I told him I needed $5,000 for a bond, he said, "No one should go to jail because they don't have $5,000 dollars." Well, he went into the bedroom and came out with the money needed. Cash! He told me not to tell his friend. Of course not, never. I was ecstatic, beyond belief.

There was cash for the bond held tightly in my hands. He had not been asked for the money, he just gave it willingly, because of our past business relationship, that was wonderful of him to do. I just about danced all the way home and when I got home, my husband thought I had slept with the man. I had not, but people will always think what they want. For some men it's inconceivable that another man would give money without wanting something in return. (My husband felt betrayed, so after this incident, he betrayed me; this husband was a real tit for tat, asshole.)

The very last time I saw Big Daddy --- we slept together. And no money exchanged hands. I felt the $5,000 was already paid, for my time. He did not expect me not to charge, and that made the act of the original gift of money even sweeter. He intended to pay, but I would not let him. He had remained a gentleman to my escort service; and as of this writing I have never seen him again.

Drug Man #2

This man had unbelievable stamina. The first time he phoned, the request was for multiple women ... four women at a time. I sent him four women to the hotel he was in. (I never figured out why four? But then, why not four? Four seemed to be a magic number for the drug dealers, a fantasy number of women to have over. This number four came up more times and I was very pleased it did. Sending four women to one man was great because the women were making money and so was the escort service.) Miraculously, after being up all night with the girls; these overworked females came to see me with the fees and told me how the night went.

Drug man #2 is on a rollercoaster and phones just about the time the girls had arrived at my home, after leaving his place. All he desires is women. He phoned the correct escort service at the right time, because at the time, there were many women working for the service. Looking at the women he just finished with, they all look like they had been up all-night and worked hard. Their eyes collectively glazed over.

I could only imagine what he had put them through. Not that they were unwilling; but "damn", they looked like he was a vampire and, took all their energy out of them, and, "spent" their "juices". You could have hung a sign on all of them reading: "Out of service." As I am looking at them I am reminded of the phone in my hand and I begin speaking again to him.

"What can I do for you?"

"Send me four more, fresh ones."

"Was there anything wrong with the last four?"

"No, they were great. Just want some new ones."

"Okay. Just give me an hour or so." As I am hanging up the telephone my interrogation of the women begins. "What happened? How much did you all make? And what can I tell the next girls; what to expect?" The need for more information was there. All the remarks are positive.

They explained he is a drug dealer in town for a short time and has a suitcase full of cocaine. From what they saw he has hordes of money on him and the money may be in a suitcase too. I was only thinking about the money and if it were alright to send more women to him.

It was necessary, for me, to send women who were trusted and during this time the service had about 40 women working. The need to be selective on which girls to send was paramount. The known thieves (or ones thought to steal) were immediately eliminated. I knew that some girls may be open to steal, so I had to lose my knee-jerk reaction to phone the best looking among the girls. Some of those women I wasn't sure of and when given more thought I was sure they may steal if given half-a-chance, so they were eliminated. And some of the girls may forget to ask for the cash; just being happy with the drugs. It was a real balancing act, and, at least one very responsible girl was sent with the other three. His request was met with a "no problem" attitude. Four more women were sent. This asking and sending went on for three days and every eight to 10 hours four more women and never the same girls twice; except for a couple of girls that he insisted come back to see him.

Possibly raw balls, from all the friction, and a great many other thoughts went round and round in my head about what he was doing with the women. The girls were happy to divulge every little detail. Some of it was your basic, "Let me see all three of you lick each other or kiss one another." Or he said, "I want to use this dill-dough on each and every one of you, is that okay?" But it seems he was more up for having sex with one and wanting the other ones to watch or kiss each other, normal stuff for escorts and clients. He finally left the hotel and the many escorts were, all, very tired and hardly any of them wanted to work for the next week. This put a little cramp in the business for a few days. But the money made by them and the service was phenomenal. The days, the women took off, were basically paid for by this man's insatiable appetite for women. He must have been fulfilling a fantasy of his and a few million other men on earth.

Every time he came into town, after that initial occasion, he asked for more women but not as many as the first time. One time, in particular, one of my best girls went to see him and she decides to take him to her place, because he is in fact, tired, and has a great deal of cash and drugs on him, and she is worried that he may get ripped off or killed if left in some hotel room. I agreed with her. Lola protects his cash and drugs for a few days; and is with him the entire time. He is sleeping this time. Lola makes some great money. Lola and the escort service felt good about keeping him safe. I found out later, that she hit the drugs hard with him, for the time they spent together. He must have really liked and trusted her to sleep.

Drug dealer #2 requests women for about a year or so, and intermittingly, as he pretends to come into town from some far off place. Then we find out he is a pilot for some drug cartels. Lola was good at extracting information and he talked more to her than any of the other women.

The fact, he was pilot explained all the money he had, and why there were no other men around when he phoned in for escorts. Usually if a drug dealer was doing business, he wanted to entertain the other men and escorts were adornments to see that the deals went well, and that everyone was happy. Because not all drug dealers use the drugs they sell, the women were wanted as a treat for those men not using drugs or drinking. An escort is a vice that few men were able to turn down, especially when someone else is paying the fees.

The very last time he telephoned, I went to see him in Sausalito at a nice hotel there. Obviously, I'm curious about him. I was not very impressed with his appearance and it was noted that, "he would have had to pay for the services he received." This was a little notation for me in the future, as I wondered what we would be doing this time.

All he wanted was a massage, and he knew that I had my massage license from conversations on the telephone over the year or two he phoned in. We had spoken on the phone for a few months off and on preceding this encounter. I proceed to give him a massage while taking off my jewelry and put it on the nightstand near the bed. He was given a very nice massage and I washed my hands and leave --- forgetting about the jewelry.

When I arrive home, I remember about my jewelry on the nightstand and phone him back. He does not answer. I try phoning him all night, and, he does not answer. I do have his in Marin County home number, so I leave a message for him to phone me, and he never does. What he kept of mine was a diamond ring and a bracelet. I thought he was a nice man until he made the decision to rip me off. Some thanks for taking care of this asshole. He never phones again using his correct name.

A few months later I recognize his voice and the girl sent to him verifies that it's him. She gave him the message that I wanted my jewelry and so he phones me back with some bullshit story that my jewelry is in a bank safe. He never goes to the safe to return the jewelry to me.

He is one man, who should never cross my path. Besides being downright ugly, he was way too skinny to hold any appeal for me. Because he ripped me off, I would suggest that I was not his type, either. There are instances in life when a woman is happy she has not had sex with someone. This was one of those times.

Drug Man #3

This man was from Venezuela and he had *Diplomatic Immunity*. (I have a "thing" about people with *Diplomatic Immunity*, but that is another story and book.) He was someone who held a very important position in the Navy. He also had a brother or cousin that was President or maybe Vice President of the country. The brother or cousin could have just been part of the cabinet. My vagueness here is because of the obvious. Other than possible hit squads and all, it would not be in any person's interest to say who his relatives were. I liked him and he was a very nice man. He lived, with his immediate family, locally. When the family was out of town he called the escort service, and I knew he also phoned other escort services, so when he phoned I made sure women were sent to him because *Professional Escort* service was his first call. Pedro did not speak English very well but I spoke enough Spanish to make our meetings fun.

Pedro loved my accent, and, I loved his money.

Pedro was a fun guy. He loved to play games with the women and this included games with me. Pedro was the type of man to blow cocaine off of your navel or put it all over his body and ask you to lick it off of him; and having three or four women with him in a big circle was the most fun for him. His eyes got bigger and bigger as the women circled each other taking turns kissing and doing all sorts of things to his body.

Pedro was the man who told me how huge amounts of cocaine were coming into our country and it was not by the border crossers (only) from Mexico. It was from his country and in huge ships that had the drugs in the oil tankers. Yes, planes were used but the large amounts of the drug were coming in to our country's ports, in their country's naval ships. "How ironic," I thought.

In the oil tanks --- amazing, because those very tanks are protected by our military in our United States harbors. I saw the ships when I visited my husband, because he was stationed in Florida, in the Navy. Thoughts, by me, about the "war on drugs" were then and are now, "there is no war --- just a war on the poor folks trying to make a buck. The drugs keep judges and lawyers and prisons in business; and don't forget the politicians." The real "war" is on the citizens of the United States and all the countries which we do business with; who in turn sell drugs to our citizens. Hypocrisy, at its best, saying a "war on drugs" exists. Laughable for me and any person I tell about it.

When I would see him, I saw cars following us, but I was not sure what they were about; he had the *Diplomatic Immunity* patch, I call it. I was not buying his drugs, so I was not sure what was going on, to have cars trail us.

One night he phoned, and, he was at a hotel near San Mateo. Pedro said he had done too much of the cocaine and was worried; and needed some 'downers'.

His face was bright red and his heart was jumping out of his ribs, when I arrived at the cheap hotel he had rented for the night. His chest was in pain, but he still would not let me take him to a hospital. I had raced over to where he was with some sleeping pills, and, virtually saved his life that night.

Pedro told me not to phone the police if he died because he was worried that the publicity would be too much for his family. I agreed, and made sure I knew where my fingerprints were that night --- just in case he died.

Note to self: Wipe fingerprints off ... anything touched.

His wife had been schooled at the Sorbonne in France. He put her through school when she was very young. The marriage happened when she was around 14 years old. This must have been some type of arranged marriage because of his social standing in the country. Social standing or not, she had been married to him long enough now and given him two children. A colossal "marriage fit" would happen if she found out what he had been doing. I asked him if I should phone her, more to tease him, and his face turned very white. He was well trained by her.

This panicking over a health issue happened another night, and, I helped him, again. There were other women with him at a different hotel and the girls were from his country. It was a young woman who was sick. This girl had gone into seizures after ingesting so much pure cocaine. I found out later from the girl that her father and Pedro were friends in their country.

His friend would have been shocked that his daughter was playing around with Pedro. Again, I helped with sleeping pills. Every time I went to see him I made sure the sleeping pills were also along, just in case. The cocaine he had been from the 'source' in his country; so it was very pure. About 99% pure and you just could not get that from anyone except someone at the 'source'.

Eventually he moved his family to another huge home in Florida. We lost contact when he moved. He will always be considered a friend. And he may feel the same way. He did say he owed me a favor; I never collected on that favor. But he is probably dead by now.

Drug Man #4

The regular run-of-the-mill drug dealers were and are numerous in Marin County. This guy was more of a low-level drug dealer. He made sure that some of the escorts that worked (from all the escort services) were "hooked" on his product, just so this "sleaze bucket" could have them for free and just for his product. Never to give them any money … he was a creep.

When I found out about what he was doing, I made sure not to send women to him, unless they were able to handle his dishing out the product (cocaine). Some women were able to use only a little of the drugs and some did not use the drugs. Knowing which women did what was sometimes difficult if the woman was new to the service. And guys like this one, always wanted the new girl/s.

Most of these men are quiet and insecure and unassuming with the women sent to them. If they use the product they sell, they are usually at a lower-level on the organization's diagram.

Except, for some that just like the product, and, do it only once in a while. Which is usually at the end of a deal they have made; then they want to celebrate.

There are exceptions to all and any rules.

Phoning for escorts was their way of celebrating.

Although, some of the drug deals were cemented by having the escorts available for the partying, before the deal was finished.

One escort who worked for the service is worth mentioning. She had been living with a pilot for the cartels and the last time she saw her man, he was flying off in a private plane that had just taken off from their ranch in Nevada.

They had a private airstrip on the ranch.

The plane crashed and she was supposed to be on that plane, but he had decided at the last minute that she should stay and take care of some business at the ranch. He must have had a feeling about what was impending. (Her thought.)

A child was also killed, who had been on the plane with his parents. After meeting her, she made it clear to me that she just wanted to work as an escort, but it was obvious that she was still in love with the man who had died. She had been told by some people who knew how he was killed that the plane had been sabotaged. These same people had virtually ripped her away from any proceeds of the drugs or money that he had stashed away. Immediately after the crash they were at her home, while she went to see the police to find out about her boyfriend's accident.

These animals took the stash money her boyfriend had kept near the bed they slept in and papers pointing to their names in some ledgers he kept. The only thing they did do was leave her alive. She was a 'shell' of a person because she had been using the drug cocaine for years. That may be why she was allowed to live, because she did not serve as any threat to them. I, of course, found it unconscionable that they had killed a child, an innocent. I told her, "You should leave them alone, that they are not your friends." Because they were giving her money monthly; she thought that they would take care of her for a long time.

Furthermore, I tried to explain to her when they were through having sex with her, as they felt they could do; eventually they would OD her (over dose) on drugs and then they would be free from any worry she may talk. From years of using the drugs she was just not right in her head. Did they do this? I don't know. All the connections or synapses in her brain were not fusing correctly and basically I was wasting time talking to her. She was drowning in the grief she had from losing the man she loved, and the drugs were leaving their toll on her face. She was aging fast. We eventually had a fight and I have never seen her since the argument.

The reason I put her story with this creep is, because of the worst case scenario that can and does happen when women become hooked on the drug dealers or their product.

Drug Man #5

This was someone who I went up to see and felt as if I should never have left my home. He had a great view of the Napa Valley, but his home was a let-down. You would think a person like him, dealing drugs that he would want to put some money into fixing up the place. There were little redecorating projects all over the place. Sort of like a remodel that never gets finished; or a drugs gone wrong reality television show.

When he was loaded on drugs he may have thought he was a carpenter or other builder because the house was a mess. Then, that night, he has arrived at his home some group of guys that are a band playing somewhere, and, not sure if this was to impress me or the band. Listened to him talk for the time I was there, and it was just talk and more talk, a horribly boring person.

The band members went to some gig they had scheduled, and I left, because he just was not very interesting and, he wanted me to stay for the evening. Some money is just not worth the time. Instead I sent a woman over who was up for listening to his gibberish all night. He must have been doing his own product, always. Areas of the home were very untidy. His most recent love interest had left him, and I did not even wonder why --- it was obvious why she had left him.

Drug Man #6

Mr. Big Cheese, Ricky

There always must be a "big cheese;" the guy that all the dealers want to know and do business with, if possible. Met this guy by working for a massage studio in Terra Linda that was called Alter Ego; he was one of their better customers. Mr. Big Cheese was overweight from eating after smoking whatever dope he had that was especially 'primo'. Not huge, just overweight.

The connections he had were unbelievable. He knew these connections from when he was once a Disc Jockey. All the other drug dealers were constantly trying to impress the escorts and me. But this guy was cold and calculating. He saw through any lies a person would throw his way. He was cold, very cold; chilly-cold to your bones. The type of person you would believe if he said, "I am going to kill you." You would never question that statement.

Interestingly enough, his closet never had more than a few clothes in it. A couple of jeans and one suit coat. He just never showed much of his wealth. I always thought where he allowed people to meet him, could not be where he lived. Ricky was rich and impervious to any one getting close to him. I know I was one of the few women he liked and was willing to have come live with him, my children too. When he asked me to consider living with him I was shocked. I did consider doing so, and was actually wondering when would be the best time to move in; he was growing on me. Maybe I was in love, I felt very close to him.

Then something happened.

I brought over a woman to massage him and she turned out to be working for the District Attorney's office. The dumb bitch told us when she was higher than a "kite." She had been snorting out of this cereal bowl that he had in the room, along with two other bowls of different types of cocaine. Each one was "coke," but one was "speedy," and one was "numbing," and one was "sexual." I only met one other person who had whatever they wanted. I believe this other person worked with him. Anyway, this baring of her soul while on drugs, he just allowed her to do; well it freaked him out and that was the end of us. Somewhere in the back of his mind he isolated me. Ricky kept me as a "mistake," that he would never do again; someone he may have liked and could love, but someone who was too loose with her acquaintances.

We had a connection and we may have been very good for each other. But we never saw each other again. That hurt. I, in actuality, liked him. Not because of the drugs, but his conversation and interests were similar to mine. He was intelligent and well-schooled. Occasionally, he would phone to see someone and I always sent a girl that I knew would not ask too many questions; not ever letting on that I knew it was him phoning.

As careful as Ricky protected information about his drug empire, he was less careful over his body. Eventually he caught a disease and I know this was because he phoned other escort services; services that did not keep a close eye on their people. The disease was herpes, and, one disease that a person never gets rid of, but you can control it. Because of the herpes problem, even I decided that when he phoned, we would just say there was no person available.

Liked him and could have loved him; not for his drugs, but because he was intelligent; we had some kind of "soul" connection. Now and then I have thoughts for him and then I rethink the situation.

Ricky never got caught for drug dealing. His connections were deeply rooted in Northern California. I am sure he had people in government to protect him. I speak of Jim as another drug dealer and I am pretty sure these two men were friends. Too many connections … connected them. (See drug dealer #12)

Drug Man #7

Billy lived just a couple of streets over, when I lived in Ross. He had a habit of wanting to show what he knew about the occult sciences and would purchase very expensive books. Then ask me over to look at them. I liked him because he was always putting his neck out to make a better deal, every time he purchased and sold his drugs. He knew I was familiar with people in his drug business. I never knew whom the people were he was connected to, but I do know that some of those people may have crossed other dealers that phoned the service. The inside of his home was an intermingling of all the studies he centered on in his psychic development. Every now and then he phoned for a woman to come see him. Not sure if he phoned other escort services or if our service was the only one he phoned.

The house he had was small for the area, but he had very expensive taste and put his money into furniture and many fine vases, rugs, and other accessories, which blended well. His time with us was short. I had trouble reaching him one weekend to let him know a new girl had joined the service; his favorite women were always new to the service. And he had asked me to phone him if I had a new girl. Then, just about the next day, another person came over to show me an article in the newspaper.

Clearly, Billy was less intelligent than I thought he was, and more arrogant than I knew him to be. He made the horrible mistake of dealing drugs in Texas. He went there to buy and was setup by the local dealers. The article, in the newspaper, did not say that he was setup by the locals, but the way the article read, it was clear that he had been turned in by the locals. He was to do many years in jail there. He may be out of jail, by now. That mistake cost him all his money and his home.

Drug Man #8

Once upon a time there was a man named Marvin, who wanted to go into business with me, but I knew he was just a wheeler and dealer. I never trusted him. He took me up to Lake Tahoe and wanted to get in bed with me. After all these years, I am not too sure if we did or did not have sex. (Small laugh here.) That is saying; if I can't remember, than it had to be bad sex and if we only slept together, that had to be bad too. His wife was part of, and knowledgeable of all his schemes, and they lived rather nicely in a huge home on the Peninsula.

One day, doing whatever at home, I receive a phone call from someone telling me that Marvin had begun his own escort service and was telling everyone that his business was affiliated with my business.

Well, "angry" is a mild word for what I was when dialing his phone number, to tell him we would be taking him to court. I got him on the telephone and was less than nice in my words. He did stop using any name references to my business but Karma caught up with him and he was busted for not only running an escort service but for selling drugs. His business lasted perhaps four months. The guy was bottom-line stupid and had come to California from some state like New Jersey. He thought that all the 'game' which was played in New Jersey could be played on people in California. The story in the newspaper also mentioned that he was some sort of molester. I think it was young women, but not completely sure. All I do know is that he went to jail and it was good riddance from my point of view. He was a con man and a transparent con man at best.

Drug People #9

The Hells Angels are known as a drug organization. When I knew them they were selling drugs and using drugs. Lumping or putting them together in this one area seems right. Did I ride motorcycles with them? Yes. And did I party with them? Yes.

Were they nice men? Yes.

The people I knew were very nice and acted like gentlemen; amazing all the stories out there about them being big and bad. Doing harm to all people who pass their way and their not caring about the human race. I call that "false gossip" and "fear tactics" possibly from other organizations wanting this organization to be taken out of business by the police; so the other organizations can take over their business. Yes, there have been times when the guys get or got rowdy together. But what group of men ever stays quiet when drinking? Police cover each other's actions and men with money cover their actions too.

I see no difference.

When I first met the Hells Angels I was just out playing pool at a local bar in Marin County. At that time there was a local chapter of the Hells Angels in San Rafael. Two of the members took me on a ride to San Francisco and then proceeded to tell me all the little secrets of the Hells Angels Do I remember those secrets? No. As quickly as they spoke I made a conscious decision to forget what these two men were telling me, about the club. The two of them had been drinking and possibly doing drugs; they were bragging about the club. At one point both men looked at me and thought about maybe doing something with me (Killing, silencing, or whatever they did to keep women quiet.) because they had talked too much. Somehow I made it clear to them, I had been drinking and all they said to me went in one ear and out the other. I am still here, so they must have believed me. What they told about was the inner workings of the club's charter and a few extra tidbits. I did not care about the entire gab fest.

The complete evening was just a learning experience, for me, about motorcycle gangs.

The interest, for me, was how they thought about life and these two men thought about life through the association of members in the club.

The club was their life.

They did not tell about all their dealings with other people, but they made it clear that women were second-class citizens in their organization. One thing each one told about was that parties they had were fronts for executions. If a person was invited to a party, he or she may be the target to be murdered. As long as I knew the Angels I never went to a party except the first one. And after that one party, I would only attend one quasi-party at a charter house that my girlfriend and I were asked to come to and watch porno flicks. The guys had cleaned-up the house and all the men there were very friendly but not aggressive. On best behavior, it seemed like; and it was odd. Years later I wondered why we had been asked to the party and why all the men were so nice. Even questioned how laid back everyone was that night. This was not a colorful night and certainly not like some events that have been written about by other authors looking for the salaciousness associated with some event and this group.

My roommate, Dee, was scared to go to this party, but I let her know that the men who invited us had given their word we would be safe. The men who had invited us were once soldiers in Viet Nam and they had joined the group out of some idea that if you loved bikes, then riding with a group was having 'brothers' with you. The type of comrades you find in battle; a men's club that was counter-culture.

Did the guys sell drugs? Yes.

Did all the members sell drugs? No.

The motorcycle clubs I knew of drove all over the United States meeting up with other club members, and members of outlaw gangs wanting to do business with them. Sometimes there were fights between clubs due to drugs gone wrong; and people not paying or the guys may be cheating one another in the various business deals. No different from other drug dealers --- who were not members of bike clubs.

Over time the Hells Angeles has changed and I would say the club is a more dangerous club than it ever was, and the club is only as good as the members that are now in it. I believe the members then were very nice, for the most part. All organizations have exceptions.

None of the members ever hurt me. Slept with four members and this was at different times and at their homes. Not unusual circumstances. No raping or anything like that and one of the guys took me on the wildest ride I ever had in my life. We were going over the San Rafael Richmond Bridge from the east side to the west side of the bridge toward San Rafael when he cranked up the engine and I was too afraid to ask how fast we were going. We had to have been doing something close to 200 M.P.H. When we got to my home, I asked him, "How fast?" He said, "The gauge don't go that high." Translation: He did not know.

He had come over my house a few months before this wild ride with some bullet cartridges that were empty. No questions were asked, but I found out that he had killed someone and eventually went to jail for that murder. The cartridges had long been thrown out. I did not know if they had anything to do with what he had done. He seemed to like drugs and had a conscience, so I was surprised that he killed someone. Maybe he was ordered to do it. He did like drugs a little too much, but was not too high on the dealing list of Angels. (Meaning: those Angels "dealing" drugs' list.) One day he had an accident with his bike (big surprise) and sustained brain damage. This accident happened when he was just making a slow turn and dumped the bike. My thoughts are that he was having some type of stroke or something similar when he had the accident, because afterward his brain was not working on all "cylinders." He remembered me after the accident, but we only saw each other a couple of times, and, we were not going out or anything like that; just some quick conversations when we ran into each other.

Another Hells Angel member who came to the house had let me borrow his truck. I was always having car trouble. When he came back a couple of days later we both went down to the truck and he opened the hood to pull out a drug-kit. (He was a little nervous that I had found the "kit.") This was a special "kit" with drugs and a needle in a black pouch with a zipper on top; sometimes called an "outfit" in drug circles. This "kit" was for killing people. I knew instinctively what it was for, and did not ask any questions. He volunteered the information and gave me a long stare into my eyes to see if I believed him.

I did.

He had been in Viet Nam and maybe it was a "kit" he had for some drug issues and problems with the gang. Our eyes told the story better; our eyes met and we both did not say any more about the "kit." He left the truck for a few more days and then he took the truck home with him. I often wondered if he stayed with the organization after his new girlfriend had a baby. He just did not fit as some biker who took orders, well; and I think he was some kind of "hit man" for the Hells Angels.

Again, I liked him.

Then there were the guys from San Francisco who were killed. (This was a man, who was President of the San Francisco chapter of the Hell's Angels; and his girlfriend that were killed in bed, while asleep.) They were nice people and were probably killed by other members, so those murdering members could take over the guy's business of selling drugs, and his territory.

The tide was turning in the drug trade and people were now "open season" if they got in your way. I had him and his girlfriend over for the Fourth of July. We had a great time at the barbecue. I was very surprised someone felt it necessary to kill such nice people.

Drugs in the late 1970s were just "blossoming" all over the country and the Angels were a huge part of getting those drug lines that connected back to California. They were spreading 'speed' around this country. Opening up "outlets" or "sources" all over the United States and some even went over to Europe; always meeting up with other biker gangs as their supply chain associates. They would bring women to sell wherever they went so those women were a cover about what they really were doing; selling drugs.

In actuality I was too old for most of the Hells Angels. Those guys preferred dumb white chicks they could put in dance clubs to earn a side-living ..... for each member who placed the girl in the club. The men took all the women's money and each woman expected to give "her man" all the money she made. Girls that did not cooperate ended up back at home or worse. The worse being truly worse, such as dead. Many of these women wanted some "action" in their lives; many of them got way more than they ever expected or wanted.

Some of the Angels paid for a few of the escort women, and saw the women at their private homes. That sounds odd, but these were men; when they had the money there were some of them who phoned the service. Just to have some "whatever" without any commitment.

What has been said here about the Angels is believed to be safe, for me, speaking about what I saw. The two things learned from them were, to say little and never betray them. Any sensible person would not want to tell their secrets.

Drug Man #10

What a different guy.

He had a little disability; he stuttered. I often wondered how his drug dealings went with people not as sensitive as I was to his problem. When he first met you, it was difficult for him to speak and you just stood there waiting for him to finish the sentence; even though you had already finished the sentence for him in your mind. This cut a little into his time with an escort. Half of the time was spent trying to figure out what he wanted and waiting for him to finish a sentence. He saw girls at his home in San Francisco, on the avenues. It was a big home and very nice. His drugs were kept mostly in his vehicle and that vehicle was stored out in the garage. I often thought that if the drug police wanted to bust him, they would then have his car---but what about his home?

On second thought, when drugs are found in a garage the entire home can be taken too.

He was around 6'1" tall and wore glasses. The man was Jewish and had a good heart. We became friends for a while, or, that is until he met the right girl from the service. That happened when he began dating Trina without my knowledge. He even took her to Europe where he left her, because he had to get back to the drugs he needed.

Yes. He was addicted to his drugs.

Once he took me to San Quentin prison for a tour. I kept kidding with him the he should take a good look at his new home. He also brought me to one of the San Francisco Zoo's fund raising party. I enjoyed his private world. And he was inquisitive about my world. I liked this man and felt some kind of connection to him. His looking for work always was difficult for him. He would have no problem getting the interviews, but the stuttering affected the outcome of every interview. He had a college degree and hoped to work in the financial world. Eventually he stopped phoning the service and possibly this was because he had a girlfriend.

Maybe it was because of the pain he was suffering from the death of his brother. His brother had worked two jobs back to back and never went anywhere and did not have a social life. Eventually the brother killed himself and left all his saved money to his drug-dealing brother.

This was a very sad outcome.

One night I was over his home and I used too much of the drug he was selling; or I was allergic to the ingredients. Another one of the escorts was there to, and, both of them drove me to the hospital.

A hospital in San Francisco where I met one of Hitler's ex-employees. This bitch came into the emergency room area, with drape closed, where the other employee had put me and said, "We don't help people like you." She had not even phoned the doctor to come down to the emergency room.

Thank God my friends were waiting in the car and then came in to check on me. The nurse finally phoned the doctor; after calling my mother.

Never, will I forget that night. People told me later that this particular hospital, in those days ('70s), had a great many DOA's to their credit. Meaning in my language, that the drug overdoses that came in were not helped and the hospital was putting on the charts, DOA, "dead on arrival."

The drug dealer phoned my mom while the nurse watched; then the nurse's gig of making me suffer was over. He knew she had phoned my mom, and he did not want my mother to worry. I still won't go to that hospital, and, I get chills when passing the place. Won't say the name because I am sure there are fantastic professional doctors and nurses working there; but that night was hell for this patient. The entire scene made me wonder what it would have been like for people of color during the 1950s in most areas of the South.

Maybe this was God's way of telling me to "grow up". I also knew what a friend this drug dealer was, because he was throwing caution to the wind by exposing himself to possible arrest charges for supplying drugs to someone.

For that noble act, I loved him.

Drug Man #11

The night was windy and rainy and this guy phoned from a home near the Russian River, which is in Sonoma County. I took the call, because it was late and I was up. No other reason, except knowing the area well.

When I arrived at his home the wooden gate was somewhat useable and a motorcycle and motor home sat next to the little cottage he lived in. Didn't see anyone else around and so I knocked on the door.

He answered and I thought he stood about 6' tall with coal black hair and sprinkles of grey scattered around his hair, which he wore long and in a pony tail. The place looked sloppy. Not filthy but sloppy and his bathroom was a stand type stall for a shower and a toilet nearby, with maybe a curtain in front of it. There was an attraction … emphatically not! I wanted to turn around and leave. When we got into bed; he was not clean, so action with him was limited to a hand job. Afterward, I just wanted to wash the old hands quickly. The guy also smelled and prided himself on wearing the same leather slacks all the time and without underwear; a real pig. I knew some Hell's Angels that were way cleaner than him.

We spoke about many things and people we knew. Not this first time, but several times afterward and a few showers, he took later, we became quasi friends; or I thought we had a limited friendship. He confided that he had been a priest and left the priesthood and now he dealt drugs. The drugs he dealt were mostly "pot" and some "speed." But he was just something 'else' and I am not positive what that was then or now.

I ended up living with a Mendocino drug dealer and that was by accident. Never knew the guy was a "grower" until he confessed when we were fighting. Anyway, this is the guy James (Drug dealer #12, one I lived with and now dead) phoned to help move me out of his house; and my things into a storage area. I saw James give him money to move me and I have never seen this creep again.

When he was a client I only sent maybe one or two other women to see him. As for our "friendship", he told me how he was on a motorcycle riding behind a friend of mine from the "river" area and he saw the handle bars of the motorcycle fly off and watched my friend die.

After so many years, I now know, he must have had something to do with my friend's death. He said how he went to the mortuary and looked over the body; just to make sure my friend was dead. I spoke about this incident in another of my books, but here is where the creep belongs. I hated him then and now and wish him the same fate he gave to my friend.

After writing about him, I questioned whether to put him as a "hit man." He belongs in hell. Well, I believe he was just a drug dealer who may have killed for the "growers" of Mendocino County. It even crossed my mind that he was a cop because Jim had many cops on the payroll.

Drug Man #12

This guy's name was Jim.

Jim and I knew each other for many years and got along well together. When I closed the business, he put his ring, literally in the "ring" to be with me, forever, in the "ring." He gave me his mother's wedding ring. She was no longer alive. He asked me to marry him. I said, "Yes." Just another foolish "pick" of a man, for me, and he moved me into his home. He was redoing the kitchen area and other areas and wanted my input. My input, because I would be the woman of the house and all decorating was up to both of us.

Then came the move … after a month of living with him; he told me where his substantial income came from. He was one of the Mendocino growers. I was very surprised. The revelation hit my like a lead balloon. I was very upset. I wanted nothing to do with a drug dealer, grower, or whatever he wanted to call himself.

After leaving my business; all, this woman wanted was peace and quiet. Not the constant fear that some cop was investigating him and then me. I enrolled in the Junior College to begin studies for my degree. He was not happy that I would be going to school. At first he was all nice, nice, but my first day of school, just by coincidence, my front windshield was broken. I came to the car and could not believe my eyes. I had to use money I was saving to have it fixed. Did I think he did it? Yes, or one of his many friends. Things of mine around the house began to look as if someone broke a piece off. Some damage could never be fixed. I have kept the pieces, just so I will always remember that I am not a good judge of boyfriends.

Well, the worst was yet to come. The night of December 31st 1993, we stayed at home to cozy-up and just have a relaxing New Years Eve. The next morning I felt odd. In the bathroom I looked at my right arm and there are track marks all up and down the arm. As if someone was trying to find a vein to put, whatever, in my blood stream. My veins are difficult to find on a good day. The person had to have just skin popped into a muscle the shot. My entire brain felt strange. I was on something but I was not sure what it was. I looked at him and showed him my arm. He denied everything. He was not going to tell me the truth. He did say he wanted to end our relationship and I was fine with that. I never wanted to see him again. The small part was, "What to do with all my things? Where the hell was I going to move too?" But my mind was not very coherent. We had an argument and he left the house. I wanted him gone.

Then, whatever had been given to me really set in and I was just floating in the house. I was still on solid ground, but felt horrible. Whatever he gave me did not affect me the way he wanted it to; I was just light-headed. I called a couple of friends and told them what was happening. I was not sure they believed me.

One of the friends came over to the house and saw a few of the things he had done. It was as if he wanted to kill me. From our conversations I knew that some people in various police departments were on his payroll. There were people all over Marin and Sonoma County who knew him and were keeping him safe; the tangled web he had woven was very large.

The drug dealer #11 that I spoke of came over to move me. What I stated before, that I felt he was a killer was stuck in my brain. He moved my things to a storage facility where the last woman who lived with Jim had her things. And Jim knew the managers, or owners of the place, very well.

When I showed up to school for the next week there were people watching me and some students would not sit close to me. I was told by one female student that no one wanted to catch a bullet. The word was out about me and I still don't know what that "word" was. I only know I had to move. What I did next brought me to Iowa. It would be in Iowa where I finished my schooling. I moved there and put the entire "Jim World" in my back mirror.

Before I had left the house, what I did take were the maps of locations where the drugs were being grown. Also, the various bank accounts he had. I was not sure what I would do with them, but I wanted to ruin his life, as he had messed with my life.

I found out later, that one of the reasons he wanted me with him, was to have me a part of his organization. That was not going to happen, so I was no longer needed. Then it was time for me to move out. What he did do was find my daughter's social security card and took it. This was used to open some bank account they had and to buy some property in the San Mateo area. I was shocked when I found there was property purchased with my daughter's name. It must have been quickly sold, because I have not seen it since when I first found it.

There was no person I trusted to speak to about him. Many of my past friends in the area, actually, bought drugs from him or people he knew. He is now dead, or I should say the name he was using shows up in the Social Security databanks. Unless I see the body, I will never believe someone, who is a drug dealer, is dead.

Drug Dealer #13

Ah love, me amour. Yes, my love.

When I was in El Paso one time, I met a man at a bar. I had just walked into the place to see if they sold food. It was lunch time and they were the closest business for a person walking.

(I did speak about this man in one other book.)

He was handsome and wore expensive everything; neat clean and gorgeous, with a touch of sophistication that empowered his education, and spoke to his need for attention. I immediately loved his coal black hair with pale skin. I had fallen in love. His eyes did not sparkle; they glimmered and shot volumes of fermions my way. I was almost paralyzed to leave. But I began to walk away and his words brought me back.

All in Spanish he asked if I wanted to go for lunch, with him. Of course I did. He gave me the keys to his car and as I was going out the door the bartender asked my name. He was shocked the man gave me the keys to his car without asking my name. I told them my name and continued walking, back across the street to the cheap motel I was staying at. It did not matter that I had a boyfriend.

This man was going to be mine.

Yes, we were perfect together.

But then the day came when I found out he was not only a drug dealer; he was "the" drug dealer. What happened next is covered in another book. No, I did not tell everything in that other book. But I did give a glimpse into what it was like being this man's woman or wife, in some circles. For me, this relationship was all I needed. Why I left him was obvious. I did not want to be part of his life that was "all" about drugs. Did I love him then? "Yes." Do I love him now? "Yes."

Drug Dealer #14

Bill. Isn't there always a Bill, who is a drug dealer? Yes, that was my Bill. He had begun dealing drugs while in high school. In a strange way I would say he paid to see me and paid the ultimate price of losing our relationship by seeing one of the many women who worked for me. Not only was I cheated out of a fee, I lost a relationship that was, at times, very violent. His moods went from good to bad....daily. He told me that when his cousin sent him some "primo" hash and weed from Viet Nam; the box was intercepted by the Drug Enforcement Agency (DEA) at the post office. He had opened the package and was smoking the marijuana when the officers came through the front door. He was so high he could barely remember what had happened. But for what he forgot, he did not have to worry; the entire "bust" was filmed. Then the DEA showed the film to all the students at the high school he had attended. It was to let the students know what can happen to you when you do drugs.

The message was, "You get arrested if you abuse or sell drugs".

Bill had not learned his lesson.

Every time he went to Chicago, his home town, he would bring drugs back to California to sell. Along with his friends, he sold to people at bars and where ever he could. This supplied money for his many habits. The main habit he had was alcohol and the second habit was women. The main habit killed him. His liver was destroyed from years of abusing every drug imaginable and he died at age 39. He actually thought doctors would give him a liver transplant. What he needed was a brain transplant.

Drug Dealers End

I could go on and on about all the drug dealers phoning the service and ones I meant along the way; but it would take up too much of the book and they are not as diverse as you would think. They relate the same to women as most other clients phoning the service. What makes them different is they have more cash and want to spend it; just compelled to spend their ill-gotten gains.

This need to show what they have and what they are able to purchase with the money from their illegal activities can always be found with each one of them. Most of these men either end up dead, in jail, or go on to becoming business men in the community. The ones working in the communities they lived in are and were also the dealers that never got caught.

Some, drug dealers, even have the audacity to run for public office.

Chapter Two
White Collar Men

"The art of being an escort comes with the ability to move the client to want more ... more of you and a desire to pay you, because you are you" D.E.Z. Butler

This chapter acquaints the reader with the men who phoned regularly and are what 'fed' the escort business. These men were the "bread and butter" clients. The nucleolus, whereby the entire business circled around. The "how" each woman fed herself and paid her bills.

These were the guys that just wanted to see someone, apart, from his or her regular mundane business life and family obligations. A little excitement and possibly the picture in the magazine, he jerked off to, that would come alive for him....for an hour. The excitement that could last until the next time he had the money to pay for the hour.

(Men mostly phoned for escorts; fewer clients were females calling for men. And even fewer phoning for same sex dating. My business did not cater to the same sex liaisons. We were heterosexual, only.)

They wanted to feel special for an hour or two. The client wanted a woman who would tell them that they were the "best" in the land and in bed. The compliments also extended to telling them that they could do no wrong; and these men needed the ego pumped up, so they called *Professional Escorts.*

Most of these men were not asking for any sexual favors which would promote the escorts thoughts that the guy was weird or kinky. Many of them just phoned on Fridays when they had their paychecks in hand. Some phoned more often than Fridays, because they had money to burn. Some were single and many were married.

The "chicken" men acted the same scared way if they saw one of the other escorts out and about at a bar, movie, or shopping. These men were the hypocrites that kept and still keep the escort businesses going. Some of these guys called while the wife and children were at church.

Some men even went so far as to meet an escort at a parking lot and have the escort get into his car, then ask the escort doing the assignment, to lie close to the floor or duck while he drove the car into the garage at his home. Then the escort would return to her car the same way. These men were afraid the neighbors would see a woman coming to the house. I always thought the intrigue was funny. The guy would even ask that the woman not where perfume or deodorant, so there was not a smell that the wife could detect. And he wanted sex in the master bedroom or children's room or bathroom; he did not want you to put any marks on his neck or any other area of his body.

These were some "touchy" guys and living on the edge. "Like phoning for an escort could kill them." It might be possible for them to die if their wife found out how ridiculous the "hide and seek" method to get laid was playing out when she was out of the home.

Having a successful business does have its perks. Besides the pick of the "crop" in clients; many times I could go see someone, and that person just wanted to speak to me. No "hanky-panky," just some great conversation. Loved those phone calls; I was paid to just enjoy another human being without any sexual tension. Even some vice cops would phone and only wanted to speak to me at their location. The money was exchanged but not for any sexual favors. Yes, there were exceptions to the rule, men in the vice department … are men.

I remember this one time in San Jose. The drive from San Rafael was long and all I wanted to do was relax. The San Jose Vice Department was very good at what they did and I knew that fact; they were always on the "job."

When I got to the apartment, from the directions the man gave me, it was easy to find, but the area did not look too great. I knocked on the door and a great looking man answered; he was tall and built. Looking just like I enjoy my men; he scanned me up and down with those gorgeous eyes of his and we walked to the bedroom. (Nice spot to go when you are tired.) As I surveyed where I was; the only furniture in the room was a bed and one dresser.

Just seemed natural to lie on the bed and he lay down next to me. We were laying there and he had not paid me yet. It was not my policy to ask for the money up front with a man I suspected of being a cop. Just knew this man was a vice cop and truthfully I did not care. His body was firm and our eyes met and that was it. The attraction was too great. We wanted each other. We were making love when I asked him if he was a cop and he said, "If I was, it is too late now."

That remark was a "yes" in my lingo.

Afterward I picked up my cash and left, he was smiling. Never did he phone again, to the best of my knowledge. But I would have seen him again if he had phoned. This guy was a pleasure in the bedroom. The apartment was stark. Very little furniture and I doubted that any person lived there. Nothing in the apartment looked like anything he would have purchased; except for the escort in front of him, for one hour of extreme pleasure. I can still smile over that encounter.

Side Comment:
{Just wanted to add, that most people have no idea how many men or how many executives love having a woman over to the office, after hours. Then the man wants the woman to either massage him or have sex with him on the executive board meeting table. You know which table. The one that is usually very long to accommodate many board members. This was just a little visual to keep your minds busy at the next meeting.}

Man#1
Herb was a long-time customer. The first time he phoned I went to see him at his one bedroom apartment. He was so adorable and funny. The luck of a healthy body he did not have, but he did have a wonderful sense of humor. For many years escorts saw him and they just enjoyed his intelligence and the way he looked at life.

Man #1 may have been married many years before we met but the marriage did not last long and there were no children. He was a computer person and worked for a government office in San Francisco. He did not stand tall, just the opposite, he was short, because his spine had a very bad birth defect. Herb was shorter than me and so that means he was a little less than 5' tall. Herb wore glasses and drank like a drunken sailor returning to port after being at sea for a couple of years. He drank every day.

He always came to the parties I gave and he loved being there. He was not embarrassed to say he used escort services. We would take his checks. He did not write bad checks. A couple of the checks may have been written before his paycheck hit the bank. But overall there was never any huge issue over checks with him; even if he wasn't pleased with an escort. Sometimes I would send a new escort to see him and he would know that she was new and to "break" her in, so to speak; he answered the door naked to give her a shock.

Then, just like a little Gremlin, he danced around his apartment to make her feel more at ease. After the initial shock of his nakedness the woman would ask him to put on his robe or some slacks at least and he would comply.

One of the ladies who worked for *Professional Escorts* went to Hawaii with him. Of course, they never told the service and the service never received a fee; but with him it was all right.

He had enough problems in life.

Herb was always trying to see women without the escort service's knowledge or consent, and away from the service fees, but he was one of our most loyal customers and always phoned around the holidays to make sure the women had their holiday money.

One of the last times I saw him was for dinner during Christmas week. A very nice restaurant he took me to, it was on the San Francisco side of the wharf. He had to use a pillow to sit on --- just to reach the high table. We had a lovely time and somewhere in the back of our minds, we knew this dinner would be our last dinner together. I can't explain it, but possibly it was how we looked into our eyes and for moments did not say a word. Very sadly he died next to his yacht, which he had bought to live out the rest of his life on.

The month was February and just two months from our last dinner. It appears to have been an accident and I phoned the coroner to make sure it was true, when someone told me he had died. I was very sad about his passing. This is a man who I still miss and he would be happy that I put him as number one in the book and dedicated this book to his memory.

Man #2

Another favorite client was a Navy guy and I considered him a friend, as I did the first client. He was someone the service could depend on to see the women first, similar to Herb, and I knew these women were safe with him. This man had served our country in the Navy and now he is Mr. Annapolis in the book <u>The Madam's Escorts</u> and in this writing. He had been on a submarine for his Navy duty and I still marvel how he could have been under water for so long and in what I call a "tuna can" to live and breathe. This takes a special type of person and he was "special" to the escort service, as he was to the Navy.

The first night he telephoned the service, I was not very sure of him; and if it were all right to send someone to see him. He asked many questions and seemed very educated, but intuitively, I thought he worked for the government and could be a cop. We spoke for a long time that first night, before I sent someone to see him. True, he had worked for the government, but it was in military service; so I was sort of correct. He spoke about the many books he had read and seemed well-traveled during that first revealing telephone call.

Mr. Annapolis was a difficult man to understand. His conversations were very general and he did not allow people close to him; to know the real 'him'.
Whereas some clients just want to talk all night about themselves; he just wanted the women to come over and have a drink and then off to bed with him.

A ... "thank you mum" ... guy.

After he dissected the woman's worth as a conversationalist, he then would make the decision to see her again or not; and I always suspected he was looking for an intelligent woman to be with him, permanently.

There was a "type" of woman, or shape he wanted, which is similar to all or most men want. Their own fantasy woman. In this respect he was no different. Men just get hung-up on certain attributes that some women have, and, many a time, I went to a man's home and his Playboy magazine was out, and he had "ordered" a busty blonde; just like in the magazine. Other escorts had the same experience of looking at a magazine, which was turned to a page that had a picture of a woman who looked like the escort. This man was no different and he did have his "type" of body, the type of woman, who was perfection for him. His "perfect" preference were women who were young and with dark hair, sporting a tight-figure; the athletic "type" woman. But, as most men are, when he was "in need" of a woman, just about any woman could be sent to him. He seemed always to be a very matter-of-fact guy.

Respect---he was genuinely 'in respect' for the women going over to see him. We never heard him disparage a woman to anyone. Maybe, he was not thrilled with some of the escorts, but gross conversations about any woman were not his style. Even when at one party at his home, an employee was having sex in his bathroom. He just made mention of it because this behavior was crude for his style.

Everyone agreed with him, about the woman; and, thankfully I was able to let that female go within a week of the party. "Fired!" I should have said, "Fired for being rude and stupid and a slut!"

Side Comment:

{She was the girl who answered the phones for me, at that time. She was not an escort. She had come out of the bathroom with her nylons all torn and for some reason felt behavior like that was "okay," because the women there were all paid escorts. All the other women were dressed well and acted like ladies. For some reason women, who do not accept a fee for their sexual favors, believe looking like a tramp when around professional escorts, is how everyone else perceives the other women to look and behave. Which is far from the truth; all the men at this party were respectful of the women and would not dare share some crude insults with those present. This behavior, she had, is usually handed out by the very young man or woman who finds getting cash for sex to be wrong. This woman having sex in the bathroom, on the toilet, was her impression of escorts. I was able to understand better why she was under or had been having psychiatric care for many years. None of my escorts ever acted, as she did, at any of my parties.}

Mr. Annapolis's home was all bachelor pad, and, he fit the place like any sailor on shore leave. It would be surprising if he ever married. (Although, I would have had his child. I know, strange, but I liked his gene pool.) He also had a sports car which went along with his bachelor lifestyle. This home had been featured in some magazine showing the homes of bachelors. The style of the home was free and easy with a spectacular view of the San Francisco Bay.

When he phoned, and wanted to see women, it was as if he just wanted to take care of a physical need, nothing else. If someone told me he was a hired assassin for the government. Well, I would have believed the news. He blended in when you saw him with a group of people. He could have robbed a bank and many descriptions of him would have been given.

Plus, he had the coldness needed by an assassin to do the job.

His loyalty was "blowing in the wind" for just one escort service. If the service (my service) did not have anyone to send him, well for him there were other escort services. He even helped one woman who had worked for *Professional Escorts;* obtain a home in Marin County. She and her sister needed a house to have their own escort service. Tacky service at best, where men would come to the house, and, Mr. Annapolis probably preferred going to a house to see women, so he helped her. There had to be a benefit for him in doing this favor for her.

Because he was with my service, from, just about since the beginning; his fee was kept to about the same as when he first began phoning. He could also write checks. I liked him and wished he could have been less uptight, or not so concerned about what the neighbors would think…this was the way he approached life. He was cognizant of how other people perceived behaviors. He never stopped wanting to have a deal or some perk, because he was a customer, so long, with the service. And every time he phoned, he wanted a new girl. This was common with regular customers to want someone they had not seen before. I always wished him well. This man was an officer and a gentleman, a man our country could be proud of, and, I was glad I knew him.

Man #3

When speaking of this man, all I have is respect for him. He just commanded respect. I went to see him at his professional office, to give him a massage. His office was in a historical building in San Francisco. He owned the company. This meeting happened when I worked for *Yumi's Massage Parlor* in San Francisco. After a few times seeing him at his office, he remained a customer for years and a person who called me directly. Eventually our relationship evolved and I was going to his home and gave a massage to both he and his wife. It was all very innocent. He wanted to be faithful to his wife and I admired him for that loyalty. I enjoyed knowing him. I would be lying if I said we never had sex. We did, but it was just something that happened, not something we wanted to go farther with and into a romantic relationship. He worked in the movie business in some capacity and I can't say too much here, because it may reveal who he was and I don't want to do that; even though these days the big 'thing' for books is to have an escort bare her soul and almost a "need" to reveal names of clients just to sell a book or two.

I loved when he joked with me about the business (my business), and, how he thought I should go 'public'; meaning, to have the business on the stock exchange. We would laugh about escort services being on the stock exchange. I saw him in Beverly Hills when he was in town. I was clear with him; less money was not an option. He had to pay the exact amount of money asked for; I always had to massage him. He was an executive with "class." I bring this up because it was the only time we locked "horns", so to speak. It was over money, and I had to be firm with him about my fee.

Side Comment:

{Many times men like to get close to you, by making you or any woman feel special, just so they can take advantage of the situation. This is a common occurrence with women working as escorts, masseuses, hookers, prostitutes, and street walkers. The women working feel their time and energy is worth every penny. I even trusted this man to have my sister's phone number and he phoned her apartment. That is how we got together in Beverly Hills. My sister and her husband were surprised I even knew him. And with him telling them what a great person I was … too bad I was not there to see the looks on their faces that a person they would have liked to know … knew me … and liked me.

I would prefer to think that maybe things would have gone further if he had not been married. But that was not the case. Still admire him and always hope for the best for him. At this writing, not sure if he is even still alive. Sex with him was very pleasant and because he was usually drinking, he always wanted me to accept less money. But I feel and know our bodies are worth something and men just want to treat them as they would their wives or girlfriends. The meaning here is they all want "it" for free. That never happened for him. No free, ever.}

Man #4

This is another customer that I thought of more as a friend. Randy and I never saw each other on a professional level and I believe that is because I was just not his "type." We never had any sexual contact with each other. Surprising as that may be, he and I had a business relationship aside from his using the escort service. He would see women every now and then from my escort service. He probably was seeing women from other escorts services and massages studios in San Francisco and may have even said so at some time, to me when we were just chatting. He liked the very sexy, small dark-haired woman and women who looked great in sexy negligees.

What I mean by business relationship is that he contacted me one time about my business and advertising in his monthly paper. I advertised with him and knew him a long time. That is how we first met. Randy had begun his newspaper business just about the time *Professional Escorts* began. We both learned about our businesses and the various ins and outs of catering to people interested in meeting people --- at the same time. My ad was usually the last page of his paper. Which means prospective clients would turn-over the paper and see my ad; this was a perfect location for an ad to be in. The business grew because of his paper. I was so lucky he allowed me to advertise in his paper. Because of our business relationship my business flourished.

One day he came over to my home and told me about a venture that he was going into. He offered me a piece of it for a small sum of money. Dumb me. He ended up making a great deal of money and began buying homes in San Francisco. Lucky him and unlucky me; his business flourished and for him just about every business undertaking he went into was run well by him. The man had and has the "Midas touch." The business he offered me a piece of was phone sex telephone lines. See, I was dumb.

Randy is another man who was trusted with the women I sent to him, and, I would be very surprised if he ever marries. The single life was and is preferred by him. Every woman sent to him said he asked her to wear sexy negligees and he loved the women to strut around the room with high-heels and garter-belts. Randy was a visual person and is called "voyeur".

This imagination, my imagination has him surfing the Internet and loving all the websites out there now. Nudity galore! He must be in heaven.

Porn heaven.

One day he phoned and asked if I wanted to go see the *Rolling Stones* concert. The deal was that I supply the limousine service to the show and he had backstage passes. We were sharing costs and were to have an unusual time. Every *Stone's* concert then, came with the 'buzz' that it would be their last, so people would come, I suppose, for that reason.

The opening act was *Carlos Santana*'s band and they were great. Mick Jagger showed up late and arrived by helicopter. I think this concert was in the early '80s. I could not believe how skinny Jagger was and all I could see was his backside. (If you want to call "it" a backside) The backstage passes "sucked" or "suck," where I am concerned. I wore this cowboy hat and some cool clothes, complete with a long blonde wig. People kept coming up to me asking if I was his current wife or girlfriend Jerry Hall. How they got to that conclusion was a mystery to me, and way off base. She was or is tall and I am short. To top it off, the concert by the *Stones* was just not great. I think the recordings are better. The warm up act, *Santana* band was far better than the *Stones* that day, as far as I am concerned; even looking back on that day, I am sure that *Santana* was better.

After the concert, it took forever hooking-up with the limo driver.

Finally, we did find the limousine and went back to my place. Nothing happened between us, but our friendship found a new level that night, by doing something fun together. In a way Randy was maybe afraid of being with me in a sexual way. I could be "off" about that, but he just never made any "moves" on me. Must have been because I was not his "type" or we were friends, only. Not a bad thing, but there was always this thought I had that he was the one that got away. It was just a thought from someone who cared.

Man #5

Putting this man higher-up the number chain, means nothing to me or should it to you, the reader. He was a "pig" --- an absolute "pig" and a lawyer to boot. When he phoned, the women cringed. He would want to see them for hours and even days if possible. Bruce was a drunk first and a man of the 'bar' second; his only "love" was drinking. If we took a check from him it may bounce. But he would spend money. When he was spending and straight with us, "Straight," meaning he was not drunk and knowing he had to pay the service fees, he spent a lot of money. I would, always, have to phone the bank to make sure the check was good, provided that was how he wanted to pay, because he was too drunk to get in his car and use an ATM machine.

When you arrived at his condo on the Peninsula he was always drunk and still drinking. The type of drunk where you have to listen carefully to make sure you understood what the hell he was saying. There was no way in hell he was ever going to get 'it' up, due to the large consumption of booze. But he would want the girl to 'twang' on 'it' for hours.

Bruce was another one of the guys that thought he could impress you by saying he had, once, something to do with the CIA. He spoke about this in depth and we just blew him off, because he was always telling a story of how he thought he once was, when he was in the military. The stories could have been true, but they did not matter. The escorts were there to make money, not hear bullshit stories.

The condo would be a mess cluttered with old pizza in the cardboard boxes they came in, along with lawyer 'briefs' all over the table tops, in his home. And sometimes he was wearing only soiled briefs, past worn or they had seen better days; and, Bruce was usually working on a case when he phoned and/or had just finished one and wanted to be rewarded. The women were his reward.

Just to get him off the phone, I had to tell him I was going to begin looking for someone for him, who he would just love. Ugh! I wanted to throw-up. The worst case scenario would be when I would have to go see him. Why? I hated passing up the money --- more than I hated him.

The backstory, for him, was tied to the first time I met him. It was when I worked for *Yumi* in San Francisco. She had a massage business on Sutter Street. He had phoned there and was seeing, what I thought to be, an old woman; of course, now I would think she was young. She was a very professional woman and had the furs to prove her worth. He loved phoning and asking only for her. I would just roll my eyes to the other women, as they rolled their eyes back to me in complete agreement.

Bruce usually phoned all the services and most of the women all over the Bay Area knew his name and never wanted to hear it. Bruce was an Irish man and proud of it, and, that is not a bad thing. But when he drank he also began to cry. Nothing is more distasteful than to watch a man who cries when you are listening to all his legal encounters and life encounters that are not going well for him. Crying real tears and staring at you to see if you cared. Ugh!

This man needed a live-in psychiatrist.

One night of horror was when he asked me to marry him. I said, "Fine, let's do it now". I challenged him. Then I told him I would not do anything with him unless we went to get married.

That was all he wanted to speak about, that night, was marrying me; such a boring conversation. He had been married and had children and his wife was lucky to have gotten rid of him. (He asked many of the escorts to marry him. This was not a special honor for me.)

In thinking back, his only redeeming qualities were when his checks cleared the bank. To make matters worse, sometimes he would say that he did not remember the night before; and then he wanted to tell me that he paid more than he should have paid or the girl ripped him off or some other shit that was not true. This may have been true sometimes.

Bruce was so believable when "yarning" his tales, that it was hard to believe he would not or could not remember the night before; when someone sent to him or even his time with me. The women sent to him did not have any interest in "ripping him off." They just wanted their money for any check or checks he wrote for the extra favors he wanted from the woman or women, as the case may be.

Most drunks can't get "it" up, so sometimes the woman has to do all sorts of things to help him. This guy was nothing but work. The girl had to yank and pull and possibly suck on him all night just to get a dribble out of his lousy "dick." The only thing I worried about with him, besides the checks clearing, was if he would die with one of my escorts. He drank himself into oblivion and was not getting any younger. Every now and then Bruce wanted two women.

Boy was he dreaming! All I could say back to him was, "Really?"

He couldn't do anything with one woman, so it was unclear how he thought he could handle two women. I sent the women to him and they said he just wanted to watch them together. This scenario worked out fine that night because the girls sent to him, well, each liked being with women.

Another area of concern with him was disease, because he phoned so many other services; no telling what disease he may have contracted.

When the business finally closed down; I thought of him, and, how happy I was not to have to hear his voice ever again. This was the only client that thought came into my head. He was really that bad.

Man #6

This doctor phoned from Napa. I sent one of the girls who had been a cop in Florida, the state she came from and surprise, surprise, they ended up living together and she never told me. Found out from other people. Doc had called a few times and then never phoned again. It was due, in part, to this woman's disloyalty.

I was informed by other escorts that he was affectionate and loving and was soliciting other women to go and live with him. Sue should have told me, so I could have informed her, he was just always asking for a live-in. She was not the first, but this was the end of her working for me. If you cannot trust the women in escorting, then you have to let them work for other people, or your business would dwindle, could dwindle, and definitely did dwindle from the client thieves. It was a business move not to give her anymore calls.

Susan was a person I liked as a friend, but as a worker for my business, she was bad news. I think she thought that she was special. It is as if she really believed the clients when they told her how great she was. Damn, I thought she knew better and I am sure I told all the girls that the men tell everyone of them the same thing, and that is how great they are. She had lived in San Francisco and would go see just about anyone who she was asked to see; sometimes driving long distances. Mostly, that is what I liked about having her work for me, the fact she was available for calls. Susan had natural red hair and was very average looking but had a nice personality. I just could not see her as a cop. Never heard if the two of them married but he was lucky to get her. Another side note about her. The reason she was no longer a cop was because of the sex she was having with her police partner, on the job and behind his wife's back.

This girl's morals were, always, questionable.

Man #7

Mr. Harvard or Ben if you like real names and that was his name. This man phoned one night and I decided to see him. He was very nice on the telephone and seemed well-educated. He lived in San Anselmo, thus, my decision to see him. The business ended up sending him many women over the course of the time he phoned the service; and he spent a great deal of money on the women.

Ben was in mourning.

His wife had left him for another woman, after only a few years of marriage to him. She was not his first wife. The first wife had four daughters by him and they all lived on the East Coast. I saw pictures of his daughters and I amused him by saying they all looked like "cookie-cutter" girls. All their faces looking the same and favoring their mother. This second wife had torn his manhood from him.

The bitch flaunted it in his face, her need for this other woman, and tried successfully to seize his masculinity away from him. She took the last bit of self-worth he had for himself. He could barely function. Ben was devastated by her leaving him and going to Maine to live with her new lover--- a woman.

Ben was unable to sustain an erection, if, he was lucky enough to get one and then he would urinate on the woman ....allowing her to think he had "come." It was all a little revolting.

Slowly, Ben was exhausting his bank accounts and was throwing all caution to the wind. This everyday phoning for women was just depleting any savings he had. We began to distrust his checks and each woman insisted upon cash from him.

Finally, he sold his home.

Then he was living out of hotels and eventually he rented a small cottage in the Napa Valley. A nice place with a kitchen and living room tightly put together and one bedroom; almost living like a Monk; and very different from his home in Marin County.

Ben was a Harvard graduate and an ex-Presbyterian minister. He had been fired or demoted or whatever they do with ministers who are drunks.

One day he phoned to tell that he had been kicked out of church---all he had done was show up and they asked him to leave the church. He was crying over the phone and I did whatever I could to console him. His drinking continued non-stop. The church had given him, his last straw to hang onto life, and now that was taken from him.

Another day he phoned from Bermuda. He spoke to me for at least an hour; he wanted me to go there and stay with him for a few days. I was reluctant to join him, but he convinced me that he was sober and we would have a great time. Wrong. The flight took several hours to Bermuda from San Francisco, and just to find out that he lied. Ben was drunk and the hotel staff was happy to see me. They were worn-out from dealing with him and his many antics when he was sloppy-drunk. I was charging him $1,000 a day and he tried to complain but my retort was, "You are lucky I am not charging you mileage." (This was the price we had agreed upon before I ever told him I would join him. The plane ticket was paid in advance and I had an open-ended return flight paid.)

He got a chuckle out of that statement.

Mr. Harvard, my Ben, paid for the round-trip ticket and perfume and whatever I wanted, plus the fee. The only trouble was I had to take him to the hospital because he had fallen the day before I arrived and had a ghastly wound on his forehead that needed stitches.

After the hospital visit, I made it clear to him; I could not stay a week, as planned. He was on a 'binge' and I was sleeping on the floor to avoid the occasional spraying of blood from his wound, when he would pick on it and take off the bandage.

Surprisingly, we almost married while in Bermuda, or that is he asked me to marry him; but I decided against it. This happened during one of our shopping trips to purchase gifts. Because he was constantly asking to marry me; I thought why not? He was due to inherit a many millions from his ill mother living on the East Coast. But I had met my soon to be husband; so I decided it was better to just forget about marriage with Ben. We had great conversations when he was sober. Too bad he had to drink. He was one person who the service helped, because he needed someone at a crucial time in his life and he was suicidal.

In looking back about what I thought of him; I know that he was depleting his resources, because he did not want his ex-wife to have any money. I am on the fence as to what was right or wrong with him throwing his money away. It was his money to do with as he wished. Ben was a good man who just "lost it" when his wife went *Major Lesbian* after so many years of marriage. The man was difficult to be around, but his wife could have been nicer to him. He was not a bad human being. Some of the other women I sent to him told me he would urinate a little, just, so the woman thought he had come. Disgusting, no other way to describe his inability to ejaculate correctly. When a man has to do that to feel alive, it is time for him to cash in his chips and yes, Ben is now deceased.

I did get to see Bermuda for free, so I will never forget Ben.

Man #8

The priest: Ah, well this is a man who phoned one night and not again, to the best of my knowledge. I had nothing to do that night; so I went to this call in San Francisco. When I got to the address I wondered if it was a fake call; a fake call was one bad part about doing calls, because sometimes people would call the service just to watch the person show up and look for the address.

I went around back of the church and knocked on the side entrance door. Yep. It was a good call. The man was a priest and was getting ready to go fishing the next day.

I spoke about this man briefly in Bellflower Boulevard. Dee had told me that I was going to hell because I had been with this priest, and my only retort to her was, "Why? He had the money." She laughed, but was putting a cross up in front of her face with her two fingers at me, as if I were a vampire. My opinion was that he was a man before he became a priest, and he was an older priest--- probably getting ready to retire. I did not think much of the encounter because he was not ready to hear my confession and I was not ready to give a confession or hear his confession.

The Priest was very nice and he did not appear to feel guilty at all for phoning and having someone come over to see him. I was there maybe ten minutes and can barely remember his room; but I do remember seeing the fishing pole.

(Amazing what a person remembers.)

Side Comment:

{*Opinion Point*: All churches should allow the men to marry. My thoughts are that when a man has chosen a religious life, there should be no reason to take sex away from him and/or a family life. The man will be a better listener to his parishioners, if he knows what other families are going through, because he also was worrying about his wife and children and going through, possibly, the same problems. The Catholic Church has an agenda in refusing to allow men to marry. Tradition is no excuse for the modern world and how a church should evolve for the people believing in that religion. The

Church must think that the money the men bring into the coffers would be mishandled if a woman were around. The reasons priests don't marry have been written into the vows a man takes to become a priest. I believe those vows should be re-thought. Now, in the 21st century, men should be allowed to marry. I am positive; I am not the only person who thinks priests should marry.}

Man #9

This was another lawyer who saw people at his office in one of the sky rises in San Francisco. He was very good looking and I saw him first, before I would send anyone to see him, because of the location where his office was. I never knew what was going to happen in a sky-high, high-rise.

Cannot say a great deal about him because he had a well-known family name and why I bring him up is just to state that we went to the tall buildings in the city. The escorts had to dress as women would dress who worked in offices during the day. Always---the impression to give when stepping into one of these business areas was that we belonged. He did surprise me by calling several times over a year to see women. Perhaps he was newly single or just shying away from any commitment. Because of his good looks, he really did not need to be phoning an escort service for women, so I would go with my first inclination that he may be just a man not desiring a commitment.

Man #10

Mr. Banker: Cannot say where this man was living in a 200 mile area from where we had our main office, because he owned a bank and had thousands of acres in his county. He is one client I did not check to see if he was deceased yet. He liked or loved the power he could garner through his money. He may have had money but "jerk" is the only word I remember calling him.

Mr. Banker also liked going to cheap hotels/motels and watching pornography or possibly meeting up with other couples in the hot tub areas. I considered him a borderline freak. This is the type of man who could be in a room next to a truck driver or hooker and put a glass up to the wall and listen; and he wanted the rooms with the mirrors on the ceilings, so he could look at what was happening between him and the woman; who he always wanted on top of him.

I went out with him a couple of times but preferred to send other women to see him. He insisted on going to some motel in Oakland that had porno films playing in every room. Seedy places to meet where his distasteful thoughts could melt in with the scenery.

The rooms of the cheap motels he rented, were consistently dark, dingy, and with red paint on the walls. Those misty mirrors on the ceilings in some rooms completed the picture of cheap sex; even though we charged him top dollar for his kinky ways; each woman felt cheap and sleazy after seeing him.

Thankfully, he only called about every three months.

When he did phone, he wanted service and wanted it like yesterday. He demanded a great deal of time, and, I made sure we charged for things such as traveling time, gasoline, etc.

A person would never have thought from the clothes he wore, to the car he drove, that he would ever phone for a woman to see him. His clothes were expensive and immaculate and his car was top of the line. Nothing about what he wore said, "Women, the sleazier, the better." Yet, he loved sleazy women and surroundings for his trysts; for one night or two. For him it was going to the gutter to phoning an escort service, and yet not all the way to the gutter, because he would not think of picking up a street-walker.

He preferred classy women and wanted them to dress well, yet he would bring them to raunchy hotels/motels. He just had odd behavior. We took his checks if he wanted the person to stay longer; he always paid in cash; especially with a woman he was meeting for the first time. The checks, he had, revealed who he was, and he did not want any of the escorts to know his real name.

The first woman I sent to him was an escort, who was going to live and work at a nunnery. This must have made his day, to have someone so innocent looking and speaking, dragged off to some creepy sex hotel, he picked.

If I had met him first, I would never have sent her to see him. She just lived closer to him than any other woman at the time, so I sent her. This lovely person only worked for the summer one year, and, I wish that all the customers would have wanted to just go out to dinner or movies when she was ready to work. I never wanted to send her to a creep like this man.

When I saw him we went to a golf area near highway one. We didn't stay there but ate close by. I think he wanted me to know that he could be nice and take a woman to dinner, if he liked the way she was dressed. Afterward, he balked about paying me for going out to dinner with him, because he was paying for the dinner. He did not get the concept that I was escorting him to dinner and that was my job and he had to pay.

Yes, he paid me but with a frown on his face.

I think he was a big baby who was use to getting his way, all the time. I felt sorry for his wife and children. But I charged him mileage and had a minimum due, if I was the one driving to hook up with him. A minimum due to see me, was my way of letting him know that I was special. Just as special as he thought he was. I always received my money from him and I am sure he paid because I knew his real name. I would have not wavered to enter his bank and let everyone there know he owed me money for going out with him.

Man #11

This man was very, very nice, and, very French. He was a top-notch chef and owned his own French restaurant. His home was immaculate and he had a wife but she did not live with him. We never figured that one out. She lived in another state. Women sent to him said he was always cooking for the escort, and he would usually have the person to his home for a few hours; just a very nice gentleman. Mr. Frenchman was also good looking. Very good-looking man and I liked going over to see him but I was not his "type" he wanted or liked women with dark hair.

Sex was not the only reason he was phoning. Mr. Frenchman enjoyed the company of the person sent. He loved to discuss his family, his restaurant, and food with wine. The time I spent with him was so enjoyable; he was truly one of the best clients we ever had. He phoned for possibly a year and a half. Each woman sent to him had to wear garter belts; this was his only request. He loved the look of women in stockings.
I was sad to know he left the area and move to another state. He sold his restaurant and opened one in the state he moved too. He is remembered calling me a few times just to keep in touch but eventually those calls faded.

Side Comment:
{Many men who are married to a person with blonde hair like to see a woman with dark hair or even dark skin; this is just how men are. Maybe the same hair color bothers them or they think about their "one and only" love; which can be distracting … if he is having a fantasy. And most if not all men are into "fantasy" play and that is why the porno magazines do so well. Everything is in the mind.}

Man #12

This guy loved seeing women who were escorts. He was a business man who phoned all the services and that troubled me. I would try to make sure and have someone available for him but he had a strong appetite for women. At times he was doing drugs and when he got on a 'roll' he would phone for women; sometimes one woman right after the other; just about a line-up would make him happy. His love of alcohol out did his love for women or even his business. His father had money and their family name was well-known in the Bay Area.

After a few years of his seeing my escorts he telephoned me one night a little perplexed. The very first time I ever heard him so serious. The news was full of the killings of some escorts and how this policeman or ex-policeman had an escort service with an attorney. I had not sent someone to this person who Man #12 knew and, he had used this guy's escort service.

He questioned me as to why I never sent a woman to this man's address or even liked his telephone number to phone my service; I was usually rude to the guy. I wondered for a second or two how he knew that I did not send someone to the man. Then just pushed that thought out of my mind. Because he used so many other escort services, Man #12 probably had heard from someone; that I never would send anyone to this other escort service owner when he phoned for women. I knew something was wrong with the man calling. Flat-up right. The vibes on the other end of the telephone when the man phoned were straight out of some chainsaw movie. Damn straight there was something wrong with him and his buddy. They were killing women in some warehouse after torturing the women.

The women killed had been strung-up and horribly treated until they died. Luckily I was correct about not giving out the call to one, or any of my escorts.

The client was amazed that I knew not to send someone to this guy.

I wasn't amazed.

I was just doing my job ---- keeping my escorts safe.

I never heard from him after that phone inquiry. Maybe he wanted to stay clear of escort services and possibly the murders sobered him up. And now when looking back over our conversation; maybe he had more to do with this guy than he let on; but that is none of my business. He never phoned my service, again.

Man #13

This was another Chef who lived in San Francisco. He was in a home that he recently purchased. This man made very good money as a Chef. He was overweight and self-conscious about it. I went to see him a couple of times but mostly sent other women to him.

He would phone after working a long night and it was usually after midnight when he wanted someone to come over. He liked the service and enjoyed a good massage.

Massaging large men takes energy. The time of night when he was calling for a woman, made it was very difficult to drag myself out to see him, or even phone someone else to see him. The women who massaged were not always available after midnight. There were only a couple of other women working that massaged, and, had their licenses, so he had to wait until daytime sometimes and that was the best I could do for him because he wanted a massage. The other women did not want to massage after midnight.

Men, who are Chefs, are very fond of their mouths or chewing and eating. They have an oral fixation. He loved eating a woman and making her come to climax. If a woman is very tired from working all night or not getting enough rest, well one escort told me she fell asleep during his chomping. She was laughing and said he took it all in stride. He always had a little bag of food he made for the escort, so she could savor his food at her home. This was thoughtful of him to do for the escorts and masseuses.

He eventually moved to Nevada because he kept having issues with owners of restaurants he worked for and possibly it was because he was very overweight. Maybe it was because he was a perfectionist at his work.

I ate some of his food and it was delicious.

I use to joke with him, if I ever had a "cat" house, I would hire him to be the Chef. He was up for that work. After he moved we never heard from him again except one telephone call to tell me where he was working.

Maybe I should have phoned him just to say hi; but I was always so busy. I wished him well. He was truly a nice person. Not a bit judgmental about working girls or escorts.

Man #14

Every escort service gets one or two "sickos". My meaning here is by societies' standards a person is mentally ill or has sexual thoughts that go out of the normal as to what society accepts.

We had this guy that cannot be called anything else but Mr. Pervert. He was sick. I mean sick. The first time I went to see him I just about laughed myself wet. He wanted me to dress up in this maid's costume and pretend to be flirting with him. The costume was ridiculous and the vision of me pretending to dust was even worse. This was just the beginning of his thoughts and dressing as a maid was not sick.

Many couples use a maid costume routine for their sex-play.

I saw him a few times before I understood his problem.

He lived in an apartment complex that was nice but not over the top. There was one bedroom and the usual living room and bathroom and kitchen. That was normal too. Then he decides to confess to me the truth about himself. He liked little girls and knew he had a problem. He confessed that his daughter was a victim and there had been other victims.

Well, I have strong feelings about men hurting little girls. But what was I to do? He had chosen a time to tell me when it was close to a holiday and there would be more children in the area of his apartment, and, he was concerned that he would take one and do something to her.

When I looked at him … inside my head, I was killing him. His thoughts about children were hurting my ears and my soul. My feelings almost got the best of me, but I realized that he was phoning the escort service so he did not act on his sick thoughts. And maybe he was lying so we would always send an escort to him.

He was old and perhaps the confession was good for his soul.

What did I do? I pretended to be young for him.

Yes, I had to pretend to be young.

Also, any other woman who saw him after me was told about his problem and she could make the decision to "play young" and keep the children safe from him.

One time he phoned and it was Halloween. Many people have parties in the Bay Area on Halloween night and the escorts were scarce. He made it clear that he was on the verge of taking a child who may came to his door for Trick-or-Treat. He sounded serious and I did not think it a ploy to get someone over to see him. Yep. I had to go because nobody else was available. I would not let him be without seeing someone.

When I arrived, I still had thoughts of just shooting him or something. He revolted me, but killing scum like him would not do my own soul any good. I kept him away from the door that night, so he could not even look at children.

I was there long enough, that he got tired and was going to bed as I was leaving. He must have known I was upset with his craving a child. That may have been the last time he phoned. It was definitely the last time I saw him. And as I said, he was old.

Maybe, just maybe, God did him a favor and allowed him to die.

Man #15

Nothing like a drunken guy who has a very important job; airport traffic controller and a person who guides planes into the landing phase of the trip; telling pilots it is safe to land and take-off. He was always a fall-down drunk when he phoned for someone to come over and keep him company.

Maybe he was phoning, so there was someone there to protect him from himself. I was amazed that he held down the job, he did, and for as long as he did. Eventually, President Reagan fired these workers across the country, because of a strike and they were public workers, which meant they were not able to strike, so he fired them. He was one of the men fired at that time. His phone calls stopped, but not after a few long nights of him being upset with the entire situation. He gave me the entire "scoop" on how the other people felt about being fired and at the time, I agreed with him. This did not stop me from flying but when I would fly any commercial plane out of San Francisco airport (before the firing) I would phone him to find out if he was working that day. Just a little added security on my part.

If he was working,

I changed my plans.

Man #16

This customer was older and had never married. He was a person, whom I could not figure out. Now, a television show now called Monk is televised and this man was similar to the lead character on the show Monk.

He was very meticulous about his person and his drawers in his bedroom were in perfect order. He showed them to me to let me know he had order in his life. Odd behavior for a man to think I would love to see his dresser drawers.

I agreed with him that there was order in his life. (As I rolled my eyes and thought about my drawers back home; wondering if I folded everything like he did, if I could squeeze more into mine; just saying he had me thinking.)

Each time he phoned, and, I would send women to him, they were never perfect enough for him. No telling what type of person he wanted to spend his life with, but at the rate he was going there would not be much time left to find someone, given his age, which was about 55 years. He voiced to me that he wanted a wife and trying out escort services was another way for him to find one. (I would disagree, but I never told him that trying to find a wife from an escort service was the preferable way to locate lasting love.)

The house was in San Francisco on a very family oriented street, complete with front lawn that was green and groomed. The inside was neat, but the outside lawn was near perfect.

I thought he wanted a nuns' character with a whore's interest in bed. A little exaggerated for him, but the truth. Some men want the same and will settle for a semblance of love. He was not going to settle for anyone who was not perfect for him. Eventually, he stopped phoning, because he just did not like the increase in fees. I was not going to give him a deal because he was not an easy person to be around. He was very disparaging about paying for services rendered, and from the moment the woman entered his home, he had his eyes on her, as if she were going to steal something if he turned his back to her. What this man did do was introduce me to another man, over the phone, which was a private investigator.

The person was on the tarmac at Jonestown and was fired (guns and bullets) on by some real crazy people. He had been hired to save or bring some of the children out of the settlement that Jim Jones had brought people to in Guyana. Many people died that day and this man was still psychologically involved with what had happened. He told me a few details that were not in the newspaper and it sounded bad. Eventually, he brought me to Charles Garry, an attorney in San Francisco at the time, so Garry could do some legal work for me.

I believe Garry was also there for some reason in Jonestown. That is where their personal bound came from and when you sat in a room with the two of them, there was the incident fresh in their respective minds, as if it had happened just the day before.

This investigator did end up being a boyfriend for awhile and I liked him but he had trouble with some other issues that did not sit well with me. Not to have a long-term relationship. We stopped seeing each other after I declined his many offers of marriage. We did not have a sexual relationship and not sure why not, other than the attraction was not there for me. He is now deceased, or so the news accounts were, that his wife killed him. I was shocked to hear he married, and then married someone who killed him. He was a nice man and I knew why he was this other man's friend. They both were better off not marrying.

In his case I was definitely correct, given his final outcome after marriage.

Man #17

Mr. Mechanical Wand (Mr. Wand) was a professor at the University of California at Berkeley. The day he first phoned was on a Friday and early in the afternoon. He liked to plan his evenings. Being it was a Friday, there was not going to be a woman available until about 7p.m. that night and possibly later. As the boss I decided to take the call rather than lose it. He did not seem too picky as to the type of woman he wanted. I was thankful that he gave me very careful instructions on how to arrive at his home.

The drive over, to his home, was the usual traffic jams and I arrived close to the time that he wanted me to, which was about 7p.m. The house was a very neat and trim one with a long walkway up to the front door. The door was at the end of the right side of a small porch which was painted red. I knocked on the door and rang the doorbell. He answered and smiled at me as he invited me in. I think he was happy that I was not too young.

When inside he offered me something to drink and my beverage of choice was a soda at the time. The house looked as if his wife had just left to go shopping and told him to have a nice time. All the rooms were very neat and clean and many feminine items still all over the house.

While speaking to him, as I sat on his couch; he told me he was a widower and this would be his first time with a woman in many years. (Gee, a virgin, almost. How lucky was I?)

"Well Mr. Wand, what do you do for a living?"

"I am a professor of (blank) at the University." (University of California at Berkeley was the name of his school.)

"How long have you been teaching or should I say profess-ring?" Trying to be cute and get a smile out of him, which I did receive.

"I am a tenured professor."

"Okay, what does that mean?"

"What it means is that they can't fire me."

"Nice position."

After some more small talk we proceeded to the bedroom. He went into the bathroom and then lay down next to me in his bed. I was accustomed to being ready, willing, and able when the man came out of the bathroom, and this time was no different. In negligee I lay upon his bed, ready to give him a massage.

He already had the lotion he wanted me to put on his body, sitting on the nightstand next to the bed.

Then, as he climbed under the covers, I asked him to put a towel down so I could give him a massage. This was always a good beginning to an hour of fun and frolicking. While I was just massaging him a little and kissing him, trying to encourage a little foreplay, the next thing I know, he is doing something to his penis that I never saw a man do before, he is yanking and pulling at his penis and then he turns over and asks me to just lay next to him.

"No problem", I thought. Then, just lay their silently and Mr. Wand continued his pulling and whatever he was doing to all his "family jewels". I was beginning to worry about him. It was like a dog just licking and sucking at his penis and, until raw and, the owner worries what or why the damn dog is doing that to himself. I was now picturing him turning the poor "thing" red and raw and useless.

Finally, I do ask him, "What are you doing?"

Mr. Wand tells me, "I was cranking up my penis."

Immediately, I stop massaging to hear more. Amazing! Never, ever heard that remark before, and, now my mind begins running with many jokes and a big smile or smirk comes over my face. He continues with his story, apparently, trying to stop my mind from thinking up more jokes to tell the girls when I get home.

"Well, you see I spent about $15,000 for this device that makes my penis hard."

"Really, I never heard of such a thing. How do you do it? Is it safe?"

Mr. Wand then proceeded to hold my hand over the area where he was manipulating some sort of lever and I could feel the thing. Never have I been too squeamish about medical devices. This touching him felt odd, all the maneuvering under his skin. He said it was not painful.

(I definitely learned something that night and from a professor.)

After a few cranks, with his nimble fingers, this magical "wand" of his was up. When lying on his back it was easier for him to crank it up. I can fully-state for the record that "it" was "up" the entire time.

Since I had and have been with men who have used the pill Viagra and other pills, which endanger their blood pressure and medical conditions; this "wand" or whatever it was named, is better for a man's health.

{All men considering using pills should look into getting a device implanted.}

The evening went well, and, I left with a smile on my face. As for him, I think it was all a bit much for him. He was not over his wife's death and seeing another woman, whether for money or not, was a kind of betrayal to her memory. He may have phoned another time but he never turned into a regular client.

Although, I have to say he gave me a great story ... forever.

Man #18

This man was a real life doctor. I liked the man but he was very fragile. He phoned many nights and I sent him many women. I went to see him a couple of times but he was more interested in the younger women working for me. It was always difficult to fool a medical doctor about a woman's age, including my own age. Many people then and now do not believe my age as older than what they think I am. There "thing", so to speak. Not mine. I feel over 100 years most of the time.

He had just been diagnosed with a terminal illness and was very weak. His work week was shortened and ultimately he stopped working as a doctor. The home he lived in was in San Francisco and was small, yet comfortable. It was always dark inside the house and may have been for some reason due to his health. I did not know, nor did I question him about his lifestyle. He was so reserved and probably was a good doctor; definitely, he was well-educated. I enjoyed speaking to him.

Unfortunately, you could feel his pain on the telephone. The pain was evident in his speech pattern that was slow and a soft voice. When I went over there, he was just so very quiet. His eyes always had a faraway look to them and they just appeared to be vacant of life.

His ethics were always in place.

Many of the medications he had --- he would not give to anyone. They were for him only. But he would buy some illegal cocaine for the women. His phoning the escort service went on for less than a year and then he stopped phoning. I assumed he died. But for a few months time he was able to see some very terrific women and have some semblance of a life. Because he was a younger doctor I believe he had been studying all his life and now he was coming to the end of his young life; a life that had never experienced a great deal of fun with women or for that matter, people. And no --- the illness was not Acquired Immune Deficiency Syndrome (AIDS). I liked him and, so did the women I sent to him.

Man #19

Paul was a person who loved watching MTV when the person arrived at his home. His eyes never left the television except for a few moments of "tender care" from one of the escorts. He was over 6'3" tall and his body was slender. His face showed some wrinkles and he owned his own business, which had something to do with construction, but he was more of a white collar client at this point in his life. He was doing less of the hard work and was more the paper pushing person now. Making sure his men were working.

Paul always phoned after or close to midnight. He was one of those men who wanted to have or be with a woman before he went to sleep. But there were still the drugs he was using to stay awake, so his lifestyle of using drugs with the escorts made little sense. If you want a woman so you can sleep, then why use drugs to stay awake? His bed was a waterbed and looked to be king-sized.

Paul did not cater much to the escort by offering drinks or drugs to her, but he did have more money to give the girl, if he wanted her for more than an hour. A woman coming to his place after midnight seemed to be just part of some game he was playing. Most probably thinking to him, "I am in control of her and her actions. No marriage, just me and her and whatever I want to do." That was all my fantasy thoughts that he could be having.

This was an easy client to be with and all he wanted was to hold the woman and possibly have some sex. Not always sex, because he was not able to function well for some reason. (Dah, drugs, maybe?) His back always hurt and his nose was red from doing the drugs. He liked the escort to watch MTV with him; similar to going out to the movies, except you were in his home.

Paul lived with an older son and he was funny by asking the escort/s not to make any noise and more or less tip-toe through his home to his bedroom.

The lights in his room were always low or not on.

The entire house looked as if a woman had not lived there in years. Little home improvement projects were scattered all over the place and you wondered where he got his money from, because he phoned almost nightly. His business must have done well for his pocketbook.

Paul's mind was indifferent to the escort, but not rude. He liked women but did not want to involve himself again with just one woman. He appeared to be hurting, emotionally, over some past romance. If anything, he was consistent in phoning for an escort and what we knew of him was little. He did not like a lot of conversation.

When the service ended, he was still phoning to see someone and did not seem to care if the service ended or not. This was a strange man; but a safe man, to send women too.

Man #20

Jerk, bastard, creep, self-entitled, ghastly man; who felt any woman coming to see him should come for free. Harvey owned a lot of commercial property in San Francisco and elsewhere. He liked flaunting his wealth. I think this is because he probably grew up without any money. He reminded me of a sewer rat that made good. (No offence to sewer rats.)

I saw him and I had sent women to him. He always wanted to write a check. Yes, he was someone who loved having me call him and tell him, "The check is no good." Then he would say, "Just put it back in, it will be good." My response always was, "Why wasn't it good the first time?" I was just perplexed why he wanted to play this stupid game with us. He would say, "I wasn't sure the girl would be okay." Sometimes he would say, "My accountant made a mistake." He had excuses for every time a check would not go through. The last person to see him was me and, yes, I still hold a bad check from him. The account was one he closed. He just wanted to be a jerk. I have no idea why he would do this to us and if I did not think I would be sued, yes, I would put his name in this book.

Man #21

Ride-um cowboy was a man from the state of Washington. He had phoned the escort service to have a woman go with him on a trip to Mexico. He is very clear that his aunt will be going with them and everything is all on the up and up. Translation, the girl will be just fine. He only wants a companion on a trip. I explain to him that it will cost him money for everyday and he has to pay in advance. Plus, he has to give the girl a round trip ticket. When the girl sees him she will ask for his driver's license and I will have her read the numbers and relevant information about him, to me, before she boards the plane. He agrees to everything and the date is arranged with Jeannine. She is a tall blonde and that is the type of woman he asked to phone him.

Everything goes well and they stay in Mexico a few days and have a wonderful time. When Jeannine gets back she clues me in to how everything went. In public all was well, and in the bedroom he would ask permission to have sex with her. She said he would say,

"May I mount you now?"

We both laughed at her being a horse.

They went on a few trips together and she even traveled to his home to see him. I suspect she saw him without telling me a few times. That would be after she felt safe with him. I guess he was more of a teddy bear than an angry horse.

Mr. Cowboy was an older man about in his fifties. His money came from the lumber business.

Man #22

Trying to get your fee out of some guys was, painstakingly, time consuming; and then you do the song and dance they want and they give you what they do for a living. The creative guys wanted you to think "all" they did, in their craft, was perfect and people would just die for the chance to be with them or have their merchandise.

In this case, Mr. Photographer did have some great stuff. He was a rock and roll photographer that had taken outstanding pictures of some of the greatest talents during the 60s and 70s. I saw him in the late 70s, I think it was and I was given a signed photo of Janis Joplin. He gave me a choice of her or Jimmy Hendrix. I liked the photo of Janis, so I accepted it for payment. It is a black and white photo and she was so colorful, I was surprised the picture was not in color. But I guess he liked black and white, or from what I remember him telling me, he preferred to do black and white photos. After all this time I forgot the "why" he had that preference. We had done some "coke" together and he wanted to pay me in a check for my time. I did not believe the check would be good, so the unframed and signed picture was the next best thing. Rather than leave his place without anything.

The next time I saw him, I took the check he offered for payment and it was no good, but he did make sure it went through the bank, okay, after I told him I would send someone over to collect.

I liked this man because he had documented artists when they were just getting started. His "eye" with the help of his lens was perfect. He was not too great to look at and when he was "high" he was awful and just could not keep his mind on anything for very long. Everything in his life was put in fast forward. He shared information about his photos with me and told me the signed ones would be worth something someday. Recently I heard he had died. I hope he was happy before he went to meet his "maker".

I had sent him other women and the women would have to drive him to an ATM for their money. No more checks from him. Now I wonder if the photo he gave me for payment is worth anything. I had it professionally framed the year I saw him and it is still a picture I like.

Chapter Three
Blue Collar Men

The Blue Collar guys were the funniest men who phoned the service. You, the reader, know these guys. The ones in the bar that say they will never pay for "it." The guys that go home alone after being out with the boys all night and phone the escort service after their friends leave. Or better yet the ones that phone when their friends are nearby to have some protection for themselves, because they are not sure the woman or women coming over will be to their liking; and if not, they have comrades to joke around and say that the women or woman is not to their liking.

These are the guys at the bar that tell everyone they don't care about picking up any woman because they have someone already setup to be there when he arrives home. Yeah. He made the call to me halfway through the night because he knew "scoring" that night was just not going to happen for him, but his "horns" got up and he needed to see a woman.

Thus, he calls *Professional Escorts.*

Usually, when a Blue Collar man phoned, he was alone. Very alone --- the wife or girlfriend had hit the road and he was ready to drink himself or drug himself into oblivion and, he wanted company. No problem. The escort service sent him a woman to talk to and possibly hold. Some of these men were so nice you just wanted to wrap them up and bring them to your home and take care of them. All were judgmental about phoning for an escort. It was going to hurt their pocketbooks and that is why they resisted, so much, to say anything nice to their friends about making the call for women.

Phoning for an escort was used as a "last resort" by these men.

The man did not want to phone and pay for a woman. He was always opinionated about why women would want to charge. Primarily he thought women in the business of charging were stupid. He had little respect for the woman he was paying. But damn, he always remembered the number. On the other hand, he did phone the service with such regularity, that the service was able to count on him for revenue.

Count on him we did; and the service was able to send a new girl to this type of client when we needed the money. His mind was confused, yet he found the money and time to phone us. Yes, he was, frequently, polite to the woman. But he was conflicted. Normally, he would make use of his time with the escort, speaking ill of his wife or girlfriend. Secretly, thinking the ex-wife should get a job like the woman in front of him, that way he wouldn't have to pay so much support to her. I actually had more than one man say those very words to me. "My wife should be doing this."

If the man was drunk, it was even worse. Many times this man would want to write a check; because he knew when he sobered up he could call the bank and make sure the check did not go through. We were ready for that type of rude behavior and childish antics.

Many of the white collar men had blue collar mentalities; possibly because those men had come up the chain of command by first having blue collar jobs.

Cheating on their wives was all part of some rite of passage which was earned. The men phoning were, numerous times, partying at some bachelor party. The party was over and the guy had been worked up by the X-rated movies watched or, there was a stripper and only the future groom got her; so the other gents from the party had to phone an escort service. Maybe, by a dare being made from the other members at the party; but no matter how the person was prompted to call, he did call, the phone rang and they better have the cash. I was always clear that the women wanted cash. You could hear it in their voices. All the men sounded drunk from the party and, these guys always sounded like they were ordering pizza when they phoned the service.

"Send one over. Send one over now."

"Now? Who are you?"

"I'm the guy that has the money. Send a blonde over and make sure she has some tits."

"If you are going to speak that way, I will not send anyone over." Then I would hang up the telephone. The phone would ring again.

"Hello."

"Did you hang up on me?"

"Yes."

"Why?" Perplexed that any woman charging, would have the nerve to hang up on some possible "big time" money.

"Because of your mouth; if you want to speak right, I may be able to talk with you."

"What?"

"You know, no saying tits and stuff like that."

"Oh. Well anyway, send me a girl over."

"Where are you located?"

"Hey, Charlie! Where the hell is this place?"

"Look, when you get to your home, call me back. And make sure you stop at the ATM, so you have cash. Cash only!" And I'd hang up again.

Believe it or not, the guy would phone back when he got home. The first thing out of his mouth would be that he had the cash in hand. Some girlfriend or wife had trained the guy already and I was just refreshing his memory as to how the game was played. Money for playtime; there was no other way to chase the "tail" he wanted.

Then, I would make sure he was not too drunk. Because if he was too slobbery, we ran the chance of him being asleep when the girl got there; and he would not be able to answer the door. Provided he could sound like he was going to be awake and there was a woman close to his place, I would then call her and she, in turn, phoned him to see if she even wanted to take the risk of going to see the man. Many of these guys would say,

"The door will be open, just come on in."

"No, you have to answer the door."

If we knew the guy, maybe the woman would open the door and go inside. But, I did not want any person flipping out on someone entering his home, especially if the guy was waking up with a mini-hangover.

Most times everything worked out just fine. There were rare instances when the guy would be asleep when the girl arrived or he would forget he phoned and then there were the men who could not count. The guy could be short a $20 or $10 dollar bill. Not usually a large number, but I always had the woman get a check for what money was missing, and with the usual threats if the check was to turn out to be bad; and threats, such as, "we have some big bad collectors who have no problem coming to your place of work."

That reminds me of one time a guy with a blue collar mentality that had a job as a white collar guy. For the purposes of this book, we will make him the first blue collar guy to speak about.

I also wanted to say that many blue collar men would have un-cashed payroll checks in or on top of their dressers. I actually saw those checks because the men who had them wanted me to know that they could afford the service. The customer would pull the stack of checks out to show me. I could not understand why the men would live in dumps and have enough money to move or, the very least, buy some descent furniture. These guys were head scratchers for me. All I wanted to do was scratch my head and drive them to a bank to deposit the checks. One or two of them needed to sign a check or two over to me.

Man #1

Ah, this man was a "pretty boy" and felt he did not have to pay for the escort. He was the typical man, who considered in his dreary life that he was God's "gift" to the human race and especially women. Mr. Stockbroker worked for a very well-known brokerage in San Francisco. The office was in one of the newer buildings in San Francisco and the people working there were very conscious of how they dressed. Mr. Stockbroker phoned one evening late and I decided to go see him. His arrogance was all over his personality and general attitude. Yet, he had no problem ravaging my body. His hands and face were slobbering around and over my body. Finally, the couple of hours were over with and, I left with a check in hand because I thought it would be good considering where he lived in Marin County and the job he had. Nice home usually meant he had the money in the bank and did not want any trouble over a bad check.

Let's get back to his job.

Stockbrokers take other people's money and invest in the 'market' on Wall Street, and most of the people working as stockbrokers think fast and would like their clients to believe that they are in a position to know where to put your money in the 'market' to make money.

These are the high-finance gamblers of the 'market' universe.

They can do no wrong, according to them. My feelings are, that putting your money on a black jack table or a craps table is just as good. The money may go faster, but at least you had a little fun putting the money down.

The Wall Street guys have all the fun and the money lost or gained takes longer to win or lose. Either way, the money is not in the person's bank account or under the mattress at home. Where the money is, a lot safer and free of the greed these 'animals' have to devour everything you have worked hard in life to acquire.

The next day after seeing this white collar guy with a blue collar mentality, I went to the bank. Go figure. The check was bad.

Well, I have always had a few tricks up my sleeve.

The moron had given me his business card to make sure I took the worthless check and, also. In case I wanted to be a client. Or see him on the side … not by phoning the escort service.

This was usual talk coming from most guys, but when it was the owner the person was speaking to, this owner disliked the person from day one. Trying to get around the service was a no, no.

I went to my clothes closet and took out a short skirt and went to my dresser and took out some black fishnet stockings, then slipped on a pair of stiletto-heeled shoes. Stopping ever so briefly at the bathroom and exaggerated my makeup with plenty eye penciling and huge amounts of mascara. Darkened my lips with the reddest lipstick found in my makeup bag.

Then the top; I am very busty, so I put on a blouse that dipped rather low in front and enough to show off all my cleavage. Yes, I looked like a streetwalker and finished the look with some gum, found in my purse and promptly put in my mouth. I took another look in my floor length mirror and was sure the "look" was sufficient to get my money from this swindler. Got into my car and was off to his place of work, with the check in hand. I had phoned and found out he was at lunch. Thinking, "With any luck, I could arrive just as he was coming back from lunch." When I got to the building, rather than park in the garage, where I would have had to pay; I took a chance and parked illegally in front of the building.

After all, I was just going to be a minute.

I walked to the front area of the lobby, where the receptionist sat behind a curved desk and slithered up to her. She was nice looking and dressed in the usual basic office-wear. This "costume" of hers consisted of a suit and a teddy partly showing under her white blouse. Just enough cleavage to say, "I am available," but you better take her to dinner first.

There were windows everywhere.

This major brokerage house was on the street side of the huge building and there were many people coming and going, because this was the first floor and everyone had to walk past all the glass doors, to get to the elevators.

When I approached this receptionist, the girl's eyes went from smiling to huge as she looked me up and down. Then I went in for the kill, so to speak. I asked if so and so was in and kept speaking as I drew the check out of my messy purse with other small papers flying out on the well-waxed and shiny marble floor. I could tell she knew him and he must have put his best moves on her in the past. I picked up some of the papers that fell on the floor, making sure I bent over, so all people coming and going could see my bountiful ass and almost glance at my underwear as I picked up each paper, individually.

Then, after popping back up to face the girl, I explained very loudly that he had given me a check and it wasn't any good. Now, I wanted to see him and I wanted my money. Further explaining, that I had done my work and he should make the check good. She was flustered. Her eyes were looking all around for some help and security began to move closer to us. People were now looking in our direction and, just about then, he walked in through the front door, from lunch, with a couple of fellow stockbrokers. His eyes were worth the drive to the city from Marin County. He was mortified and I was smirking at him.

He signaled security off; that he had the situation under control.

I showed him the check and he just about began to stutter in order to let me know he would take care of the check. He told me to go home and, he would call the bank and, I could go into the bank in Marin and the money would be there. I smiled, as he showed me the door and by now all the people were looking our way.

I made sure the conversation was heard by all.

Then, to top it off, as we got to the door I said, "I need gas money or I will have to wait here until you get off work." He just about died as he reached into his pocket and just gave me all the cash he had on him. I smiled and under my breath told him, "This check better be good or I will bring more girls with me tomorrow and they will be dressed the same way."

He said, "Yes, yes, the check will be good. Good bye." As he pushed me out of the front door. By the time I arrived in Marin County and arrived at his bank, the check was good. He even phoned me, to make sure that I got my money. I told him he better never make that mistake again. He was more like a puppy then, and, agreed he had made a mistake.

Gee I loved my business.

Sometimes guts or intestinal fortitude is all we had. People like this man would try to get "over" on us. He probably believed he was better than me and all the women working at the escort service. He was wrong and underestimated this working woman.

Man #2

Well, I will call this man the swimmer. He was a construction guy that lived in Marin County and, worked for the family business. His father owned the business but this son of his was the only boy and, would eventually take over for his father. He normally phoned at night, when he was so drunk he could barely speak. I saw him first, but decided that other women would be better to send to him when his calls came in, in the future.

Many times I went first to a call, just to make sure the client was safe and, also, to make sure that I even wanted him as a client.

The decision was made by me, that he could phone us and I would send women to see him.

Many times #2 would write a check and these checks were always good. But mostly he gave the women cash. There was an accountant who worked for the business and did his books too, so he did not want the accountant knowing how he spent his money. Some of his habits were using drugs when he paid for escorts. Most, if not all, drug dealers want cash, as do escorts.

The swimmer had phoned my service for a few years and I got to know him and more importantly, I knew his voice. When clients phoned they enjoyed the fact that I knew them by just hearing their voice and, I could recite back their telephone numbers, for them, and, sometimes addresses. Many people thought I had a computer next to me and, that was not what I had. It was just me trying to get my memory back from the bad car accident I had in 1976. I memorized all that I could, just to improve my own mind. This included phone numbers, likes and dislikes of clients, and voices. I was better than any electronic device for voice recognition.

Over the years Mr. Swimmer liked a few of the escorts and played it straight about phoning just my service, rather than call all the other services.

He had enjoyed a great many of the escorts. It was surprising when one day an escort phoned me and asked me if I had read the newspaper. I was way too busy to read the news. In one section of the paper there was a news clip about Mr. Swimmer marrying, and we joked about how short a time it would be before he began phoning again. "Once a customer, always a customer," was a saying I used quite a bit. Next scene, the happy newlyweds went on their honeymoon. The newspaper wrote the couple was scheduled to take a cruise. I thought that would be nice for him because I know he was having financial trouble and I thought it a bit odd that he even married. He had phoned telling me about his dilemmas and maybe there was IRS involvement too. Can't remember all the issues, but there were issues. About a week later, the same escort phoned me and said, "You've got to see the paper. He's dead."

I said, "Are you kidding?"

Because he drank so much, most people did not think much about him falling overboard on his honeymoon and he was not found. Well, I told the escort that, with all his problems, maybe this was not such a bad thing." Then I thought better of what I had said to her, and told her, "We should say a prayer or have a drink for him, maybe both."

I put the news and this man to rest in my mind; another customer gone and lost revenue. A few months go by and, late at night a man phones and asks for an escort. It was him. I did not call him on it, but it was his voice. If I knew anything I knew voices. I sent him a girl, one who was new and she just described the same guy.

"Did we read the newspaper wrong? Was the paper wrong?"
I had no idea. But this man gave a different name, and he was living in a different town, in Marin County, but I knew it was him. Same requirement for an escort, as to appearance; but mainly it was the avoidance to speak to me for long or ask too many questions, that made it obvious, it was him and, he was trying to avoid my knowing it was him. Same drunk voice and I am sure it was him. Mr. Swimmer is what I call him now. Either he swam away from the boat or he did not get back on the boat from a port of call. I never told anyone about this man and am still a mystery for me; but I know I am right. The Swimmer phoned one or two times after he returned to the area.

Man #3

Mr. Glass-man was a guy that seemed to be doing well putting in glass windows at businesses and homes. No telling how much he was making but he was blue collar all the way. I saw him a few times, but mostly I sent other women to see him. His appearance, for a description, was, he usually wore work clothes when he called; and those clothes had his company name on the front and back of the shirt. I am sure he had a wife, so we saw him in the daytime when she was out of the house. Yes, he was one of the guys who wanted you to come to his home. There isn't much to say about him, other than he was a nice run-of-the-mill type of guy. Typical of the man working, who finds time to be at home in the middle of the day and wants to see an escort, while the wife is out of the house. No real kinky thoughts, just wanted to be with someone other than his wife.

Years after he stopped phoning the service, one of my sons crashed into a truck of his and the truck was at fault. My son settled and probably never knew the guy who owned the business was or had been a client.

Man #4

Most people would not think that the Mafia or Organized Crime guys were on the West Coast. Well, they are and, or were. Let us call this guy Homer. He was big and round and must have been at least 6'5" tall. A large boned man and his belly was always full of something and he smelled from garlic. Homer had black hair and olive skin color and his face was pitted.

Forgot how I met him, but I did meet him when I had my massage service; he knew about my service and he wanted to use the service. I saw him and I sent other escorts to see him. Meeting him was always at various hotels in San Francisco or a little motel in Marin that was once owned by the Mafia.

One night he phones and asks me to go into the city (San Francisco) with him. I had nothing to do, so I said I would meet him at some cocktail lounge in the city. That changed and he picked me up at my house. I do remember him picking me up at my house each time we went out. He always paid me for my time. Getting into bed with him was like … my eyes and hands were rolling around looking under the sheets trying to find the pizza he had to have stashed somewhere. He always had the odor of food on him.

There was this one weekend that stood out from the other times we had been together. This time I met him in the city. When I arrived at the lounge there were two other men with him and one was a man I use to call my cousin; because of some heritage we had back in Europe.

Homer had some work to do and 'my cousin' was going to meet up with us later. Homer told me after 'cousin' left that he had to pick up some money. I thought it was a little strange that he and this other "bodyguard" type guy wanted me to go along. We all got into the large Cadillac Homer owned and drove to North Beach in San Francisco. When we got there, he parked at this Italian restaurant parking area and we all got out of the car to walk down the street; which was still all right with me. The other man I just met and he had a gun with holster under his jacket. Still I didn't think too much of anything. I was enjoying all the lights and the walk.

We kept walking down the street and going into the strip places and everyone would come over and smile at us and look me up and down. One place I went into the bathroom and a dancer came in and questioned me about how long I knew Homer and other questions. I was very good at being dumb and answered with a 'bubble gum mind' statement. Could have been, "A friend introduced us."

I met a well-known "plastic boob's" dancer that night and thought her breasts looked terrible. They were blue. She was some big attraction on that Broadway strip; too much surgery. From that place we went to another and another place (bars) until we had walked the entire area.

This was in the '70s and there was plenty of action going on down Broadway Street. After we were finished going from place to place Homer went in someplace by himself to use the bathroom.

The man with him stayed with me and asked me if I knew what was going on. Of course, I didn't, and I told him so; then he told me that he was the bodyguard and all the cash from each place that Homer had to collect from was now in the trunk of the car.

Dumb I was and I just looked at him. He was trying to impress me and this did the job. Homer came out of the club and we left. I wasn't asked to go anywhere that night with him or to a hotel. I suppose that night was just so I would know who the hell Homer was and what he was doing there.

Possibly to give him some semblance of life with a woman or girlfriend; or better yet to have the women in those clubs know that he could get a nice looking woman who was not dancing. He did pay me for my time.

(The 'cousin' spoken of here was driving a Rolls Royce and lived quite well in Marin County. Eventually he was arrested by the IRS and he called me to confide in, because his wife was very naïve and had no idea how much trouble he was in at the time.)

Eventually, with the passage of time, I never saw any of these men again. I often wonder how long this went on and how much money he collected. "My Cousin" did tell me the man died and that is why this little story can be told.

Man #5

Loved this guy, he was from Italy. My little Italian friend, we shall call Fred. He lived in San Mateo and phoned for years. Fred was about 5'6" tall with black hair and black eyes. His skin was olive toned and he was a very average looking man. Fred was an engineer, but goes in this Blue Collar category because he disliked white shirts. Fred liked coming home and working on his projects that were here and there, in his small living room. Some projects involved aluminum cans and were strung on the walls. The house he had bought, years before, was basic sparse and austere and had, it seemed, used furniture in it. Not a great deal of any furniture and definitely no high-end pieces. Some large flat piece of wood was in the living room area and could be used to put a train set on or some other device that moved on the flat wood.

His mother was still living in Italy and would never leave there to come and live in the United States. Every now and then she visited, but as time went by Fred had to travel there for visits. He spoke of his mother with a great deal of respect and when she died I know he was unhappy. He sent money back to her for years. He was an interesting man and I know he kept financial care of his mother in Italy. His heart was in the right place. And he was a pleasure to have as a client.

While Fred used the service, I never heard of him being drunk when he phoned and using drugs was out of the question for him. He was a quiet and reclusive type person and the only expense he ever had was seeing women from escort or massage services. I don't remember him ever telling me he had a date with a woman for dinner. A woman, who was not working for an escort service or any other woman for that matter; he just liked to tinker with his projects and was a steady worker for a company as a mechanical engineer.

When he saw that I was hiring men to work as escorts --- well he volunteered, just as many clients, occasionally, asked; but I never asked them to be paid escorts, it would have changed the arrangement and I liked the clients to be the ones paying. If Fred had male friends, I was never told of them. He liked speaking to me and the conversations were not long. Just how are you doing? What is going on with you? Never anything to say about any other person; except he would tell me if I could trust a girl or not and he would say if he liked the girl or not. Occasionally, on holidays, he wanted a girl to come see him and I went one year. He was just the same, nothing fancy for him, not even a dinner that was extra special. Sometimes he would tell me about his job and work. Not many details, just if something was not going too well that week.

This man phoned my service regularly for many years and he never married. Perhaps he is married now, but I doubt it. He preferred phoning for escorts and when I did not have anyone available, he would phone other escort services and this did not bother me. I liked him and liked the fact I could send a girl to him and know she was safe with him. Many times he would see a new girl first. Fred liked being the first client to see a new girl. A girl that had never been seen by anyone else yet and I counted on his opinions. This worked out well for both of us. I got needed information about a new girl and he saw someone who had never worked before. Because he did not pay a great deal, the women were reluctant to go see him. But he was someone they could count upon when they may be broke. I could call him and ask if he wanted to see an escort, usually a girl that needed some cash.

"Safe" is a relative word to what is happening at the time. For all I know he was an ex-hit man from Italy and was hiding out in San Mateo. This was a hugely private man. He never wanted to have a problem. When I was having some police issues he told me about them phoning him and asking questions. I was sure that he did not say anything that the police wanted to hear. Such as the escort service was a front for prostitution or whatever else the police in those days wanted to "call" my escort service, or thought the escort service was. The last thing Fred wanted was to end up in some police case. I know he phoned other services but he liked my service best. He was a great source of information as to what my escorts were like and what other services were doing. You might call him a spy, someone to tell me if the women being sent were loyal or not. He just fell into that position because he enjoyed telling me about the last woman sent to him, and her likes and dislikes in bed and, when meeting him how she came across; if hard or sweet, or trashy. He was always very accurate and that is another reason I kept his fee the same. In a way you might say he worked for *Professional Escorts*.

In the bedroom he was strictly a "missionary" guy.

(Meaning he liked the usual style of having sex; man on top.)

He had first phoned when the rates were less but I allowed him to still pay the smaller hourly fee because he was reliable and safe --- and as long as the woman I sent was okay with the pay for that hourly rate.

Those phone calls to his mother must have put a big dent in his wallet.

I even phoned him after the business was over and he was his usual nice self. A year or so later I phoned and his number was no longer in service. That was sad. It was unusual for him to have a disconnected telephone; and I thought either he went to Italy or Fred was now dead. I often wondered why in those days he was in the United States and so alone. He either died, went back to Italy, married, or moved. Not sure what happened to him.

Man #6

Bus Man was someone from one of the tropical islands, called Hawaii, and a martial arts expert. He stood about 5'7" tall and was stocky. The type of person he "was" made up for any money or wealth he did not have.

Bus Man was always friendly and a kick-boxing enthusiast. He did not have the money to phone and have women visit his apartment in San Francisco. Phoning and seeing someone was a luxury for him. Eventually, we just became friends and he stopped having escorts over to his place.

One time he asked me and another girl to San Francisco for dinner. We met at his apartment and went out from there. The food was very good and at an Asian restaurant in Chinatown. While we were walking down an alley I told him we should stick to the sidewalks to walk for safety reasons. There had been too many muggings in the city. He explained that most people knew who he was and his friends and would not dare to pick a fight with them.

The friends he had were all from the martial arts world in the city. I met a few of them before this night. Over a couple of years our relationship advanced into a strong friendship. He and his friends were bodyguards at one of my parties for me. He was very firm that I should have them there to make sure there were no fights and I was safe. Meekly, I agreed ... but I believed everything would be fine because most of the people coming were quiet people. Not rowdy. Clients able to afford the escort business and some people who just wanted to take a look.

After the party our friendship continued and it was difficult sometimes to tell him when he saw an escort from my service that he had to pay. There were those times when men just did not have the money, but were too nice for us to turn them down and I did not want to hurt his feelings, because phoning for women was a cost he should avoid.

Eventually, I sent him a school teacher who was working and they hit it off. They did get married and I was not invited to the wedding. I believe his wife was jealous of me and she had some issues possibly with people finding out how the two had met. Not that I would have ever told anyone at the wedding. But people, I have found, worry about things and sometimes err to caution, way too much. They would rather be safe than sorry and, not having me there was the solution for them. I never heard from either of them after they married and I thought it was rude of the both of them. These two people had me feeling I was used. They had met because of me, but damn if they would even say thank you.

His wife picked a fight with me the last day I ever saw her and later I figured she did that because she did not want me to know they were getting married.

Truly, shallow people; I was annoyed with him for pretending to be my friend. Once again, the typical blue collar mentality. Not that blue collar is bad, but that judgmental "thing" always seems to come into play. I spoke of his wife briefly in another book and it was because I was surprised at how many clients liked her; given the fact she was one of the least attractive women who ever worked for my escort service.

Man #7

This man I shall call Mr. Hairy. He was anything but hairy. I saw him first and thought there might be something odd about him. Then after watching too many CSI television shows; those programs made me think that maybe he was some sort of maniac; and, he always decided not to do anything to me or the other escorts. The first time I saw him, Mr. Hairy, he was striking to look at and this was not because he was some great looking guy. He had absolutely no hair on his body. None, I mean none. He shaved all the hair off of his head, under arms, legs, arms, back, stomach, and crotch. No hair at all. And he would slick himself down with baby oil. Freaky! And sometimes he would use baby powder on himself or the escort. He must have liked the smell of the powder.

Because I had seen a few men who were odder, I did not think too much about his method of taking care of his body. He told me that he was allergic to hair. Yep. That works. But if I were to see him now…I would be looking for more clues as to why he did not have any hair. He only phoned the service a few times and each escort was amazed as to how he was able to reach his back to shave. His arms were very flexible and able to reach behind himself and abracadabra, a shaved back. Mr. Hairy always saw women at a hotel. No idea where he worked or who he was and when writing about that now, it seems even scarier. When he stopped phoning, I was a little surprised. His appetite for women was just as manic as his shaving ritual. What was even more interesting was the fact the women did not want to speak about him. It was as though that was the way he was, end of story.

I always wondered about him.

Chapter Four
Hit Men

"Being scared is relative to the situation you are in; never will a person hurt you who needs you." D.E.Z. Butler

The mornings were usually quiet for "legitimate" callers wanting escorts. Most people phoning in the early part of the day wanted jobs. By afternoon the customers began their huge flux of phone calls. Then by nightfall, the phone was dancing off the hook. Everyone was calling and all the escorts and clients were ready to get hooked-up.

How the slang "Hit Men" came about, I have no idea. But "hitting" someone on a playground is far different from what real "Hit Men" do. They kill people for money. The movies are full of these men. Some movies even make these men out to be a person you could admire. Really, how the hell do you admire someone who kills for a living? I suppose it is no different than a military person. But, killing is killing, and it is final. Hitting is not killing and it only gives you bruises. If a person is trained to kill ... I still find it difficult to believe that we get the slang "Hit Men" to mean killing.

Why not paid murderer?

The following men knew me and called the service. Did I like them? One I did like and he was a torn man; a man who was conflicted about what he had been doing his entire life. Not some guy who should have been idolized in some movie. A man, just a man and only he was able to look at people as if they were "game" in a cement jungle. A hunter and a thinker, who did not care about any person, not even himself.

Man #1

The business had just begun, and, it must have been the second month when Mr. New York phoned. That would make it about 1977. Perry sounded like the client I had always wanted to phone or hoped would phone the escort service. A customer who was interested in seeing the San Francisco Bay Area sites, a real tourist, and, the reason I had just began the business.

Oh, was I right and wrong about this man.

We decided to meet him at his apartment and discuss where he wanted to go in the area and what he wanted to see. He was living in Tiburon and his apartment was easy to find.

The parking lot backed up to the building and there were many other units in the various buildings, on the hill. His building was set off from the main roadway and the building was quiet. When you entered the unit it was from the back near the parking lot. After entering the apartment, there was a living room on the right and to the left a small eating/dining area attached to the kitchen. You walked down a hallway to the bedroom and the bedroom had a view of the water and all the many buildings or homes in that area. The bathroom was off the hallway too. Nothing else stood out except for the small patio off of the living room. A small, yet efficient, unit and everything a bachelor would want.

Immediately, I was happy that he looked nice and was a gentleman.

Perry told me what he wanted to see in the area and I suggested other places to go. But first things first, he wanted to have a little play time and that is what we did.

This is where it gets interesting.

I liked him.

"Damn this was going to be a problem." I thought.

Here was a guy that looked Italian, but was using a Jewish name. I had no idea why he was doing that, and, I only cared that we could possibly have a relationship and I had only recently begun the business, so I was not that into charging money for my time. Yes, I did charge for the 'massage' he just got, but I was more into making him one of my suitors, rather than keep him as a client. A mistake all working women eventually make and I just had decided to do that and not because he was so great in bed. It was done because I just liked him. Really, I liked the guy and maybe even loved him.

Just blowing caution to the wind; I decided I wanted to be his friend and lover. Although I never stopped charging him for the lover part; it was a little foreign to me not to charge for my time and 'favors'. I still kept my head about me and did charge for the time in bed. This was done because I was unsure of his feelings and I did not want to feel "used."

Together, we went all over the Bay Area and I even let him pick me up at my house, or that is my mother's house. He met my children and was a man who I was incorporating into my life. Usually, with first meetings of clients, I would put my psychic mind on them and visually scan the guy to find out who or what he was and with this man I did not do that until a week or two into the relationship.

When I did the whole "mind" concentration thing about him, I was over his place and sitting on his couch. I held his hand and looked deeply into his eyes and almost jumped back. There it was right in front of me and I had not seen it at first. I was slipping by not doing this "mind" scan over him the first time we met. Wrong! Way wrong!

I should have done this the very first time. Boy was I kicking myself.

His eyes were deep and full of something dark. I began to tell him that his name was not his, he had a different name, that the apartment furniture was rented, and I kept going on and on.

Yes.

Perry was impressed by my accuracy.

I was becoming cautious with him. Not afraid, just cautious, instantly after reading him. He was the man, who, when I went to his car (Mercedes) one time, I backed away and he said, "If it blows, it will get you there too."

I smiled at him and we both knew that I knew something.

After about the fourth month I came over his place and he excused himself and went to the bathroom. I looked around for something to read and saw newspaper clippings on the table in the dining area. Of course, I got up and went over to them to look. All were killings done on the East Coast. Each killing was done a similar way. A way that I cannot tell, even now; it was his "signature."

The stack of newspaper clippings was big and had not seen it in the room before or after. Perry came out of the bathroom and looked at me and then to the stack. He was wondering if I looked. Our eyes met and I told him "yes" with my eyes, but I never mentioned the stack; nor did he ask about the clippings.
He had just let me know who he was and what he did for a living.

A few days later I was on the telephone with him and told him I could tell him his real name. He was already impressed with my abilities and so I began. (I always wanted to impress some people with my psychic talents.) I asked him to think of his name. A little playing with him but also wanted to let him know I could do it. I could tell him his name.

I started with the first letter of his last name. Right! Then the next letter until three or four letters and he told me to stop; he was adamant I stop. He was serious and I stopped. I had just breached some sort of security he had. Mr. New York, my Perry, did not want me to speak about him on the telephone.

After that little show of dominance by me in the psychic game, Perry and I stopped seeing so much of each other. Our relationship was dwindling. He did have me over his apartment a couple of more times; but I knew that --- I knew way too much about him and his dark past was overshadowing our relationship.

We were getting serious.

When in bed I would look into his eyes and he was the coldest man I ever had been in bed with or to have sex with; his eyes looked through me. He was a self-admitted manic-depressive and took pills for the mental condition. He told me that if we had met when he was younger, maybe we could have been together. But his life's path was now formed. There was no room for a family.

Our relationship was over and I was hurt. I could handle what he was, but he could not handle what he was or anything about himself. He was torn.

Mr. New York was at a crossroads in his life. Perry had been raised in the "Little Italy" area of New York and came right out of Canal Street; but his wish for his life was to be different.

Yes, he had regrets.

I believed that about him and at times he told me he wished his life had been different. Maybe it was the way he killed. He had compassion. Perhaps he worried about me and my family if we kept seeing each other. But business is business. Through my hurting I sent him a bill for services rendered while escorting him all around the Bay Area. After all, I was an escort and doing what I had always wanted to do; show tourists the area. He phoned me after he got the bill, which amounted to the thousands. He was laughing. I laughed too. We got over it all and I sent him other women.

But I never saw him again, because we were too 'involved', it would have been more emotional than I wanted or needed.

Some people would wonder why I dare put this man or any man who killed people in this book. I dare because I was not afraid of him or any of them; and this was so long ago, he is no doubt not alive any more. I would be surprised if he were alive. His business did not keep men like him alive.

This was not a "staying alive" type of employment.

Perry was very, very good at what he did and maybe he is still alive. I could be wrong. Alive because he vanished from the area where he did his work or because he was so good at what he did, that those he worked for never came after him. I don't know, but I do know leaving him out of the book would be wrong. He was a client and that is what this book is about. The back of my mind had me fantasizing, at times, that he was my protector. Somewhere and sometime, if I needed him, he would be there.

Just a thought, not something that happened; or did it?

Man #2

Ah, this guy was a real "pretty boy." Very nice looking and someone, who, a person would not believe was a killer. Because of the first hit man I knew, there was an instinctual need for me to always check the men out that I saw. And many times I would see a new client first to make sure the women could be sent to the man, later.

This was another afternoon call by a hit man. He was living in the Contra Costa area and the house was beautiful. The home was on a cul-de-sac and the neighborhood was very quiet. You could hear the birds chirping from the trees when I arrived. Just a picture perfect home and gorgeous looking man.

I pulled into the driveway; got out of the car and walked up to the door. The usual procedure and then the door opened. He had been watching out of the massive front window with the drapes opened. His eyes were a sparkling blue and again, very deep.

This man put me off-guard as went through the front door. The home was so nice I thought at first a woman had to live there. Then, I looked around a little more and there was absolutely nothing to show a woman lived there. The colors matched very well, but possibly because a decorator had furnished the home. The back of the house had a huge yard which was nestled between many "shouting high to the sky" trees; trees that had branches which were very full and a spot where the birds were happy living.

This was a two-story home and he walked me up to the second story of the house. The bedroom was there and then he decided to go down to the first floor. Leaving me to wonder what he was up to and I thought this was a little suspicious. When Blue Eyes had come back upstairs, before we went downstairs, he held me in his arms and I knew I had to use my ability to find out what he was up too and who he was.

Yes, he was a killer.

"Was he going to kill me? No." He only did contracts.

The answers were all there. All there inside my brain.

He was 6'2" tall and built very well. He only stared at me. I have no idea what he was thinking but I did know I was safe. He had brought me up to the bedroom and then down again because he wanted me to know he had a bedroom, but for our purposes he was more into using the couch. He wanted to be spontaneous. This was just so odd the going up the stairs and then down the stairs. Because he was so good looking, I was thrown a little off guard and truly putting my instincts 'on-guard'. Mr. Blue Eyes, also, was not much of a talker.

He hardly spoke two sentences.

Just about when I thought I was safe he put his hands over my throat.

"Okay! Maybe I am wrong." I thought, almost speaking out-loud. No it was his style of having sex. He wanted his hands over my throat as a "sense" of 'real killing' for him. Keeping his eyes open the entire time. Just like Mr. New York. Even though I was safe this time, he wanted to think ahead. Did I show fear? No way. I was not going to let him have 'fear', the 'fear' that comes with the thrill which he likes to see when he kills. I was reading his mind and trying to keep some scenes of his life out of my mind.

I was the mouse and he was the cat.

We had our quick session; I collected my money and almost danced out of the house. He was so silent that I had to use my abilities and those abilities saw how he killed and why he killed and that he was now on a small vacation for about three months. He wanted to relax.

The intensity this man had and all contract killers have, is something a true psychic cannot --- not --- see and feel.

He had asked me if I wanted anything to drink and I declined when I first got there. This experience was right up there, as one of the strangest men I ever saw. The house almost looked like it could have been a model house; it was too perfect. He was too perfect looking.

Everything was wrong about his calling an escort service.

This man could pick up any woman he wanted. Because of Mr. New York, my Perry, I knew what a hit man was like when he looked into my eyes. This man looked through me just like Mr. New York. There was that same coldness. The body was there, but the mind was a long way from being in the moment.

Mr. Blue Eyes never phoned again, to my knowledge. To say I am glad he never phoned again is an understatement. In good conscience I could not have sent someone to him. Perhaps he would have killed me --- thankfully, I just was not his "type." If I sent someone who was more his type … who knows what could have happened? I did not want to find out.

Man #3

Gee, speaking about Lonnie is a little too close to the core, but he was at one time a client and then a boyfriend. (My meaning here for "core"... he was close to my heart.) He was about 6'5" tall and was African-American and looked meaner than bulldog in hot pursuit. He is called a client because he loved bringing me drugs to use and then proceed to have sex with me. All I can say is this was the very best this body had ever had, then or now, or ever. He may disagree that giving me something made him a client, but it did in my mind. I would have rather he not give anything to be with me.

Did he kill people for money? Yes.

He was a mercenary, and, had been in Viet Nam for more than one tour of duty and then contracted with the government to kill in Africa and other places. He confided in me that killing his "own" people bothered him and maybe that is why he was doing the drugs; to forget. Because I liked him so very much, well, that is all I have to say about him.

Conclusion

This is a chapter which will end early because of the, subject, people. The other men known to kill would be upset if I allowed others to have a glimpse at whom or what they did for money. I can say that many men who come back from a war are prone to kill and have no problem being talked into a life of crime that involves taking lives. Your next door neighbor may be a contract killer and how would you know?

When I was a teenager (about 18) in Phoenix, Arizona there was a young guy I knew and dated a few times. He called me up and asked me to go to lunch with him and a friend. This guy always wanted to impress me, so I would sleep with him or see him more than what we had been doing. Which was, we were just friends, going out every now and then but uncomplicated.

We arrived at the diner or restaurant at noon when it was very busy. The orders for all three of us were put in with the waitress and then we just began talking about many things. I asked what his friend did and they both looked at each other and the floodgates of information came out.

"What I do? Hum. Should I tell her?"

"Yeah, you're just in training anyway."

"That's right. Now you have to keep this to yourself. I mean no telling anyone. Do you promise?"

"I promise." (Rolling my eyes to the mystery they both were set on telling me.)

Each one of the guys was about two years old than me at the time and you could tell they thought they knew everything.

"Well, I am in training to be a hit man." He waited for my reaction, which was close to, no reaction. I looked at him with some surprise and said,

"You? How can you be in training to kill?"

"There are some people from New York who come out here for the training camp."

"No way ... a training camp?" I was extremely puzzled because in my very naïve world, at that time, things such as what he was telling me did not exist.

"You two are nuts." This was a statement I felt strongly about then. Immediately, they looked at each other again and said, "It is the truth. I can't tell you the details but I was chosen to learn because I wanted too."

"Okay, I believe you; I have heard they bury bodies in the desert. Growing up here there have been lots of stories about people being planted in the desert."

After this little confession, I looked at my friend and wondered, "If he were in the same "club" to learn how to kill?"

This is one story which ended that day. I was leaving Arizona at the time and I never saw either one of them again. There was more talk than what's written here, but I know they believed what they were saying; and they were bragging and trying to look "big" for my attention. Even looking back on that day, what they said rang with words of truth, what his new job was going to be.

Chapter Five
The Disabled
"Lean on me," means something different when escorting the disabled; with the lines a little blurred as to whom is helping who."
D.E.Z. Butler

The men phoning that were disabled gave the escort business a credible reason for being in business. These men did not have any other means to have or find female companionship for a short time. Many of them were nice and there were a few that were rude and wanted the entire world to feel sorry for their condition.

The first time an escort would see a person in a wheelchair or lying in bed without any means to be ambulatory ... just had the woman choke-up and she would tell me how she felt about this type of client. Some of the women, usually the younger ones, could not see a person who was unable to move or the person had some affliction which the girl was afraid of catching. This may even be a rash that was just from lying in bed too much.

Most of these men also wanted to always write checks. Clear enough why they wanted to write checks, but that did not make it any easier to explain to the women, because it was difficult for the man to get to the bank, that we had to accept a check or just not go to these calls. We went the extra mile to be accepting of their various conditions. Most times, the checks were accepted and with my fingers crossed that they would clear the banks.

This was a small battle to overcome for the women and some did just fine with visiting the disabled. The one thing I would never do is give them a discount and, many of them wanted a discount. I just could not do that, because the women had to usually be talked into going and it took a certain woman to handle the handicapped.

Not all the women working for the escort service were nurses.

It was great when I had a nurse who worked. But, some of the nurses, because they did deal with people who had disabilities, just wanted to have a good time and seeing a person who was disabled did not help each individual 'nurses' mood. Clearly it was like being at the hospital.

Even escorts want some fun.

Seeing the disabled after working with them all day is no fun for the women, who were nurses. They told me this with funny stories and some stories not so funny. The nurses did help me understand certain conditions and I did give one or two of the men who were paraplegic a discount.

These men were not mobile and the women could usually only give a "hand job" or just some great conversation. Their incomes were very limited.

The work was not rough on the women, so a discount could be in place for some of the men. Yes, there were many men who were disabled calling in and after the men knew we could be trusted they kept calling. Because of their vulnerability, trust was needed for these men.

I will begin with a man who lived on the peninsula and was a client for awhile. He would like to know that he was first in this chapter.

Diary Comment

Jay was a respectful and polite man. The first girl I ever sent him called me back immediately and asked me if I knew he was confined to his bed. Not knowing what she was speaking about, I asked her to explain the circumstances of the call with me --- in detail. This she did and I verified with her the feelings she may have over someone who was unable to move. Jane felt she could handle the call and I agreed that she was the type of person to handle a disabled man. Jane then phoned the man back and received very detailed directions how to get to his location. She was to proceed to San Francisco and then take the freeway south to an exit in San Mateo.

Upon arriving at the house she was greeted by a very nice lady who asked her to please come inside. The lady then handed her a check and led her into a bedroom where Jane saw, lying in bed with tubes and all sorts of medical equipment, a person unable to move around. A man, frail and smiling was looking at her. She said this man was totally incapable of movement other than a small turning of his head. I then asked her what had taken place with him. She said that he was mostly interested in female companionship; and then he explained to her that he had been disabled since high school.

Jane said they spoke for a long time, even longer than the hour which his mother had paid her before she entered his room. This was one of the more touching encounters that the escorts were to be exposed to over the years. His mother was open with Jane and truly wanted her son to feel as though he were having entertainment. Just as other men his age have.

More than anyone really knows --- I have wished all people could be as open and loving as this one mother was and still is at the time of this diary entry. This is the type of call that should not only be allowed but it is also why I feel services such as mine need to be in business. (Not all the women could handle calls such as these, but those that did, found the rewards given to their own character more beneficial than money.) After many years of service to Jay he wrote me a very warm letter. I wish to share it with the readers.

Letter from Jay

Hi friend. Well it's me again!. I'm sure you remember who I am, but in case you don't after these last 2 years, I'm the disabled guy living in -----, who enjoyed the service you gave me for so many years. I imagine your still with Professional Escorts Diane, and if you are, could you please put me in touch with a lady, what I'm looking to pay is from $100 dollars to $150 dollars for an hour to an hour and a half or $350 for a 6 hour date! Give me a call, or write. If you call, give the information to my mom or nurse and I'll get back to you, and arrange a date with the lady. So many things have gone on in my life since I last was in touch with you. This is one of the reasons for my writing and not calling you on the phone. Nowadays it's not as easy for me to speak as it was before. I'll explain why as I proceed with this letter. What I'm writing for is to ask you if you could put me in touch with a cute sexy lady, who would be kind enough to share some fun and intimate times with me at a reasonable price. I'm looking for a lady with a curvy figure, who likes wearing cute dresses, nightgowns, sexy underwear, and perfume. It's a turn on to me seeing ladies wearing nightgowns. I love perfume also! I'm just wanting to have some TLC and some good sexual fun and would like to meet a sexy, loving and compassionate lady who can believe in the idea that a disabled man such as I deserves to have sexual pleasure and the companionship of a special sexy loving woman in his life. What is most important to me is to find a lady who can forget about my being disabled, and bring me the same pleasures any other guy wants. I want to find a sexy lady with a cute sexy figure, about 5'5" to 5'11", 120 t 140 lbs, not a heavy drug user or drinker. Who likes French kissing, giving head, who wouldn't mind oral contact, kissing, and licking my nipples and body, and having easy going intercourse, as well as touching and hugging. I'm pleasant, fun, easy going, not hard to be around and not physically demanding so the date with me would be enjoyable, and not a pain to be on. I will treat her as a loving friend, not as a worker, and with respect *always! It would be great to have a sexy lady to spend quite times with where we can cuddle, hug, kiss and make love, (safe sex) and just spend quality times together. 2 years ago due to complications I had to start being fed by a small tube into my stomach. It's not a bad problem, and not to be worried about during sexual activity. It needed to be done, due to the fact I was having a problem swallowing and I was aspirating food, and was no longer able to eat. I also had to have what is called a talking trach put in. The problem with this is that in order to talk, someone has to assist me by putting their thumb over a small tube about 12 inches long leading from it. It's not hard, just an inconvenience. This is why talking over the phone isn't impossible, but is difficult. So I try to write more often, with the aid of my computer, which I operate with a switch that is activated by my mouth, and uses the dot dash system of the mores code to operate the computer key board. This allows me to run some small businesses with it also! I also stay in bed, and I'm unable to leave my home. So I need my friends to visit me. I hope when the knowledge of my disability is known that your ladies are not turned away by the fact. For I'm wanting to get as much out of life, and I truly need a sexy lady to have some sexual fun with in my life to make it complete. Please know, that even with my disability and limitations, that I'm still as horny as every! So to be able to find a loving lady to share my sexual fantasies and romance with would be fantastic. I may not be able to come and go as I wish, but in my mind and soul, is an enjoyment for sex, life, and romance that is never ending, and I'm always wanting to take it even further. By the way! My health status is the same as before, except for my added attractions. Also being in the hospital for the 5 month stay, I was put through full blood testing, and my tests are completely negative. So please tell the person you put me in touch with, not to worry. I do understand peoples concerns nowadays, so I want to make people as much at ease as possible! If you can help put me in touch with a loving, understanding, and trust worthy lady Diane, just phone me, or write to me at the above address. I will be very grateful for your help Diane. Looking forward to doing business with once again. I enjoyed it before, and I know I will once again! Sincerely yours, Jay*

PS. By the way! I also have 24 hour nurses now thanks to a grant from Medicare. The nurses are also great friends, and their also very open minded, and feel it's a great idea that I deal with one of your escorts. So your ladies don't have to worry about any problems or hassles in fact if the lady wants to leave a message with my nurses

for me, she can.
[The letter was put here without corrections.]

Man #1

(Yes, the person Jay mentioned above, this is the man's first encounter with our service.)

The first time this man phoned, I thought he was kidding. Not because of his disability, but because his mother got on the telephone and told me that she would be answering the door and that, not to fear, she would not be coming in the room while the woman was there with her son.

This mother's love was complete. She understood her son needed someone else other than her to give him comfort and whether she approved or not, she allowed the women over the years to enter her home and see her son in his room.

I had to speak to a couple of women before one would say, "okay" to make the drive down to his home. Most of my women then were living in Marin County and it would be a distance for them. His mother said she would be paying for a couple of hours to have the drive worthwhile for the girl.

After a long speech to the first girl who would make the drive, she was on the road. When she arrived, she was to phone in to say if everything was fine with the situation and make sure the guy was an invalid. When the girl arrived she phoned me and said the woman, his mother, had given her a check and I asked, "Do you think the check is okay?" Business always is the bottom-line for us and she assured me that this was a legitimate client.

When the escort left, she phoned me again and told me what the "skinny" was there. He had a disease that was crippling and he would eventually waste away. His mother was there and he just wanted to feel like a man for a few stolen moments. She said, "Everything looked fine and he will probably be a customer for a long time." He had hit her up for her private telephone number to circumvent the agency, but she declined and had told him to reach her through the escort service.

(Later the girl told me she cried on the way home.)

After many women and years later; I was very impressed with him and his mother. His mother for being such a selfless person and him for trying so hard to be a confident man and man able to express himself so well in writing. He would write to me and thank me for sending him women and he always asked each girl for her phone number.

Over the years, I am sure, one or two of the women gave in and wrote down their telephone numbers, but he liked variety. No matter how much he may have liked the girl that gave him her telephone number, he still wanted to see a new girl, more often than a woman who would give him her telephone number. He had a certain loyalty to my service. And even told me when a woman gave her telephone number to him. This always gave me a laugh. Many customers told me when women gave them a phone number to reach them by; but the customers must have thought telling me would endear them to me. Even though the guy must have bugged the woman for the phone number.

Over time his health deteriorated and I am sure at this writing he is no doubt deceased. But I would like him and his mother to know that I never did go see him because I wanted to always treat him just like all the rest of the men phoning. If I had seen him I may have wanted to feel sorry for him. (I believe he had the same affliction that has ravaged Stephen Hawking's body.) And I believe he would have preferred me to not have any pity on him. He knew what I looked like and he sent me a photo or two of him. Somewhere I still have a couple of his letters and a photo. If he did die at least *Professional Escorts* had a hand in allowing him to feel and be manly for at least once a month when his Social Security check came. Since this writing I found out he has passed away and I hope that he rests in peace.

Man #2

There always has to be a nasty old man in a wheelchair. This guy, Howard, phoned one day and I went to see him. He was very loud on the telephone and I had to make sure he was not some cop or nut case; so I went to his apartment in San Rafael. He had to be hard of hearing because he was yelling into the telephone receiver.

When I arrived, Howard answered the door and led me into his apartment. I sat down on his couch and began to listen to his every word. He had many thoughts scrambling around in his head that wanted to get out and tell or ask me.

First things first; I asked him, "How did you get this way?" I was curious.

Howard began by saying he was stupid. I would agree if it were his fault on how he lost his legs.

"I got drunk in the snow back East and fell down and passed out. When I woke up my legs were frozen and I had frostbite so bad they had to amputate from my knees down. Then another surgery for infection on this here leg up past the knee." Yep, he put his leg up and the smell of urine had me wanting to vomit. "Not so high." I thought to myself.

With the smell he had, I was not about to massage him or anything else. I was nice to him and told him he had to pay me for the hour and I would see if any other girl could come out. Letting him know that I had another appointment and because he was in a wheelchair, I would want him to be squeaky-clean and that would take a little too long. I wanted him to bathe before any person saw him. I also explained that because he was new; I always checked the men out and there was going to be a cost or the fee for an hour. No exceptions. He was mortified that he would have to pay more money.

Ultimately, I had to give him a hand-job, so he would not feel ripped-off and yell to whoever would listen to him. That is what he threatened if I did not give him something. Even a hand job was after a trip to the bathroom to clean him and this bought him a few minutes. I could not think of touching such a smelly guy. I washed my hands very well before I left his place.

He phoned the service later that night and I told him I would try to find someone to go see him. The fact he was on a limited budget did not matter to me. If not my service he would phone another service and pay the fees there, for those services. The bad part was that he wanted to pay by check and I was just not going for it.

I got a hold of this black woman who worked for my service at the time and who was also a nurse. You know what I am thinking here. A nurse is use to the smells of dirty-old men. She went to see him and everything was fine. Then kept him as her personal client and I were not happy about that, but in some recess of my brain, I could have cared less. He was filthy and belligerent and it would always be a battle to have someone sent out, to go see him. Over the years he phoned, and, especially after this first time, he always wanted this first girl or asked if she were working. This was because if she was not answering her phone, then he phoned my service. He also told me she had given him her telephone number to call her directly.

In phoning my service, he was just checking up on her, to see if she was just avoiding his calls. Howard had no loyalty to my service and I had ongoing trouble with him, each and every time he called. The phoning of the escort who gave her telephone number to him was painstakingly difficult, because there were too many phone calls, back and forth, with him trying to find out where she was and what she was doing. I really preferred that he just call her and forget about telephoning my service.

Usually, he was drunk and wanted to write a check, and, sometimes the checks were good and other times the check would not go through. Eventually, I had to tell him I would not send anyone to him. And then to make things even worse between our relationship, he threatened to go to the police. That is how nuts he was, and, drunk he was, when he related to me or any of the escorts. If the escort service would not send him someone he wanted to tell stories about the service. The police knew his game and even they did not want to hear from him.

Sorry, but every time I think of him I laugh, because he kept telling me he is going to call the police and they already told him they don't believe him and they even said if we were so bad, "Why do you keep calling the number?" I only know what the police said to him because he told me. He was funny and a huge pain.

Man #3

There was this man in San Francisco I will call him Mr. Leg. Sometimes when women go to see a client, the man may be calling just because he has been drinking or doing drugs. Not always would the clients' telephone because they had the correct amount of money needed to see an escort. That was the issue the night Mr. Leg telephoned. He had the same problem about losing a leg in whatever snow bank there was, that year in his home town when his leg got frozen. Then the amputation and now he was a dedicated creep. Not just any weirdo, he was a "vocal offender."

The first girl, I sent, got to his place sometime in the early evening and he stood about 6' with his one leg on and without his leg on he was limited to a wheelchair or a cane for short distances in his home. He was very average looking and worked for the government. The girl said he had brown hair and eyes with a ruddy complexion. His body was not overweight but he did have hordes of hair on his body. This night the girl I sent to him did not ask for her money up front. I suppose it was because he was without one leg. Well, Mr. Leg wanted her for a couple of hours, and, that means the amount of money he was to pay now doubled. With the first hour up it came time for her to ask for her money. Very simply, he did not have the required cash or check. She gave me the telephone, so I could let him know there was someone out there that could make sure she got her money.

Basically, I pleaded with him to pull out his check book and he refused. Some of his jokes were pointing to his lack of an appendage as a reason, or we were charging so much. I assured him that was not the case. Our fees were not as high as they could have been. One thing led to another and the telephone was handed back and forth a few times still talking about the fee. I explained to him, he should have not phoned if he did not have the money. When he called he asked what the fees were, so he cannot claim ignorance. Our remarks and the tones in our voices went to upper registers. We almost began to shout.

Finally, he got the idea that the money was to be paid. And most ridiculously, he offered her his leg. The prosthesis that he had been wearing and said, "You can hold this until tomorrow when the banks open."

I asked her, "Is the leg marketable? Can we sell it?" By now she was trying very hard not to laugh, but she did begin to laugh. Then I began to laugh. The only one not laughing was our client. He was serious and we had not realized it. The entire episode was ended when I told her, "Tell him you will take the check, but it better be good or we will be back for the leg. And don't laugh; be serious so he believes you." Yep. She took the check and it did go through. He got to keep his leg. Added benefit was I had another true story to tell to people and put in this book. Lol, lol, lol.

Man #4

When this young man phoned, I did not have anyone to send to him. He was living about 50 miles from my house and he wanted two women to come see him. I explained that the cost was double, if I had anyone to send, and he did not object to the fee and cost for two women. He further explained that he was living in the house behind the house and that the door would be open ... this door open thing happened many times, so I did not think much about it. I was going to go see him and another escort was at my place and she said that she would go too. We got a map out because this was long before GPS service or MapQuest. The trusty flashlight had to come with us so we could see the map at night.

When, we finally found the place it was located in a nice neighborhood near or around the Stanford University campus area. I thought he might be a student there because he sounded so young ... I had to ask him if he were over 18 years old.

He said, "Yes, I am 22 years old." With his age established over the phone, I knew that we would still have to see his driver's license when we got there.

The house he lived in was around back of the main house and there were some big stones to walk on as we made our way back to his house. The worry right then was not to break our heels.

I knocked on the door and he said, "Just come on in."

"Hi, are you Dave?"

"Yes."

"I really have to see some identification."

"It is over there on the table."

"Is there some reason you want me to get your wallet for you? I mean, I don't mind, but it is dark in here and I am not up for any misunderstandings."

"I would get up but I am a quadriplegic."

I look over at Shelly and she looks at me and we are both thinking the same thing. "How the hell or why the hell does he want two women?" Then I look back at him and begin to ask more questions.

"Why didn't you tell me on the phone?"

"This just happened about six months ago snow skiing and I am not use to telling anyone about my condition."

"Why two women?" I was flabbergasted that he could even think of having two women.

"Because I thought it might stimulate me more. Up till now I am not sure if I am getting erections or not. My mother leaves the room sometimes but won't tell me why. They live in the front house."

Now I was over the shock that this great looking young guy was basically a basket-case and could not move anything but his head. He began to tell us what he wanted and it amounted to the other girl sitting on his face while he fondled me. This was getting into a perversion place I did not want to do, but because he was so damn cute, I went along with the program.

Then dumb me, I tried to move his body a little and he was just like a rag doll. It was scary. I was concerned we could hurt him and I told him; "One woman should be all for you at a time;" his body could be hurt if two women are circling him, trying to give him some pleasure.

Even though his driver's license said 22 years old, he was like a very old man with his body and, his mind was like a teenager. He began to give us the details of the accident and we both had tears in our eyes. Yes, I still charged him for the two of us and this was because he had just received a settlement, and, if not us, another escort service would have the money he wanted to spend.

Not exactly cold hearted on my part but, just practical. We left and could not stop chattering all the way back to my place. Both of us were in agreement, that he was too nice looking to be in such a way and his body was still firm and athletic ... as it was before he had the accident. He phoned a few more times, but I always sent a younger escort and they would come back looking very sad about him. Eventually, he stopped phoning or one of the women I sent him, became his private girl. I did not know and if one of them was his private woman, it was fine with me if he got one of the women to see him away from the service. He needed someone.

Man #5

This was a night with the wind blowing and rain was falling down from Marin County to Oakland. It was a dark night, and, no moon was shining.

I parked the car near to his apartment house and rang the correct bell for his numbered apartment (The number he gave me on the phone). A call from a man who sounded "black" on the phone, he spoke with a soft southern voice or drawl, and, I had taken some drugs just to get my ass out of the house. After all my pressing the buzzer for him to respond, he finally pressed the buzzer next to the door in his apartment and the outside door, of the apartment building, opened and I walked to his apartment, which was on the first floor of the building. Robert answered the door and he had not told me one or two facts about himself; he did not have legs. It was okay with me, his not having legs; because the escort service, by now, had seen many men with a leg missing or in various stages of loss of limb, such as arms, etc. Robert did not have prosthetic legs near him, but he did have a blanket in his one room apartment. The first thought, I had, was, "Can he afford this?" It was the first of the month, so I figured he had Social Security to depend upon, and, that is what he would be paying me from and, I asked him if he had cash.

"Yes, I got the cash. But what pills would you like? I have all kinds of drugs."

"Let me see what you have?" This was in the 1970s and I loved taking pills to get me through the calls. He had some powerful stuff, of the drugs I recognized, so I took a few and swallowed them down with a beer chaser.

Yep. I was high on pills and booze almost immediately.

Robert let the effects of the drugs and beer catch hold of me, before he told me what he would like to do. It seems when he was in Viet Nam he lost his two legs and his third leg. (His penis.) I tried hard to understand.

He said, "I want to fuck you."

"How?"

"Like this." He said as he was pulling up some contraption which was put around his waist and had a penis attached to it.

"How is that going to give you any pleasure?"

"By giving you pleasure, I have pleasure."

This is where the drugs were happy to be in my system. Nothing like this had ever happened to this escort before and, I was not sure what the hell to do. Being as "fucked-up" as I was, well

I thought, "Okay. I'll try anything once."

Hard to say what happened, I was in and out of consciousness, until the drugs wore off a bit. Then it was time to leave. The room was lit with a small nightlight plugged into one of the wall outlets not near to us. The floor was hard and so was the device. I remember his face and how he wanted to be a "man" again. He tried very hard to please me. Did I fake it? Some was faked and some was real. I never saw him again, because I just could not bear to see the pain in his eyes and face. He was hurting and hurting to a point of suicide. Somewhere in this mind of mine, I never wanted to forget him.

When life became difficult; yes, I would think of him and many of the men who phoned who were disabled. These numerous men were worse off than I could ever be. He was a real man, not some poster showing men going off to war. He had the worst wounds a man could have from combat, and, for him, and all the new amputees; this is why I put him in this chapter. He did not want pity, but he wanted something the escort service could never give him.

Man #6

God knows this man should be here. His name was Bob and he was one of our oldest clients. He lived in a residential retirement building in San Francisco and may have been about 80 years old. What he wanted when he phoned was to have a massage. He liked to think about sex but was long past doing anything for the urges he occasionally had. The year was 1974 and I was doing most of the massage calls. About 10 calls to every one of Dee's calls; she liked answering the phone and I wanted to do the calls. Actually, I loved to massage people. It was fun and I loved making people feel good.

Bob had lots of drugs at his little studio apartment because he was old. The doctors always seemed to give the old people hordes of drugs to take. Then, the men would phone someone like me and "share." They would "share" all their drugs. We could even ask them, to ask for our special drugs, the drugs we really liked. The men loved watching a woman become uneasy and more susceptible to their advances because she was "high" on drugs. Bob was such a man. He wanted his massage, but he also wanted a hand-job after the massage. The basic "easy call" and not a lot of work. With all the advantages of "extras," such as pills to pop, which helped the masseuse stay focused. Oh, she had to be without clothes for the massage. Somehow he got his "kicks" from seeing a woman naked. Many clients had the request of "no" clothes for their massage. I obliged.

Then one day Dee phoned to give me another call and he spoke to her and asked if she could come the next time I came over to his place. (The time for the next call would be the first of the month when he received his Social Security check.) He asked her what kind of pills she liked. The night came when he phoned to have me over and requested me to bring Dee. We both took off our clothes and I began his massage as he massaged her. He was disabled and could not walk very well and with all the drugs they were giving him, it was clear he had more health problems than just not being able to walk straight without his cane. For whatever reason he got up off the bed and walked over to his pills to do one or two and bring us more. In the meantime, Dee began to kiss me and I was more than surprised; but not as surprised as Bob. He began screaming and yelling at her calling her all sorts of things. Mainly a "dike" and too many other things to mention here; and by now we were both on our feet just looking at this crazy old man go nuts; then he takes a revolver out of a dresser drawer and points it at Dee.

Being the natural heroine, who I am; I stepped in front of the gun and Dee. He had pointed the gun at her abdomen and was hell bent on shooting her dead. The drama was loud and had me standing in front of and between the two of them; of course, I would be the one to get hurt. He flung the gun upward and caught my chin. The bottom of my chin still has the scar from saving Dee's life. We dressed quickly and I phoned him either that night or the next day to tell him he still owed for the two of us. And he paid when I went over to his place just one more time. Bob felt sorry about my chin and I never wanted to see him again. He was taking too many pills and was nuts, just plain old-fashioned nuts.

Dee repaid me by turning over a letter I sent her, on how much money I was making a few years later, to the IRS; asshole friend.

Chapter Six
Judges, Elected Officials, Attorneys
"The Lady is always a lady when she has Mr. Justice on her side."
D.E.Z. Butler

Faith, hope, and charity are how the escort business survives the police and all those members of government wanting to escape to the other side of the law for an hour or two. Many people have asked how the business stayed "alive" for so many years. The answer was an uncomplicated one, but most people wanted to think the "mob" or some other nefarious people were behind the business. Even though most of the women saw a great many lawyers, few of them ever realized the truth about how our business stayed free of guns blazing through the front door.

The answer is and was easy.

Lawyers grew up to be judges. Amazing how I figured it out and the people, asking, could not put it together. Not one judge, living, wants to be found in a diary or book of an escort service. The judges are the people who sign the warrants to enter for a "bust." The diaries kept for *Professional Escorts* were not complete and only served as reference points for the owner, me.

People then and today want to keep all their records on a hard drive or one of the travel memory gadgets.

Boy, are those people stupid.

When I first arrived in Marin County there was not a lot to do but go out with men. Many men asked me out and I liked going out. The escort business had not crossed my mind yet. I began to date a huge variety of men. Some had money and some did not. Some worked for the county and some worked for the state and some worked for the federal government. Many of the men were just "making their bones," so to speak, and none of them were married at the time. Because of what happened, I will speak now about one police officer. We met at a bar and liked each other. Went out a couple of times and definitely slept together. Then we moved on with our lives, but kept in touch.

My job at the time was as a store detective (loss prevention these days) and occasionally we would come in contact and have a drink or something like that. The relationship was long over. When I stopped being a detective and moved onto working at a massage studio his "angle" of looking at me changed. I was now part of the "other" people. The people he would arrest. My thoughts were just to make money at the time and the legality of the entire business was just not where my head was at the time. My needs were more important and food in the refrigerator to feed my kids was a top priority. Not the men I was or had dated. I could have cared less about the law then. My material needs and those of my sons were number one for me.

Eventually, he married another cop and she was out for my hide. Crazy stupid woman, he was actually horrible in bed, so I could not figure out why she was so messed up about me. Perhaps it was because I knew what a bad "lay" he was. Now, let's get away from the '70s and go forward to the early '80s. She is crazy and wants revenge for the lost honor of her misdirected husband who once had an affair with me, long before she was even in the picture. Gee, makes you want to know what sweet nothings he said about me in their matrimonial bed. The way she got to me was by telling a judge I had over 500 pounds of cocaine at my house and that I was selling drugs to the guards at San Quentin, so those guards could, in turn, sell them to the prisoners.

All lies.

Yep, the dumb judge fell for it and there were no less than 100 cops from DEA, local, other federal cops, etc., etc. He signed the warrant for them to come in and arrest me for a bogus charge of selling drugs. Unfortunately, the house held a small amount of cocaine for personal use with friends. Which they thought was enough to have me on a charge for sale with intent to distribute; or something like that. The scale I had "got lost" when I told them it did not work and I had it at the house for any gold dust my sons and I would find when we went gold hunting. The boys had played with it and the thing did not work. No reputable drug dealer would be without a working scale; so the police got the damn thing lost from all the evidence they confiscated.

Meaning it was not available for my defense in a courtroom, which came to play several years later.

I phoned the next day, after their "bust", to complain about a shipment of wine the cops took which had the name *Professional Escorts* on all the bottles. Assholes were not in to get my phone call and I told the receptionist, "I wouldn't doubt it; they are probably drinking my wine." Never got the wine back … thieves. The newspapers, the next day, especially the local paper, had me on the front page and the second page. A Saturday paper that had a large distribution for the area. My collagen was in vials they found and the paper said those vials were heroin. Not true.

The next page showed San Quentin and a couple of guards in handcuffs. I never met them in my life.

The person I did know the day the "army of idiots" came into my house was an ex-guard, who was now my personal exercise coach and that day we had an appointment for exercising. He says to me that he had to step out for a minute and as I waited he was being arrested for selling "coke" to someone a couple of blocks from where I lived and then the "army" came into my house. This was all a little funny, if it did not end up costing so much money and, I actually thought a jury would find me not guilty. Wrong. What hung me was they wanted to show the jurors a picture of one of the guards I knew, which was the fitness coach, and had been an escort for the service. This was a naked photo and had been taken at the first party at Mr. Annapolis house. I thought because it was just him standing there against a wall and nothing lewd was going on that no one would care.

No. I was wrong.

The jurors were not a jury of my "peers." Convicted!

Then I had to go through the hoops to eventually have the thing expunged from my record.

The above was just a little side comment to show how some relationships complicated my life.

The massage studio, Alter Ego is where (My first place of employment doing massages, before getting my massage license at Yumi's massage place in San Francisco.) I had lots of guys who worked at the government offices in Marin County and were coming in for massage. Massage was not a dirty word for sex yet.

This chapter will have the clients in it but the format will vary because of who these men were and may still be remembered in the community. My meaning here is that I will not give direct descriptions of these guys. When certain clients came into the massage studio, we were alerted if he worked for or had an important job with the county. I saw so many of them some will not be spoken about due to the sheer numbers involved.

Mr. Government elected official #1

This man (will be called "John" because many clients said their name was "John") was older than me by about 20 years and wore glasses. "John" was of average height and weight and loved to have a massage with me leaning over him and his face became a victim to the "hills of softness and pleasure" that I had. "John" came into the studio every week and sometimes twice a week. I actually liked him and now everyone knows what he liked.

Then one day I got arrested for some ticket that was neglected (was actually quite a few tickets and I always thought if the cops don't show up the judge is to dismiss; well that did not happen; the judge made everyone show up the next week and the courtroom looked like a sea of blue; yep I was going to jail for ticket avoidance; I was allergic to tickets) and was told that two weeks wasn't too bad at the "farm."

The "farm" was where offenders who were not dangerous could spend their time. Because I was a person "allergic" to jail; even the "farm" was not where I wanted to go. So I did the next best thing. I called "John" to come see me at the jail. All I wanted was to go home, but when I saw his red face, the truth was that I would be hurting someone who had been very nice to me.

"John" said, "What you want ... to leave here ... suspended sentence ... what?" He was almost crying and I felt like the "big bad wolf."

My answer to him was, "No, I'm sorry, just maybe later."

Later meaning, I would pull this favor in, some other time; a time when things may be worse. "John" left and all the jailers just looked at me and I was almost immediately sent to the "farm." No one wanted him to be irate with them. Another girl was scheduled to leave for the "farm" but I took her place. (Damn it would be nice to say who he was; but even though he may be dead, he still has children living.) This was a lesson and one learned well. Never call in your "marks" too early. It was '74 or '75 and the business of escorting was just beginning a huge push in the Bay Area. *Professional Escorts* would not begin until 1977. My hope was that he would remain in his elected office, long enough to call upon, if needed.

Elected Judge #1

Now let us move forward to about 1980 give or take a year. One of the escorts comes leaping into the living room where a few escorts and I were talking our heads off about whatever. She exclaims, "I just saw a judge."

"Ho hum." Was the reply, moaning or uttering from most women in the room, made to her excitement; except me? Me? Well, I brought her to another room and asked her what he looked like and if she got a name. She did not have a name but I knew who he was from the description. He was a Marin County Superior Court Judge and one of the best ones to have used the service. This was because of his position. The call was a "slam-dunk" for the service. Years later an attorney, who once worked for *Professional Escorts* and knew many judges, told me, "You have at least 12 superior court judges all over the Bay Area and they are concerned." This was after another little legal problem happened and we will get to that later. Actually, the number was higher and he did not know that fact and I was not about to inform him. He had been told by another judge and this is when "deals" began to emerge for my little legal issue. (Too many "dicks", so to speak … in a "sling". Lol lol)

Elected Man #2

The time, when I heard about this man using the service, was from an escort named Cynthia, who saw him and she was surprised he had phoned. This woman had been in politics in Washington D.C.; and maybe she learned something and perhaps she did not. When I would go on vacation, I asked her to watch things for me and of course she would steal clients. And this must have been one of them. This client, again, the name will be called "John", was someone elected to his position and he went to Washington to do his work (Congress) and now is elected "locally," meaning in California. And yes, he is getting old.

Cynthia told me he used drugs and when he was "high" on something he would phone. I think she kept him as her client … maybe … to protect his job. This could be the reason I did not know much about him until the late '80s when Cynthia finally informed me of his activity in phoning the escort service. She then gave some big confession to me about him using the service with lots of drama that he was drunk or on drugs every time he phoned. Without knowledge of him, before she told me, I can't say what he liked except I know he had phoned and she saw him. Mostly they did drugs together and she never told me what he liked to do in the bedroom. Knowing her, it must have been to smoke "pot" and then have some food which would help them both in the "missionary" position which she liked so well because of her bad back. Cynthia is now a displaced person.

Elected Man #3

The call came in and it was a couple who were staying at an expensive hotel in San Francisco. They were sent a woman who liked other women because that is what the couple wanted. The woman, I sent, was liked by the wife. The escort told me the woman was the main customer, with the husband watching every detail of their lovemaking. What I wanted to know was who the couple was and the escort told me they were from some Southern state. The man was the mayor or held another elected position and this was their getaway weekend. The escort saw some written information to confirm who he was in that part of the country. They only phoned the service for that one night and the next night and that was all they phoned. But again, the escort may have given her number away, so they could phone her directly. This is what I suspected.

Conclusion

For the sake of reputations, the judges cannot be named. They did take care of me and it would be rude to violate some hidden bond we had over the years. When the little problem my husband caused exploded in Contra Costa County; the men were worried. I felt so sorry for them. And even sorrier for me as the door to the condo was busted in and my place was destroyed by some "hot shot" detective who wanted to earn whatever they give such rude, arrogant swine, which he was and will always be.

No person was ever arrested as an escort while working for *Professional Escorts*; but when I was trying to sell the business and my husband and I were having issues ... he went to the police to say, whatever, he thought would allow him to win. He did not win. (He is dead too.) At first the case was public and I hired this attorney who was more arrogant than the detective. He wanted to just walk into the court and have me plead to everything they were throwing at me. I began to plead in front of a full courtroom and when they got to registering as a sex offender, I stopped; looked at the judge and said, "Your honor, I rescind my plea." Gee that felt good and I heard a prisoner in the holding area say, "You can do that?" Yep. I did. And shit-canned the attorney, who, I had to fax him untold messages asking for my money back because he was doing nothing for me and a public defender could have and would have done more.

The next time we went to court, not one person was in the courtroom. Those present were my attorney, who was being paid in "sex" and one of the district attorneys and a judge who made it clear that he was coming out of retirement for the case and was from Sacramento. We did not have any judges in Sacramento to the best of my knowledge. I took a plea and the district attorney asked, "Why?"

As I ignored my attorney; and spoke directly to him with all ears listening attentively, including the judge.

"Simple, no matter who you have to speak out against me, my ads will kill me in a court of law." (Still remembering my last stint in court and the jury was tainted by a photo.) My ads had become more provocative over the years and before a jury it would have been made clear, without a lot of words, what the escort service was doing. The person they had to speak up ... and the only person ... was Cynthia. They had tricked her into thinking they had a lot of other escorts to be witnesses against me. To the end, the women, who had worked for me, were grateful and in my corner. Or they just did not want their own lives upset. Poor Cynthia, as smart as she was; she was really the dumbest escort I ever had. And yes, this case, also, has been expunged.

"Lawyers do grow up to be judges and professors and clients of escort services." D.E.Z. Butler

Chapter Seven
Famous and Not, so, Famous
"The music never stops just because the musician does." D.E.Z. Butler

Client #1

My friend was first a client. Not too sure who the escort was that he saw for the first time, but I do remember what she said about him. "He has this God awful smell about his body." She was right, he did. When I, eventually, met him; I found the smell to be very strong. It was all the drugs coming through his skin as he perspired. Mr. T.T. just loved women and wanted company when he did cocaine. He would have the woman over his home for at least a couple hours, and, sometimes all night.

The first few times he phoned, the women went to his house and then he finally divorced and saw most of the women at some hotel. He would vary the hotels or motels. I was never sure where all the money was coming from, but we suspected because his mother was in politics that she gave him the money. And it had to be a huge amount of funds, because of what he consumed in drugs and all the money he gave to the women. He was singing professionally and his band was looking for a good music contract. That could also be where the money was coming in from; it is widely known or what you call "common knowledge" that there are many music companies willing to pay the artists, who want it, in drugs.

This "doping of artists" has been going on for years and I defy the record companies to say, "It's just not so."

Mr. T.T. ended up a victim of one recording company because they took a song of his and gave it to a well-known singer, which was recorded and a hit was made. Then the company was trying to stop a lawsuit by Mr. T.T. When T.T. was "high" he was telling me all about the crap he was going through. It was very upsetting for him. Aside from those issues, when he saw women the sex was almost there. Unfortunately, he did too much of the "coke" to be very good in bed. (Sorry T.T. but the drugs did have an effect on you.)

The story of an escort going over to his home and, was there for about five minutes, when his wife came home, is one of the classic stories for *Professional Escorts*. The girl had to climb a backyard fence with clothes in hand, less the fee, and phone from a telephone booth, (this was before cell phones) telling me what had happened. She got back to my location and we both had a good laugh. He did pay up the next day. (I did give a note to self after this: Self make sure the women you hire are physically fit to scale backyard fences.) As the escort told it, his wife had been screaming, "A prostitute in my house? How dare you." And the words got worse from that starting point.

Must be one of the reasons why the divorce happened.

Mr. T.T. and I went out one New Years with my boyfriend and some other people in my rented limousine. This was after I knew him for a few years. We were friends but he was also a client. I had asked him to sing me a song one time and he said, "That is how I make my money. I charge."

Put me in my place. We charged too.

Anyway, he wanted to introduce me to a friend of his who was recording that December 31. We drove to Sausalito and a recording studio there and he told everyone in the limo that they would not be going in; this was just for me. When we went into the studio, he introduced me to Rick James who was miraculously "straight" and recording an album; breaking in the New Year working. This was very nice of my friend and I enjoyed the special treatment. Mr. James was nice to me and played just a little of a new song they were putting "tracks" to that night. I know years later there was some shit about James, but what I saw was a very nice guy who was serious about his music. At this writing I am not sure what happened to my friend. The last time I saw him was at a hotel in Corte Madera and another girl was there. The two of them were higher than any imaginary kite I saw flying. I know he married, again, and it may have been this girl. They had a child together but he was an addict. She must have been doing something for him because he stopped phoning for escorts.

Wishing him well just does not seem good enough. He was a very good guy and one of the few clients who ever had my heart feel true friendship for him.

Client #2

A man from Mill Valley, who had so many gold records, platinum records, and honors on the wall it was difficult not to ask who he was or stop in front of one of those records to see the name on it. Another guy just wanting to be called "John," and I was the first one to see him from my service. He actually did not like me at first look. The bedroom work convinced him I was fine. But he obviously wanted some younger escort. When he phoned back I had to hear from the younger escort all about who he was and the records on the wall. Already knew, but what the heck, it was nice to let her go on and on about him. "John" wanted her to wear all the gear that comes with buying sexy outfits and then prance in front of the guy.

No big shocker here.

He was another "missionary" guy, who was a voyeur.

(Voyeur, a person who likes to watch.)

Client #3

Way too many people know this band, so I will try to skirt around them and just tell some facts about the night. This night I received a phone call from a past friend of mine; a man who worked for a big promoter of artists and his office were in San Francisco. The year was possibly '75 or '74 when this friend phoned me. He said that a group was in town and needed some "speed." At the time I was selling "speed" for the Hell's Angels and worked the outcall massage business as a sideline. The "speed" was excellent and a few people, such as this friend, knew about the drug I had. He told me the group was throwing up from some heroin they had and a concert was to be worked the next day.

"Okay, I will be there in a couple of hours."

He wanted Dee to join me and I thought that was odd.

I arrived at this hotel near the wharf area of San Francisco and entered the hotel with instructions to ask for so and so. Magically, I was waved through to the room where the band was puking up their guts. The introductions were made to the lead singer and he looked me up and down. As I looked him up and down, with my eyes noticing one guy hanging onto the toilet vomiting and other members of the group laying on a couple of beds in the hotel room. The drugs were already paid for and each member was using the drug as he wanted. Meaning a couple may have been shooting up the drug with a needle. The lead singer was now more interested in me. He asked me if I would take $100 for each person and the roadies. And the same amount would be given to my girlfriend when she arrived if she looked as nice as me. The compliment was a good one but I was there for one reason and not the one he wanted. I had never heard of this band before and they were even asking me if I wanted to be backstage the next night. I declined.

(It was '76 and a bar in El Paso, Texas when a song came on recorded by this group. I asked the people I was with if that was really this group's song. "Yep". What an idiot I had been not to go backstage.) Dee showed up and we both declined, again, and then left.

The next night after the show, two members of the band came to my house to buy some more "speed." They wanted me to sell it to them on the road. I declined. Thank God. Half or more of this group died tragically. I loved their music.

There were so many groups who used the service; I actually think I would offend a few of them if I spoke about one group and not the other. So I have to leave off the groups that used the service; and the solo artists; just not fair to them. This is definitely a time when it would be easier to ask what groups we did not see in those days.

Chapter Eight
The Marrying Kind
"A golden slipper you will never have if first he finds you with your hand out." D.E.Z. Butler

Man #1

Some men, you just instantly fall in lust for and, think it may be love. This was the case with Harry. He was refined and just plain nice. His eyes were thoughtful and loving, mixed with a lot of knowing what you may be "really" like. There was not one bone in his body which could scare you. He stood slightly over 6' tall and wore clothes that spoke to his job. He was a horticulturist and was part of an established family in Marin County. Because he had grown up with money all his life, he did not think to drive the newest vehicle to show off his wealth, in any way. It blew me away that he even phoned for an escort. I saw him first and sitting at his kitchen table that evening, was as if I had known him all my life.

There is not one memory of being in bed with him and, what I remember was seeing him and, holding him, which was as natural as drinking water. A gentleman and he was a gentle man. Over the years he saw many of the escorts and between us a limited friendship began. This friendship was in the way that I could phone him if I had a question about something, but not a friendship where he would come to my house and we would chat for hours.

After so many years of knowing him, what I did see happening with him was disappointing. He began to use drugs and this was surprising to see. And he changed his business to one that catered to the musicians.

The very last time I saw him as a friend, he was aging and it was as if Dorian Grey, was he, but in reverse. All his sins were showing on his face. The once innocent man I had first met was now a jaded man. A man who should have stayed with his plants and flowers, the change did not suit him. Yes, I would have married him, if only I could have told him how I felt about him.

Man #2

Mr. Shoe-man was someone who should have been married. He had a home in Contra Costa County and it was a well-manicured home, which belied what he did for a living. A wife could have enhanced his life and he appeared to be looking for one; but escort services are not the place to find a wife. The women, in general, are not staying at home types. They want fun and find it for awhile with many different people. Many of the women are stable but their relationships are far from the norm.

The first time he phoned, I went to see him just to make sure the shoes he was offering were worth the trip. Plus, I loved shoes. Oh, to die for yes. He had most of the expensive brands at the time and an escort could walk out of his home with a few pair of shoes worth more than the time of an hour or two of being with him. His taste in shoes was impeccable and all he needed was the woman's shoe size and the shoes were there when the escort arrived. To say I wanted to keep him as my own is more than an understatement. The downside was how far it was to drive to his home. This man just wanted "standard" sex and was very easy to please and, he liked to see the escort walk around in the shoes and clothes were optional and as a client he was easy. I think this was because he felt he was cheating the women by not giving them cash.

The trade was far better in the long run for the escort. If he had a "type" it was not clear, even after a few years of seeing him. Shoe-man just enjoyed women. Short, fat, skinny, pretty, un-pretty, and flaky women were all who interested him. Thinking over his likes and dislikes; well there just were not a lot of dislikes regarding the women. He had shoe sizes for everyone. Perhaps he was a foot voyeur.

The way the escort service received a fee from him, if someone other than I saw him, was he would send a couple of pairs to home base. Nice, very nice and the only way to "buy" shoes; the only wish was for him to live closer to Marin County at the time. I loved having my fee paid to me in shoes. Just loved it.

Man #3

Cop-man had been on the San Francisco "team" for many years when he first called and he is spoken of in another book.

Scared the hell out of me the first time he phoned and I went to see him. There we were sitting on his bed and both naked when he informs me that he is a cop.

"Okay. Is that the signal for the police to come marching in?"

"No, just having some fun with you. I am not on duty and not in the vice department. My mom is really at a church function."

"Damn, you could announce what job you do before letting me take my clothes off."

"Yeah, but the look on your face is worth the money."

We both had a laugh over his scaring me. He turned out to be a "real" client for awhile. That is until he found an escort through the service that he wanted to have as a girlfriend and possibly marry. Not sure what day it was when Internal Affairs from the San Francisco police department phoned the house. I was still living at home at the time. Which means it was the end of the 1970s. The fellow on the phone began by telling me who he was and why he was phoning. It seems this "hag" who had worked for me was now putting in a complaint over Mr. Cop-man and his job was basically on the line. Cop-man was supposed to have tied this escort up with a phone cord and hit her and would not let her out of the place.

Well, I am usually on the escort's side … except, not in this case.

This "hag" was a liar and a thief. She had to be fired because of lying to me and stealing from clients. After my firing her, she must have latched onto this really nice Cop-man, who she had seen through my escort service.

The words just flowed out of my mouth telling the Internal Affairs man, "You should think "better" about who is telling you this story. I know this woman to be a liar and a thief and I would not believe a damn word she said. The man you are speaking about has phoned the service and was always polite and respectful with the women and I even saw him. I never had a problem with him, but I did with her. I even wanted to smack her around a few times. She is just a nut case and should not be taken seriously. If he did hit her I am sure she deserved it."

We hung up the phone.

The next time I spoke to Mr. Cop-man; he was angry with me because he did not know what I said to Internal Affairs about him. He was so angry I had spoken to Internal Affairs that he didn't want to even hear what was said. I can't remember all that he said on the phone, but he was very upset and thought I had done something to him, siding with the girl. He was so wrong. Eventually, the whole thing ended and he was cleared of any wrong doing and ultimately found out that I had not spoken harshly about him. His attorney told him how positive I was for him.

Then we were friends again.

I think he even thanked me. That thank you was not necessary, I had told the truth. With his strong Catholic upbringing this was a man who should have found himself a wife. The only issue was he lived at home with his mother and was devoted to her. Few women will want to live with a mother-in-law or deal with the competition. And the mother-in-laws do not always like the wife; I know he would have taken his mother's side if there were ever a need too. This left him to live alone. Without his income as a cop he stopped phoning for women. Maybe he met someone at church. I always wished him well.

Chapter Nine
Nerds

The men and women who keep their minds forward and focused on the work they have to do, normally, make hordes of money. Many of the people phoning the escort service had great jobs or were owners of their own businesses. The entire world knows that Silicon Valley is just a few miles away from Marin County in Northern California; so it was inevitable that men writing computer code and inventing new ways to master software, which made mankind fonder of computers; would phone an escort service.

These men had full bank accounts and wanted to share with women who could get them back on track to being sexual dynamo's and men again. Some were interesting but most of them were quiet, unless speaking about some great project they were working on, and, could possibly interest a woman who was only thinking about the guy's wallet. I was lucky enough to know a few of them who had been on the ground floor, that is, in the beginning of the push to allow all people to use computers. The home computer coming of age, and, this was a time to see what all of us now know of as "common place" in our, limited, but growing computer world and eventually the Internet.

The only time you knew these men were a "somebody" was if they had you come to their home. Gadgets abounded and the wealth was showing. The sexier the woman this was the only type of woman these men wanted. The "geeks", which all these very sexy women would not give the time of day to if in college or high school. Now the same women were anxious to fondle the body of a "nerd." Yes, I saw some and I have to say they do not change. I remember cringing when in high school and I was out with a super "geek." His hands all over my arm at the movie theater and sharing popcorn, which I had to let slip onto his lap to make him stop touching me and giving me the creeps.

Well, times changed but the men did not. Many of them were still with sweaty palms and wanting to just touch and touch until he or they just about "come" in their jeans. Surely, now there must be some men who are great to look at and wonderful to lay in bed with; but in the late '70s the guys were still in the drool stage. Hanging onto your every word, but they could really care less about anything you had to say. Get their "rocks" off and then you are "history" and they are back to building something which will cost a fortune to buy and the escort returns to men of lower IQ's.

I have to admit I was so dumb about computers in those days

that I did not even pay attention to the names of the men we saw or I saw. Because I was able to get a guy talking about his work, it did not mean anything to me as he spoke nonstop about some "program" he was developing. I just did not understand. If I had understood what all the hype was about, I would have bought some stock or traded our services for stock in some of those companies.

Man #1

Mr. Lobster was about 5'6" tall and a little pudgy. The typical "Geek" looks. He wore glasses and had an instant arrogance about his personality. Which I did not understand, given his appearance. When he phoned in the location where he wanted someone to come to, it was close to me, so I took the first call to see him. He was living on a yacht in Sausalito. The directions to his berth were very accurate and even though he wanted me to wear heels, I had to change shoes when I got there. Heels will constantly go through planks when you walk out to a yacht and mess up the expensive shoes that you had to sleep with a man for and don't want to face him to tell him how you managed to ruin the new pair you just saw him for. Could you keep up with that? Basically ruining escorts clothes was like losing or damaging a mechanics tools.

Anyway, Mr. Lobster watched me walk toward his yacht and he walked forward a few steps to make sure no one saw me and he could get me on the boat quickly. This is typical of the men calling for an escort and they live where it is very public, such as a yacht harbor. The stairway down to the main area of his yacht had the usual small steps and a narrow opening to move through and the opening that you hope you don't slip and fall through. Once down to where the sitting area is you are required to "oh and awe" at how spectacular the yacht is or you may not make the owner happy. I was more into getting to know the person, so I began with lots of questions.

First it was important to know what he did for a living. That question was easily answered.

"I'm retired."

"Well, what did you retire from? You are not exactly old."

"I sold my business; and bought this to live on."

Now this is where he became a little quiet. He did not want to give up the answer to what type of business too easily.

"Okay, may I ask what type of business it was?" Not showing

too much interest to allow him to think about the question and decide if he wants to tell or not.

"I sold a computer business." Sure, that was easy enough. I found out later that it was more than a fix it and sell it business. It took him a couple of more times seeing him to know he had sold a business worth a lot of money. Actually, I don't remember what business it was, but it made him a very rich man and he retired. He did tell me how many millions he got, when he quasi-trusted me. But his coldness toward escorts did not change. He must have been worried that he would have to like one of the escorts and think in terms of girlfriend or wife or something like that, which for these new rich "geek" men, is a fate worse than death. His morals were still middle-class even though his money was now in a huge tax zone.

Mr. Lobster was a "thank you mum," kind of guy. Nice man and safe to send escorts to, but not really into doing anything else but release his body fluids. I got the feeling that if a computer could take care of him, well he would have preferred a computer in his bed. I think I remember him showing me some photo of him in a newspaper article about when he sold his business. It meant nothing to me then or now. I still would not know what he sold all his rights too.

Man #2

Berkeley is full of intelligent people, just like most college towns that have minds that actually think. One call was this Mr. Geek who stood about 6' tall and was very thin. He wore glasses and did not have an extra exclusive apartment in Berkeley. What he did have was access to the main computers at the University (University of California at Berkeley) and was doing a project for them which this escort was able to see. He was so proud of it that he took the time to explain to me what he was doing.

The entire project was very impressive and each time I went there I asked him about how it was going. He was a very nice man but as with most "geeks" he was shy. Very polite and very shy. If he found a woman to marry, she would have been standing next to a computer mainframe handing out cookies and her phone number to any computer engineer who may want it. The guy was a rising star amongst other computer people in his field and is. No doubt, doing very well somewhere in the country. The escorts saw him for a few years and I am sure we were his only form of female contact. I could be wrong, but in his case, no. I do admit that I really enjoyed hearing about what he was doing at the university. It was very impressive and a huge undertaking. The university was lucky to have him and they did not have to import him from some other country.

Man #3

This guy was almost put in the next chapter, but I rethought what he really thought he was, so that is why he is mentioned here.

Mr. Computer Nerd.

The night was cold and rainy when he phoned and he lived in San Anselmo, at the time. I was on the phones and it was late, so few escorts were available to see him. Thus, it would be me. He told me that his house had a gate and he would leave it open, so when I got there I would not have to buzz something or whatever to get inside the area, which I think meant getting out of the car and with it raining he was being polite to tell me he would have the gate open.

I drove to his house and the gate was open as he said it would be. The house looked large but it was the cars that were in and around the property which really caught my eye. (Must have been from my working at a drag strip when I was young.) Some were old or that is antique and others were brand new and expensive. Maybe six or so were parked to the right of the house. My car was not even close to being new and for just a moment I thought, "this was not going to be great if he saw my car"; which he would see, because I had to park in front of his door, due to the rain. Then "control" took over and my thoughts were, "I could care less what he thinks of my car." Trying like hell to believe those words as I exited my car.

The outside lights were on, so I would not break my neck walking up the couple of stairs to the front door. He had been waiting for my grand arrival and opened the door as I walked forward. The man was not really tall, but there was something familiar about him. He saw me looking at him and then he showed me to the bedroom which was a little left of the hall table which held a photo of a baby. When I entered the bedroom it was green from what I remember with a bathroom attached to it and for me to change in. I went inside the bathroom, not thinking much about this man until I returned to the bedroom. The negligee I was wearing was a cream color and I thought it looked nice. He had not been very particular about the woman he wanted and when I said I was a busty blonde, he was okay with that description. We did speak a little before I entered the bedroom and actually I was nervous and joked with him. I asked him, "Is this your home", and, this is when he lied.

"No, I'm the caretaker."

"What do you mean the caretaker?"

"You know, just watching the place."

"Hum. So what do you do for a living, Mr. Caretaker?"

"I work with computers."

"So you program or something like that?"

"Yes, you can say that is what I do."

Now, the entire time he is watching my reaction to what he is saying. Me. I am actually just concerned that the real owner may show up and here I am with some guy pretending to be the Caretaker. Again, I say to him.

"Are you sure it is okay for us to be here?"

"Yes, no problem. Don't worry."

It was late, I was tired and, then I began to look at this man's face and I knew I had seen his face before. Not sure where, but his face was familiar. We lay down on the bed in this green bedroom and the bed was one of those canopy beds, but with an incredible soft mattress. I asked him what it was made of and he said, "Feathers."

It was a feather-bed and very comfortable. About now I realize that he is the owner of the house and has been jerking me around with this story. I, of course, thinking he could be a robber or something worse. Then it hits me who he could be, so I relax.

We begin to make love and he likes doing just about everything. He loves staring at my face or my eyes. Not sure which he was enjoying looking at more. But I still felt that I weighed too much for him. My thoughts were that he liked smaller women. I was just about positive that he preferred women who were fit and maybe underweight.

When we finished he was very polite and asked me if I wanted something to drink. I told him water would be fine and then I went into the bathroom. While I was changing in the bathroom he got my small bottle of Evian water and handed it to me. As he was handing me the water bottle he asked me, again, what the fee was; even though he knew … he was double-checking; and after he did this recheck of the fee, he handed me the cash, which was already in his hand. The exact amount was there and then he walked me to the door and that was that.

Driving home it hits me who this man was and yes he was into computers but he was also into making movies. He continued to phone and I saw him another time after this first time. But he really liked this one girl who worked for the service who was getting her law degree. I thought twice about putting him in the book, but because I found out he used other escort services; which for me, was a betrayal of our escort service and keeping his name safe; that is why I put him in this book. No, I won't tell his name, even now. He was a few billion reasons not too.

Each escort sent to him verified who I thought he was and, they were surprised he was calling for escorts because he could have had anyone in Hollywood. I think he phoned because we were there, and all he wanted was one thing, and… not one reason to see us again. Escorts are a onetime thing and no contracts or guarantees on either side of the fence. Actresses want something. All we wanted was the correct amount of cash and no checks. And yes, he is a computer geek and has many of them working for him. He did not lie about that fact.

Chapter Ten
The Very Wealthy

The men who phoned with huge pocketbooks were, actually, high in numbers or percentages. Some were bankers, producers, oil guys, sheiks, and the popular computer people. Speaking about them will be easy. Wanting them to storm or swarm me into taking them out of the book is why the need for no names. But it will be difficult to disguise at least one of them. As the reader, you have no idea how difficult it is to write a book about clients, when those very clients have so much money they could have lots of bad things happen to you.

These are men that, many times, have not been perfect people in acquiring their money, so harming a person telling some of their secrets would be no problem for them. Publishers want you to name them, but I won't. Not because of what I fear they could do to me, but it goes against my own "code of honor", which was when I began the business, all who used the business would be safe calling and those people working with me would be safe.

I have done my best to keep my "code".

Man #1

This guy is named appropriately, Mr. Crap. I personally saw him and it was at a party that we had to wait two days for these assholes to get their shit together. I am still "ticked" and wish I had not settled for the agreed price before we got to the get-together. The only thing nice about their "party" was the condo. The decorator was fantastic and I am sure the idiot I saw, did not pick out the furniture and decorations. He was too much of a "know-it-all" and an "I-have-it-all", to dirty his hands doing "real" work.

Spoke about this "dirt bag" in another book and to tell the truth; I was actually way too nice with the words for that writing.

The rings on their hands gave it away who they were. He was too short to have ever played on the field himself and it must have given him some great "boner" to watch the team he owned on the field of action. What did he do to get me so upset? He treated me like some piece of meat to be thrown to the "dogs" when he was through with me. Without or any clothes on he shut me out of his bedroom after our own little (Really size is not important; unless of course you can't do anything with what you do have … 5 1/3" to 5 ¾" of hopelessly less than acute stale hamburger meat; just saying if you were purchasing "it" at a meat counter.) time with me; all he did do was get it up for his "get off" time. He basically gave me…without my permission, to his lackey bodyguard. I grumbled and the bodyguard just about "killed" me. Very violent momentary scene when he swung at me. I had to go into the bedroom with the overgrown headache and make him happy. I was then through and just wanted to get the hell out of their personal "devil den." I would never have been there if it were not for the limo driver. He insisted I attend. I found out later it was because I looked like Mr. Crap's wife. Ugh!

Mr. Crap must have played this again a year or two later and the woman he put the screws to that time sued and got over $200,000 dollars. That is what the newspapers said. She deserved every dime. Mr. Crap never learned how to treat a woman and all he knew how to do was have someone cater Kentucky fried chicken. (The Kentucky chicken was much better than the "hams" dishing it out.) He had promised the limo driver we were to go to dinner; that is why the women with me had dressed-up. This was the story the limo driver of theirs had told me for two days. We were going out for some great dinner. No, they saw the "merchandise" and just wanted to get with their real intentions. Foul assholes. Anyway, even this many years later I still hate the sound of his name. I did the big "no, no" and gave my card to someone; I think it was an attorney friend of his.

The limo driver had given strict instructions not to say where or whom we were with, such as the escort service. Like women such as us, grew on trees somewhere. (My meaning here is we looked great.) Maybe the limo driver was playing some con of his own. I don't know or care. Did not care then or now.

Well, I had given my business card to someone, before I met Mr. Crap. No more calls from those creeps. They had rules. Bullshit! This is one nightmare the other escort services could have and *Professional Escorts* was glad to not have this group phone, ever, again. Some other things happened to, but I can't speak about that.

Man #2

The time came when our escort service telephone number was being passed around the very wealthy of the Bay Area. This man phoned with a very bad drug habit. No, nothing new, but the amount of wealth he had was new. Most of it was inherited and his wife had money of her own. The escort sent to him was slender and short with dark hair. Young was his "type" and she stopped working for the service after meeting him. Too afraid to tell me about him; I had to hear it second-mouth from one of the other escorts. Their days and nights were filled with drugs and he was giving her enough money to live well. She even has a mansion in Los Angeles now. What the escort service got out of the deal was the first fee and he let his friends know about the service. Maybe a win, win for everyone concerned. But the girl I sent to him was the real winner.

Man #3

Just your basic royal Sheik phoned and a tall blonde was sent to him. She received $10,000 for the weekend. The bad part is she gave him her phone number, so he could phone her directly. This was lost revenue for my escort service, but a big addition to the former escort's bank account. Many of these "Sheikee" guys phoned the service when they were in town. How they knew to phone *Professional Escorts* is beyond anyone working there at the time, which means me. I never found out how they got my number. It could have been as simple as picking it out of the telephone book. What I envisioned at the time was the phone number being written on the royal marble bathroom walls in the palaces back in whatever country these men came from. No matter how they got the number we did receive some of their money. Not as much as I would have liked, but some.

Man #4

This group of men phoned from a local hotel in Marin County. They wanted about three women to go out with. I always wanted to go out and have fun so I went on this possibly great party. I informed them that we had to have them come to the lobby and we would call them when we arrived. Wow. I was shocked to see such great looking guys from one of the Arab countries. I immediately took what I thought was the guy in charge and the cutest one, just for me.

Man #5

Publishers do have money. Mr. Pub liked me from the moment we met. What he wanted for me to view or do at his home was at first, spooky. The preparation he gave me for what he wanted was zilch. The home, as I drove up to it, had a few lights on inside and there were outside lights. Gently, I walked up to the door and this tall man who was, at least, 70 years of age asked me inside and then asked what I would like to drink. Because of his quiet mannerisms I thought a Vodka and Diet Coke would work. He went behind his bar and poured me a very nice drink. We sat down and spoke for awhile.

Not sure why I did not ask what he did for a living, but by the looks of the residence it seemed as though he would have the money to pay. While sipping my drink he asks me if it was alright for him to change into something comfortable.

"No problem. I'll just sit here."

Mr. Pub goes into his bedroom and is in there awhile and then comes out wearing a horrible blonde wig, great looking stockings and a pretty tight black skirt with lovely blouse. Yes. There was makeup was all over his face and it was almost on his face correctly.

Not missing a beat I said, "Nice legs. But your makeup needs some work."

"Well, I was in a hurry. Do you like what I'm wearing?"

"Yes. But you put a little too much makeup on." Then I found myself critiquing what he was wearing and letting him know that the skirt should not be so tight.

"Just a minute and I'll adjust."

He goes back into the bedroom for another 10 minutes and then reappears. Now he has on a different skirt but higher heels.

"Yes, that looks better."

"Okay, then it is okay for our date?"

Shocked I said, "You want to go somewhere?" I was totally puzzled. This had never happened to me before. I mean…never.

"Yes, to dinner."

Now my heart begins to skip a few beats. It is one thing to be inside with a cross-dresser, but yet another thing to go out with one.

"Sure. Where are we going to dinner?"

"I know this perfect place in town that has soft lighting and delicious food."

"Okay. Do you want me to drive? I mean the heels and all."

"No, I am use to driving in the heels."

We arrive at the restaurant where he had reservations, unbeknownst to me.

The maître d did know him and we were seated at a table rather quickly.

Not a table I would have chosen, but Mr. Pub wanted to be seen. Nothing amazing happened over dinner, except when we were leaving the restaurant; I almost jumped for joy the entire hoax was over. The hoax being on me. I assumed. This was the only cross-dresser we ever had, or I ever knew, who wanted to go out in public.

When we arrived back at his place he gave me money to purchase him some more clothes and gave me all his sizes. This was the area of cross-dressing he did not like, purchasing his "equipment". We made a "date" for the following week and I left. Yes, I did purchase the clothes and brought them to him the next week. He, in turn, gave me the wigs he had in case I wanted to use them. Yes, I took the wigs; a girl never knows when they (the wigs) could come in handy.

What he wanted to do was just a quick romp on his bed, to enable him to "come" in his new underwear. This was his "thing" to do. How I found out he was a very, very, very, big newspaper publisher was through a newspaper article about him and his photo was part of the article.

All I did was smile.

Generally speaking, cross-dressers are very nice people and rather meek. He had to have been doing this "show" of going out to dinner, for years.

Man #6

Mr. Bad Check writer and this is one guy ... I would love to say their names, and his name, in big letters in the book. What a jerk he was and they both were. We always had to argue with him over money. He lived in San Francisco and had tons of money; owning many office buildings and lots of real estate. Going over his home ... the one away from home was never a treat. He would insist he wanted you to take a check and said he told the person on the phone that he was paying with a check. Always a lie! I was normally the person on the phone. Dah! I knew that I had told him, "No!" to any checks.

Then his sexual preferences were all about the girl wearing fancy negligees just to have him paw all over her. His wife and children lived at his house and he would stay in the city just to see women. What a freak. Standing about 5'6" tall and that could be a stretch. The man kept his weight normal but his mind was foul. Lots of dirty talk to get him going and my take was that he really was in love with men and just put up with women.

I went to his office one time just to try and collect on a bad check. He wasn't there but I made it clear, we had another bad check from him. For years I kept the check to throw in his face one day. Men like this one were not why the business was fun, or why we stayed in business for so long.

Comment

It has been said that names should be put here, in this book, to make the clients more real. Well, they were real and names would only mean lawsuits.

Also, in using the escort service the clients knew that I was a private person who did not kiss and tell. Once I wanted to speak about a famous client and even phoned a tabloid. The writer came out and because of how big this client was in the world stage I was put through hell. And basically, called a liar, but I am no liar and don't wish to be paraded on television or radio and gossip circuits just to prove that someone used the service. Use your imagination and the location of where I had my business and maybe you can figure out who the clients were. Or hire a rocket scientist who is able to give you a list of all the variables.

Epilogue for the Clients

The men represented here are less than .0001%, or, a very small fraction of all those clients, who phoned over the years. Some of the sex talk was relevant to what was happening and was not put in the book to just be salacious. For those many women who have contacted me about beginning their own business of escorting; what I would say is, "Do not do something in life, whether escorting or washing dishes, unless you plan on working long hours and will devote your life to what you have chosen to do. Devotion is a word which flows easily from my mind and from my voice, when I think of escorting. A person has to be devoted to making people feel good and hopefully happy."

The escorts with *Professional Escorts* were normally well-paid and allowed people to be free from guilt. The world has a place for escorts and massage people and it is not at the highest of respectful places. This is sad, because these people do serve people and are usually happy to be escorts and they make people happy.

The mere act of dating for money has its cavalcade of ideas from experts and "Sex-pert's". In reading some of the ideas behind the experts' comments, I would say many of them have tried working for or asking men to pay them for their time. Not as a habit or a profession, but just to see what the hype is all about. If escorting is tired or done just a few times and possibly interviewed with only a handful of people, it does not qualify them as "Sex-pert's" or any kind of expert.

Well, I am an expert on dating and relationships and my world was both for money and profit. My dating for just the fun associated with getting to know another person, who was of the opposite sex, went on for many years. I loved the good and bad experiences because all of those experiences gave "growth" to my character. After 40 years of dating, I know what men want and what they dislike. The primary reason a man wants to go out with a woman is to get to know her. His wants are simple and his needs are even simpler. If he is paying, yes, he wants sex. How the rest of the relationship moves forward is up to the woman. If it is just sex, the man wants out of the relationship, and then the woman should make sure she is asking for all the perks. Meaning she should get something out of the relationship and not feel shy about asking for rent money or a new dress. This appeal to your better judgment and you should, at the very least, get him to buy some books or CDs for you. Jewelry is wonderful and should always be "hock able". But under no circumstances give him all the perks out of the relationship. And for men, yes, sex is a perk in a relationship.

When writing my books I have tried to increase awareness for men and women as to why men want to pay for time with women. As part of my own awareness of men and their motivations I have also decided that all women can benefit from a few commandments that I put in place for my escorts when they worked for my escort service.

Please find here, those commandments and utilize them in your own dating life.

The Escorts' Commandments of serving men on earth:

1. Don't steal from the clients.
2. Don't tell his wife or girlfriend. This is sound advice for all women who are dating men that have significant others.
3. Never phone him first.
4. Get your money up front. Adjust for women who are dating without money exchanged. Such as find your dinner has landed in your stomach first, or you went shopping before any other physical gifts from you were given.
5. No pity.
6. Be his instrument of fascination.
7. Do what he wants and what you feel comfortable doing with him. Never allow him to talk you into anything that doesn't feel right.
8. Don't fall in love with him. Unless you are planning a family, because love just gets in the way of your primary wants and needs for you.
9. Make sure he is satisfied with you. This one is self-

explanatory and here is where you earn your keep.

10.   Leave him smiling.

When followed, the above commandments will support the user's goals in harboring an interest in the finances and a possible relationship with the man they are dating. Maybe not all the commandments relate to your own dating world, but they will help you understand how escorts think about the men they are seeing for money and how you should think while pursuing, your man, or many men. Remember that a marriage, relationship, and a dating experience is time out of your life. Time is valuable and you should know that your time is worth something.

Prologue for Escorts

This work, (meaning book) is not an attempt to control the universe regarding sexual topics. It is not the *Hite Report*. Nor is it the *Kinsey Report* which was maniacal report. The *Kinsey* documents spoon-fed to the public the sexual morals of people with dominate and latent sexual values, commonly worked out in quasi-therapeutic circumstance. Done with socially repugnant research doctors; they collectively and independently felt they had the world of sexual fantasies solved or nearly solved. Both reports had merit in a few ways, but the way in which they came to all their conclusions was questionable.

The following is an expose on escorts who once worked for a now defunct escort service, which was based in Marin County, California. Some of the escorts are less interesting than others but are put in this writing to allow the reader, you, to find solace in the fact that you are not he or she or them. Each one was handled, by me, with the utmost compassion and understanding.

There were moments when I felt as if all hell was breaking loose. I did have, accompanying regrets for hiring some escorts, because I never gave a thought or a concern that this very person or persons (some cases) in front of me was or were really not up to the task of working as an escort.

Shame on me, because I was naïve, in thinking that all women and men were naturals at the game of dating and it was just one more step to ask for money. There were times when I had to fire people and yell at the top of my lungs so the person would understand the term, fire, and not cry or use up any more of my time than the person had already stolen from me.

Regardless as to how you read this and give it your own interpretation; it is original and truthful, and it will, hopefully, have you think about the people written with some positive discussion and view them as individuals.

Each one had left a different "stamp" on the escort service I operated for those many years. Each one, even if that person only lasted a day, made an impression on me and how I handled my service.

Chapter Eleven
The Escort Service

Most of them were gorgeous and some had the inner glow of innocence. At times there were women hired over their prime, but in primal velocity for making men happy. There were the women with 'keys' to the minds of men, and, there were those women that could hardly think their way out of the car they were driving.

The attitudes varied, but they all had attitude. You would think they were high-fashion models (some did model), or rocket scientists (a couple were doctors), or better yet computer programmers (a few were computer programmers). And a few insisted on having a driver take them to their appointments.

Some wanted to only see a client with another woman. Not because of just liking women but because the person was scared to go see a customer alone.

Those women that came to me to make money and only money did not benefit from the experiences they received, as much as the escorts that just wanted to do it 'all'.

The 'all' was having sex in every imaginable way and with all kinds of people. And seeing people that did not want any sex at all from them; which was tantalizing to find men that just wanted to talk to a person and pay that person more money than the person could ever make working at most other jobs.

The 'all' of going out to places they never would have had a chance to go, if not with a person of means.

The 'all' of being adored and, what I mean here is, letting another person worship you for a very short moment in time. A worship that was complete.

This was the magical hour a person paid for and wanted to be with an escort of his or her dreams. And this was adoration that melted the escort and allowed the escort to dream of being someone else; and to have an escape plan for another source of support, and possibly dream of owning their own business when they were finished as an escort.

This adulation empowered the women and men working as escorts.

The money gave infinite possibilities to dream and fantasize what life could be for the escorts.

The girls loved to talk about their big nights out. Mostly, they would embellish the night and speak of the rock star and compliment of awards on the walls they saw or about the drug dealer and the hordes of money he had in a cabinet, safe, or suitcase; again more drugs and money than those women had ever seen before. To be privy to business deals that the person or client knew by telling the escort could get the escort killed. It was all there, loud abrasive, sick, solitary, and many, many times depraved.

A unique life of traveling in cars and planes the escort could only dream of affording. Having clothes purchased for them that cost a King's ransom with the added benefit of never having to look at the price tag first. Living a life that many a housewife dreamed she had, and in some cases while working for me, did have. Never to let her husband or boyfriends know of the many secrets that were kept and that are still kept secret. More secret than some government files. And quite possibly are in some government files marked TOP SECRET.

The millionaires that phoned and the billionaires that saw women and have lived to keep their lives under wraps were all my clients and loved being able to phone and have one of my escorts journey unescorted to that person's home.

The judges that protected my escorts and my service along with the police that never wanted prying investigators to know that they used the service.

The attorneys that grew up to be in political office and in many cases those judges were all my clients.

The women that phoned and wanted to be discreet and only see men that would not speak of her sexual appetite and prancing her 'play' boyfriend in front of colleagues. The male escorts kept those elusive women's stolen moments quiet and did not even tell me.

The lovely high school seniors without dates to the proms and those moments forever lived. Because my escorts were there. The sick and dying patients had the availability of a person to hold their hands as the inevitable crept into the rooms. The teenagers that needed warmth and companionship while lying in bed without movement of torsos. We complied.

The parents phoning for a woman to hold their son's hands, while recovering from surgeries, we were there.

There were escorts that tipped me extra above and beyond my fee because they had never made such money before. Yes, it was for money, mostly, but it was also to experience a side of life that did not exist in their 'normal' world.

The girls wanted to survive and live a fantasy that most women will think of someday doing, but never try.

The forbidden frolic and the long walk to Satan's door and back again.

These women knocked upon that door and some became lost and entered to lose their very souls to the money they made. There were those men and women that seemed to have the keys to Satan's many rooms.

While other women made the journey that their various preachers and told them they should never think about doing, and, every night was calling out to them in their dreams. But with soul intact fell back into religion to preach the evils of the sin that escorting was to them. Torn women, who did not want to make the choice between good and evil.

Almost all of these women broke the cardinal rule of having sex without the piece of paper, well- typed, to say they were bound to one man and only one man. *The Harlots of San Francisco* is what many people called them then and now. For me they were my *Professional Escorts.*

They were all part of the new *Barbary Coast*, the new public bounty of flesh for money trade abounding all through the last twenty years of the twentieth century.

These women helped me bring escorting to a whole different level. To be paid for doing what comes naturally on a date; to feel free to express one's self as you looked deeply into a person's eyes, knowing full well that your night would be full of lust and intense and even insane passion. And you will be paid for your time, up front, not waiting until the night was over. The money was there or you were not. Something that never happened with regular dating; the dates that took your soul and spit you back into society for your pain and punishment to work out with phone calls to your friends and family wondering why the person hasn't asked you to marry, since you have given your body to him; for having loved someone that only used you. A sense of empowerment was the escort's main tool in her new found trade. She could walk away from the date, knowing that she took something back to her home that she did not have to want marriage or a relationship. She was as free as any man was, with his empowered life of hopping from one bed to the next, without regard to give finality through marriage to the person he carelessly clung to, for a few lust filled moments.

A new passion was felt by the escort. The passion of knowing she or he was worth more than their parents ever allowed them to think their time, beauty, and knowledge could be worth. This passion created a sense of style that the escort put to his or her personae and developed, while trying to hide their haunting mistrust of this new found confidence.

The range of motion to evolve as a person was there, for the escort, and, they did evolve. Some did very well, and, others were just sleepwalking through the experience. Their eyes closed for fear they may be seen. The trepidation that all people knew, who they were when shopping or attending a religious service. Yet some had absolutely no guilt feelings to impede their progress in learning.

All the passions and feelings were real. Some felt weak from having erotic feelings about men that were unattractive or only had the money to pay the fee once. Others knew that the power between their hands and legs was immense and they wanted to train the clients to phone for only them, so they explored the realms of fantasies that only lovers contrive to escape to in the marriage bed. That type of coupling, the couple could only dream of, when fondling each other in some euphoric dream of pleasure.

Many escorts blushed when coming back to me and letting me know about the first call they had gone out on. But all had eyes that were glazed over. The new experience of having sex for money was intoxicating and liberating.

The men and women, who phoned, became addicted to phoning me and listening to my programmed voice. This went for both the clients and the escorts. The "voice" that would steady the caller's nerves about making arrangements to see women or men, who were new to them; a stranger, a person on the other end of the phone, with tones in her voice, when they phoned for directions, that would bring the person, the climax, he or she wanted. It would happen soon and the clients became their own worst enemies. Some emptying their checking accounts to have the satisfaction they wanted.

The escorts were lulled into compliance by the "voice" on the phone. It was me, their mentor, their savior from their bills and mundane existences; I was a boss to help them escape from, many times over, a very bad relationship, controlling parents, and even their own fears of exclusion in society.

My *Professional Escorts* were daring and trusted me implicitly. I never wanted to betray their undying trust. Even when the Internal Revenue asked me, I would not give up their names. The truth being, in some instances, I did not know the escorts real name. I used all my secrets and cleverness to keep them safe. Safe from glaring eyes and safe from the predators that lurked on the other end of the phone; those that phoned to see them and these were my escorts and they were exceptional. Other escort services offered men and women, but did not use the care in grooming them for going out, as I did. Many other escort and dating services just gave out calls to women and did not make sure the women were safe. My girls were safe, for the most part working with me.

If someone had a problem, many times it was because they broke a rule I had in place. And yes, I did have rules for these escorts. This escort business was in Marin County and that county begins somewhere close to the middle of the Golden Gate Bridge. The public interest in county lines was somehow benefited by having the line drawn using a bridge. I would really like to know their reasoning years ago. By doing such a thing. Perhaps both San Francisco County and Marin County wanted credit or responsibility for the famous bridge.

Bringing up the bridge is not only for a visual but to tell you, the reader, that the bridge was a significant part of why *Professional Escorts* did so well, along with the use of the other Bay Area bridges. I and most of the escorts traveled it many times a day to see clients, place ads, wait at bars and restaurants for telephone calls, interview prospective escorts and masseuses, and party all over the town of San Francisco.

The bridge linked my escorts and escort service to the clients living on both sides of the historic-orange-monolithic-span, and, also allowed us to travel down to the Peninsula servicing those cities and even as far as Fresno.

Professional Escorts was the front runner for social change in dating experiences in the San Francisco Bay Area at the end of the 1970's.

The fact was that *Professional Escorts* advertised in newspapers and in phone books for the entire San Francisco Bay area, which included Marin County, San Jose County, Contra Costa County, and the Peninsula. Also. the Fresno and Lake Tahoe areas helped this service become a 'must do' experience for blue collars, white collars, government employees, police, movie elite, sports figures, drug rich, rock musicians, tourists, wealthy and those able to afford the services *Professional Escorts* service provided.

Many new citizens and illegal immigrants even phoned the escort service.

The service was a perk for executives and was even used by men with terminal illnesses to relieve some of the pain they were experiencing, and, for one precious hour, could forget. This was a complete hedonistic time for the user of the service, the "I am" of all

"I am/s." The money needed to begin *Professional Escorts* was borrowed. This business began on a $35.00 investment and mushroomed into a six figure a year big business. Much or I should say most of the money being escorts employee money. The money I was making went directly back into the business to keep the advertising going and a host of other bills both personal and business that generated monthly.

This service became the largest well-accepted escort service in the country, which had been set up at that time. It was not franchised through the 'mob' or any other illegal enterprise or organization.

It was a sole-proprietorship. One person responsible for the entire running of the business, and it was me, Dian. The business was getting a lot of attention and I suppose it could be because I did not hesitate when asked if I would interview. Many escort owners did not want the publicity, but I had the notion, that it was free advertising and I would accept anything, which helped advertise the business, especially if it was free. The program *"That's My Line"* chose my escort service as the 'straightest' service in the country and this was after they did some survey. My escort service beat out some well-known services on the East Coast for that honor.

The day came when the program was in town to film my segment and we had filmed it at a hotel lobby and restaurant in San Francisco. {The two escorts chosen for the segment were clean cut and represented the service well. One was a male escort and the female escort had some of the best legs a woman could have. Each person was attractive, as any model on television. It is too bad the show was canceled and our segment did not make it to the American audience.}

The first hotel asked us to leave when they found out that it was for an escort service. I think this allowed the person in charge to understand, better, that escort services were not always thought of as 'straight' and, that was how I wanted my business to be thought of, especially, when a customer phoned for our service. We were as diverse as any brokerage house and I was trying to eliminate any 'seedy' connotations that the word 'escort' mustered up in the minds of the unknowing. But as life and style would have it, I was unable to stop people from believing the negative remarks they had heard or believing how they wanted to think about escort services.

This television program planned to feature my service on their show, but the show was cancelled before my segment was aired. I wish it had aired because it might have allowed people to think of businesses such as mine as not so sexual or just sexual, but a service that people could use to see the tourist attractions and sites in San

Francisco and, people could have fun dates for money.

It was an uphill battle to achieve acceptance from the general public.

The regular newscaster for local news, occasionally, called me for comment. The first call came for my opinion as to how the hotel strike was affecting my business in San Francisco. Nice news for escorting. A positive news clip. Unfortunately, there was a huge spout of lava from Mount St. Helens that took away from that first interview on the 6PM news. There were other news shows and a couple of radio interviews and all were expected to get the message to the public that *Professional Escorts* was a business first, and always accepting new escorts and clients. Especially the clients, but any broadcast had our phone ringing for days with new applicants.

The Minneapolis area, I believe, or somewhere in the Midwest called and I had a live interview for their radio listeners. Locally a radio station interviewed me and I was able to promote my business and answer his questions, which were similar to just about every interview. Radio was scary. I definitely liked taping interviews. Live audiences were a nightmare.

My favorite interview was with a Bay Area back roads type of program and the host came to my home and it was a very relaxed conversation. Loved that little show and interview, which gave the service great publicity and the phones just rang off the hooks after it aired, which led to my accepting an interview for the local show *People Are Talking*.

This show was televised from their San Francisco location and had a live audience. Not one of my female escorts wanted to accompany me to the show. That was okay with me because I always wanted their anonymity, so one of the male escorts went along with me to the show, but he asked them not to film his face. He was not ready for his wife hearing all the negative talk from neighbors. She knew he was an escort, but would probably have asked him to stop working for me, had his face been seen. (I would have liked to have been a fly on their wall as they watched the show together.)

The live audience also included a woman that was there to call the business prostitution and other audience members were invited to ask questions to put me on the spot. Her name was Margo St. James. Margo was a publicity hound if there ever was one for prostitution. But I was surprised she was put in the audience to chip away at my interview.

When founding a "ball" for prostitutes every year in San

Francisco to bring in money for her agenda ... I would have to say that was a great idea. The people love that "ball" and no doubt gave her the cash she needed for all her projects. You don't hear much about her anymore. I think she has retired from most activities that have to do with prostitution.

The one time I did meet her at her home, she handed me a cigarette, which was marijuana. I hate smoking and can't remember if I took a hit or not. In the back of my mind I was throwing her out of the studio that day. Not because I did not like her, but because I can't stand the word "prostitution"; and that is the only word she knows for women who take money for their time.

Margo was fighting for prostitution to be legal and I was yelling back at the women who worked for me, telling them that it was legal. The name had been changed to escorting or massaging. We definitely had different ideas as to what was best for working women. It was a good move that the escorts did not want to join me that day. Margo would have eaten them alive.

Live shows are no place for people that want to advertise their business. Even though we had a huge amount of calls that day and for weeks after; it also attracted the wrong attention, which came from the authorities, police, and yes ... the IRS.

Since the beginning of *Professional Escorts* there has been many books written about dating, escorts, sex, massage services, scandals, etc., and very few of these books are completely accurate. Even fewer people writing such books cared, when they knew their facts were untrue. Most writers of such books ignored what the influence of these escort services have done to our generation of 'free thinkers' and 'free love- makers'. Many of these books and their subsequent writers, have been careless and not acting in a responsible manner to society, to inform the public about the truth of what was going on with the sexual habits of people, after the big push of sexual services revolution in the 1970's; which I might add was after the 'free love' era of the 1960's. Most insiders' views are from the girl working, or the male working, and he or she cannot speak to how the operation was run, except for their bias insights concerning the person in charge. They leave out the wider area of influence the services have had.

Countless, past escorts will not speak about their families and how their working affected them, or, even, how society may have treated them. Some have lost track of the acceptance they received in the 1970s. Preferring to say that the businesses were not run well or putting blame on other people and not taking responsibility for their own actions. Usually, taking this low-road, after they have played out all their own fantasies with the public, their customers, or, perhaps, even they were arrested and no longer wanted any part of the sex for money trade.

The people talking the loudest were usually too over-the-hill to be an escort anymore, so it was beneficial, for them in some way, to now downplay the escort services and massage services that were currently in business. Many had hidden agendas, which brought them in grant money to educate the prostitute. I believe it to be just a con to get money, because they are no longer "prized" stock to work in the business. That brings me back to what I always said, "My escorts were not prostitutes because they were not asking for money for sex. They were asking for money for time". Not much of a big difference to the police, but it was to a lawyer poised in front of a jury. And sex for money or time for money came in the following forms: Verbal, physical, visual, and psychological. Numerous people that worked with me never told their families what they were doing.

Instead, some of them even made fun of escorts when a conversation about escort services would be brought up - just so they would not be revealed. Sex was happening on just about every call I sent people out on. Some of the sex was just verbal. This is explained by a customer, who is only able to think about sex and not do anything, so he would get into some heavy talk with the escort. The client may even want the escort nude as he spoke to her, but would not touch her. Making her out to be the forbidden fruit of his desire, yet keeping her at a distance, as an untouchable.

The escort being paid for satisfying his quirky situation, as she took off her clothes, or, she just laid there next to him, with all the interest she could muster about what he was saying. What did she care? She was being paid for her time and only had to listen to his words and possibly say something he wanted her to say, which got him excited.

I was back at the phones and could have gotten him going and ready for the escort, who would be at his home, just by breathing heavy on the phone and letting him fantasize about the escort showing up. By the time the girl got there he was mostly done, with his sheets already wet from his excitement. Her work was easy, all she needed to do was accept the money and give him a kiss. This happened many times, because no matter what job, the client had, many were using alcohol or drugs to relax, which meant they may not be able to have lasting erections. Now with medical breakthroughs there are pills to take for the man and, it is probably better for the current escorts, they can end up being with a client for hours and, time equates to more money to put in their pockets.

Sidebar: The escorts always wanted to know what I said to the men.

When the first help wanted ads for escorts appeared in the *San Francisco Chronicle* newspaper; the phone was ringing off the hook from persons of all social standings and sexual orientations wanting to be escorts. There were students, housewives, unemployed, adventure junkies, prostitutes, curious people, drug addicts, waitresses, sex maniacs, etc.

The business was planned to run 24 hours and, I had hoped to find a pattern lurking somewhere in the timing of all the phone calls, in order to limit the hours I had to work. That never happened.

Professional Escorts was a 24 hour business. Those 24 hours of work quickly became the headache of the century for me. No time for the employer, me, to be the escort. Calls were needed to be matched and records had to be kept. My primary job had changed. Bills accumulated and needed to be paid. Just to stay on top of the business was a most extraordinary accomplishment for one person. It had to be run out of my home, because the phone gyrated all the time and, to stay at an office was not practical.

Now, in the 21st century it could be done by computer or cell phone and run very well, but back in the those days it was not feasible to sit all night at an office. Some services did it, but not *Professional Escorts*, not me. I had my family to take care of and they came first.

The sexual revolution of the sixties and the seventies brought about changes in laws and viewpoints. Disease entered the picture on an enormous scale that pushed local governments to have more restrictions and enabled the conservative establishment to push for laws that would prosecute owners of services; where the politicians felt sex was being promoted. It has to be noted that *Professional Escorts* was headquartered 15 miles from San Francisco where AIDS had became the single most destructive force for people expressing themselves sexually without the use of needed protection. No one could blame the officials for wanting to stop the spread of an uncontrollable disease. But in reality, people that worked in what can be called the "sex trade" of massaging and escorting, did use protection, for the most part, and, were not as likely to spread the disease as those individuals having one night stands, after picking up someone from a tavern.

The media has filled the coaxial cable lines with enough talk about sex to confuse anyone, who, really might be interested in what happened before, during, and after the 'free-love' generation; or should I say the 'baby-boomers' sexual revolution.

Sociologists around the world have written many half-truths concerning money for sex in the United States. Primarily, because most of their information is taken from police records and people surreptitiously involved, admitting to or giving just tidbits of what happened. The police have tunnel-vision. They scatter through just one viewpoint and that is the laws' position on sexual favors, for hire. Those very people giving out the tidbits of sensationalism usually do not want their names mentioned. The ones that do not mind being involved, are self-serving and it is most times, the hidden agenda running their motives, which are for money and their fifteen minutes of fame.

Never have I read a full report on the involvement of the United States government in all areas of the dating sector. Maybe it is there, I have just not been privy to it. The United States government has extensive research through the Naval Department on sexually transmitted diseases. Any person that has joined the Navy knows about those informational films. All Navy personnel have to view them before going on shore at foreign locations.

Most of the Navy's research was done, by using brothels in other countries and the involvement of our troops with prostitutes around the world. The Navy's web site has the necessary information for their men and women to view, at their leisure. The focus for our country, (United States) comes out of Nevada and counties within that state where prostitution is legal. The reason used in past years for our government to monitor these establishments was the (IRS) Internal Revenue Service. The one government sanctioned department that does not care how you make your money, just like the Mafia, that department wants its "cut", its money.

Many people laughed when the IRS went to the now defunct Mustang Ranch (A fire destroyed the original ranch in 2007, but within a few months after there was launched a new ranch in August of 2007.) In Nevada and kept the books in September of 1990. The IRS laughed all the way to the bank. But the IRS says they failed in that attempt. Who knows what the truth is? But I would say the IRS made some money, to pay down the taxes of the infamous owner, Joe Conforte.

Plus, the IRS learned about the sex business, first hand. Legalized government run brothels should be, and, will be in the future, on this North American continent. My prediction for the future in the sex trade, because disease has become the single largest factor for monitoring those brothels and other locations where sexual behavior may be attempted or is occurring.

All escort services and massage services should have their employees monthly tested for disease and I am not ever going to believe the statement, "My business is legitimate". That is what every owner says. Legitimate is relative and, can be anything from a licensed massage studio to contracted dating service. If I could not keep a handle on what was going on with my business, servicing the community; I know that other services cannot keep their businesses 'straight'.

Now, in the 21st century, there has to be controls.

The escort business is similar to other dating situations. Most dating experiences do end up in the bedroom and there is no moral governing body telling single and married people to obtain monthly checkups; but that can be achieved if you are in the business of volume and profit.

Counties and States can demand for the people at establishments to obtain disease cards that show their workers to be free of all major communicable diseases. Harry Reid, a senator, from Nevada wants to banish legalized prostitution in any part of Nevada. At the time of this writing his wishes have not been met. But hell if they can have nuclear waste hidden in the mountains of Nevada, why not women of ill-repute? I think given the choice, the women would come out on top. No pun intended. A computer generated card given to registered workers would work out well; then all employees would be monitored by computer if counties and states implemented the solution, as I see it. A private business computer would be programmed to tell the owners when it is time to have their employees scan their card in to verify that they are free of communicable diseases.

There once was a requirement for employees, to have x-rays, to determine if food industry workers had tuberculosis. That should be ongoing and paid for by the person who wishes to work in the massage or escort business. Sometimes the simplest ideas are able to prevent major outbreaks of disease.

When a person asks another at a bar or restaurant what their astrological sign is, those very people can also be asking the other person if the person has a card showing his or her self is free of disease. It may take the spontaneity out of sexual attraction, but it would keep the social and promiscuous dating circles safe. I have strong feelings about organizations or people that may protect those people who manipulate the minds of children. I have to say that my business was a consensual business between adults. Not children. Period!

The people working with me did not have to engage in any sexual conduct. If they did, well it was between the customer and the escort. Just like any other dating situation.

Do I condone this type of behavior? Yes and no.

Some people benefit by paying for the company of another person. Escorts benefit by having their expenses paid for and they have some fun.

Should this type of work be available and controlled? Yes and no. There will always be people paying for the company of another. So to control such behavior, shall always be in the interest of society, because when government attempts to control disease and know where to find people that need to be tested it benefits all of society.

If escorts are not having sex with clients, then it only serves to put a stigma on people that are just going out with others. Dating for money is accepted in most areas of the world. Dating with sex involved is not. That is a true statement.

Do I believe both cannot be controlled? Yes and no. Some activities can be controlled, but human behavior will win out. If people are going to go to a social function and. then home for some other type of fun...well you just cannot stop people from being themselves. If the attraction is there, people will do what they want to do. Very similar to popular reality television shows. Many of those shows have people getting together for sex. The network cannot stop them from being human.

Many times I told people who worked for me that it was up to them if they did anything sexual. What else could I say to them? Not a thing. I was not approving their behavior. But what I was doing was being realistic. Hordes of people in American society run their lives with their heads in a hole filled with pipe dreams and religious conflicts. The very people you see having marital affairs, would, most probably, not condone escorts being in their community. These people are the snakes and hypocrites to the bone and finger-pointers of the very communities they live in. Honesty was the foundation of the business of escorting that I ran. The women and men were honest that it was money they wanted from the clients. Not love and a forever dream.

Their lives were based in reality.

Chapter Twelve
The Interviews

The naivety I had expressed to my mother when I began *Professional Escorts* was found in my statements when I told her that both men and women would phone for escorts to see the San Francisco Bay area. I hoped there would be enough female and male escorts ready to work, if the demand was there. This was a time when I had underestimated what was about to happen with my new business.

The first day the ad appeared in the *San Francisco Chronicle*, it was very obvious that the men phoning for women would be out-numbering the women phoning for men by the thousands. Women also desired information as to how to become an escort, but unfortunately, the men calling tied up the telephone line wanting information as to how, where and when they could become escorts?

The fact that I used my mother's home to begin my business is not really an unusual idea. Many businesses, such as mine, were and are run out of a home and there is an even higher-rate in the United States since the dawn of the computer age and online access, there are hordes more explicit web sites on the web. Than I ever had in any newspaper.

The first and primary goal of *Professional Escorts* in 1977 was an effort to add some respectability for escorting and massaging businesses. To take away from the idea that escort and massage services were there for men only and those men were in need and wanting sex delivered to their doors.

In speaking to the people calling, I had to determine if the person was interested in being an escort or wanting an escort and, with the men it was not discernible at first. The men had more unusual questions and the women calling were uneasy and had fewer questions. All tried to dissect what type of business it was and, with that new found information, they decided if they wanted to meet me.

Those early days of operating my escort service gave me a lot of reflection as to what an escort really is thought to be, from the eyes of the general public. I had ultraistic thoughts that people coming from other areas of the United States and the world community would really want to see the city (San Francisco and surrounding areas) and all the attractions.

Wrong.

Men wanted sex or thought they wanted it.

From the beginning, I informed clients that they would be only paying for the time of the escort and, if anything else transpired, then it was at the acceptance of the escort; leaving any decision of sexual behavior up to the escort or masseuse and not the person paying for the time involved. It was my desire to take the power away from the men and put the last word about the 'date' in the woman's control over her body and soul, and thus, to empower my escorts.

Men did not catch on too quickly to the idea.

I had to inform them, many times over, that the escort was there by request and that the man was paying only for her time. Bottom line was that he had to pay for her, a minimum of one hour's time and, if he wanted or expected anything else, then he had to discuss that with the woman. He was paying for time. Over and over again that was emphasized for years. This statement could have and should have been recorded to play back, the hundreds of times I had to say it to people day in and day out.

I was never part of the discussion about what they would do together, except to make sure the first one hour was paid and, if she wanted to stay longer, that he knew he was on the clock. Those were my duties. To be the authority at the other end of the phone and, the escort had to phone in and she had to phone out. Then she had to phone again. So I knew she made it safely away from the location of the call. I instilled in my escorts, a work ethic that…time mattered and if they stayed even for a minute longer, and then they were being taken advantage of by the customer. Time was important and an escort could make more money by getting back on the road and off to another customer. Such an easy concept, but difficult to drive home and into many people's heads, but I would try.

Mom's home was literally, figuratively, reliably, and operationally running 24 hours a day. She hated the phone as much as I did. My mom's routine of eating quietly when she arrived home from her job was shattered. She could not sit and watch television with her food in front of her and relax as she wished to do, after a long boring day at the phone company. At first she tried sleeping with her radio on to obscure the sound of the phone ringing. Then she asked me to turn the ringer down, to a can hardly hear it, low, on the phone. Mom even threatened to unplug the thing (phone). She asked me to take it in the kitchen, the bathroom, and at one point I had to answer the phone outside the back door.

The call-forwarding of the phone to a public pay phone came in handy, so I could sit in comfort and wait for calls; also, stopped the shouting from my mother to me. So it was to spare my mother's home and feelings that I made a local restaurant the rendezvous for meeting the first six months of applicants, who wanted to work for *Professional Escorts*.

There was this restaurant that I used in San Francisco on Van Ness Boulevard for those escorts without transportation or some other excuse not to make the drive to Marin County and interview with me. I would always tip very well at any location I used, so the staff would keep their distance. The ploy worked and the staff let me sit in a booth to interview. And I hired or met many people at the restaurant, my office away from home in the city.

When I first met a woman that was interested in being hired, I took a quick scan of her mannerisms and colloquialisms as she spoke. It was important for me to know that she was a suitable package. Someone the client would want to see again and, she would represent the service well. For each and every person I ever met, with few exceptions, I spoke a lot. About jack-shit and I would continue, until I saw that the person was ready to leave or wondering why they had made the phone call to become an escort. My reasoning was if she or he could sit through my nonsense, then they could listen to the clients. Most clients wanted to talk. Sex was a by-product and mostly an after-thought for clients, also, something they thought that the escort expected to do. The clients were lonely and just wanted to speak to someone or hold someone.

Those escorts that passed that primary test were hired.

The typical interview went like this at a restaurant.

"Hi, are you April?"

"Yes."

"Well would you like to sit down?"

(Many waited at the front door because money was always an issue. Sitting down and waiting for me meant that the girl would need to order.)

"Yes."

"Would you like something to drink?"

"Yes. Just a coke."

"Okay, waiter"…… (The order is put in.)

"Are you from here?"

"No."

"Where are you from?"

"I just drove in a week ago from Los Angeles."

"Did you have a job waiting for you here?"

"No, I just thought I would try my luck."

"How has that been going for you?"

"Not too good."

"Okay, let me tell you a little about what we do and see if it is something that you would like to do. First of all, may I see some identification? You do look a little young."

"Yes, here it is, I am twenty-three."

"Amazing, you really look good. What type of work have you been doing?"

"Dental Assistant."

"Is that what you plan on doing for the rest of your life?"

"No, I   plan on returning to college and finish my degree in medicine."

"Do you have transportation that is reliable?"

Then some more chatter about how her drive there was, or her parking situation and, in some cases, she may have had someone waiting for her. Then I would either hire her or ask her to phone me later. Later meant she would be told that I did not feel she was right for my service. I wasn't leading the woman on ... but it was necessary to put some time between when she finds out about the job and, searches her true feelings, as to if the job would work out for her.

It would upset me, to answer the phone from so many men, who wanted to be escorts. There just weren't that many women phoning in for a man to escort them out, if any. Those endless phone calls from men would wake me from a needed sleep and many times from my constant cat- napping. I had to do something that would get them off the phone quickly and still keep the respectability of my service intact.

My next move was to the post office and put my money down for a P.O. Box. This is where the men could send their resumes and women who did not sound interesting to me. There would be another benefit for me – the escorts could send my fee there if they lived too far to come by and give the fee to me.

There was such a need for escorts that I really accepted everyone I met when it came to the female escorts. She would have to be really smelly or something repulsive, such as obvious lack of education, for me to not accept her. Without an education a woman was unable to converse with the wealthier clients and most of the clients did have money. The reason or action of total acceptance of escorts was very clear. Because there were so many different types of men phoning, each escort had to be different. Some men did not like a too pretty or too classy a girl.

Men wanted: small, tall, medium built, athletic built, intelligence, no intelligence, sexy, large breasted, small breasted, younger, older, and the list expands as our American culture moves into other countries.

The people I did not accept was because of other reasons that were different than appearance, which were sometimes obvious, if I knew immediately that they were working their own 'book' (client list) through my service; or they had a man behind them taking their money. I wanted nothing to do with those people. I wanted independent thinking women who just wanted to supplement their income and if they were able to adjust to this business and make a living full-time, that was okay too.

In fact, I was surprised to find that the women who sounded best on the phone, not pushy and firmly polite, were usually the best to hire, and many of them were nice, the girl-next-door types. Moonlighting from their regular jobs or homemaking situations, but they all had several things in common: the desire for money, and in many cases sexual appetites, that would surprise their inner circle of friends and family if known.

I was convinced that you can never know everything about the people close to you, or you work with, or casually come in contact with, and, this is because the person you know, well, that person could be leading a double-life. It was not fiction by any stretch of the imagination.

The story was very real.

Women wanted to be respected for who they felt they were inside.

If that respect came to them, by a man telling them how beautiful or sexy they were, for a few minutes; then---damn---that is what they needed and wanted to have and was sought out by the working escort.

Eventually, the women knew truth had nothing to do with the story each one told, but the better the story the better the money. Factually some, if not most of the women were working through a psychological issue and being paid for who they wanted to be. Someone who was not a working mom, a dedicated student and friend, a person using drugs or hiding the child abuse, and who she was could be put in the closet for an hour or two. The woman could free herself from all the worldly troubles she had. This was every woman's dream. A paid for escape from reality. The money, in some cases, was just an added benefit.

Some situations, the escorts did not want anything from the man but money and, were tired of hearing how beautiful or sexy they were, because they knew the man was not serious and, the escort had heard it all before.

The escort was only in it for the money and gave the many men, she saw, their fantasies. She would work like a machine going from one man to another with her supply kit. What did she have in the supply kit? What she wanted or felt she needed.
They may have brought:
•   Candles and matches for dropping hot wax on clients' genitals or to remove hair for them.
•   Whipped cream
•   A fresh change of clothing and underwear
•   Whips, handcuffs, ties to be prepared for that unusual customer
•   Scarves
•   Sexy negligees in a variety of colors and lengths
•   Perfume
•   Toothbrush, toothpaste, mouthwash
•   Personal videos
•   Wine or other beverages
•   Sex-gadgets or apparatus
•   Massage oils
•   Movies, photos, or still films and projector
•   Cameras
•   Hairdryers
•   Lubricants
•   Credit card machine
•   Condoms
•   Soap

Various times, all these items were brought, just in case the client wanted to pay for the entire evening. Some girls even brought wigs of different hair colors if the client wanted a blonde, brunette, or all the various other hair colors and lengths of hair. She was prepared to be his fantasy.

Handcuffs could turn into a dilemma, but some escorts did have them.

Preparation was everything, and, I insisted on it. I did not want a phone call from a girl saying that the customer wants her to spend the night and she forgot something. So my idea was to head it off at the pass and, I demanded or explained that the girl bring it with her; what you feel you need to have with you to make the most out of the evening; was my lecture to a new woman.

Some girls brought their own liquor or soft drink or water. No one wanted to be "accidentally" drugged by a customer. I always told them to make sure they snap the lid off of the drink instead of leaving it up to the client. You cannot trust anyone. You never know when a client has lost all his money or is suicidal. Be prepared, was not just a motto for me. In order to live, the women had to breath safety first and money second.

The girl could have seen the client many times and he always had the money, so she would wait until she left to collect her fee. She has relaxed her business attitude. Then woops, that one time when he is ready to leave the service or is tired of seeing her; he does not have the money, so he writes her a bad check and it is after bank hours, which means I am unable to phone the bank to verify the funds are in the bank. She has now spent the entire night or many hours with the man and she still has to pay me my fee. If she made the mistake of breaking a cardinal rule, by not getting her money up front, then she must still pay and, I will most likely try to get the money out of the client for her. I did this usually by threatening never to send another person to him and that ploy worked most of the time.

When that arrangement produced the desired result, it was great, but sometimes it just did not and the woman was without her money for the time spent with him. Not really her fault if he had decided paying for the service and her was not in his budget. He may have lost his job and was too proud to tell her and writing worthless checks, to a trusting person, was more akin to his psychological disposition. This was just cause for the escort to never be caught in 'hindsight' mode.

Now, in the 21st century an escort could have a debit taken from his account through her employer. This would rule out any surprises, by taking a check. Also, with the advent of the Internet, there are web sites that display photos or videos of the escort and the customer can now choose, who he wants.

It takes the guesswork out of phoning a service. But it also diminishes what I actually did, and that was to match people and convince customers to see someone different or out of their comfort zone, which worked out very well and many times. I call this modern matchmaking by a woman who enjoyed "hooking" two people up.

The phone company, you would think, the company was working for me at the beginning of my business. "Ma Bell", (The phone company in those days.) made it easy for me to advertise in the yellow pages. But the prices were high. Some of those ads could cost $500 or more a month. A huge business cost and, in today's marketplace, the ads cost huge amounts.

The old phone company made it easy for me to not only

advertise but to expand my business into other areas of California and Nevada. The ads were sometimes large and did attract business and very rarely did I have an escort out of the business calling plan that "Ma Bell" reached. Many times potential escort would phone from a distance and this was wonderful for business in those outlying areas. Plus, the phone company had prefixes that cost the business owner big money when phoning them; they were out of the local calling area for the business. And the escorts hated phoning a client out of their prefix. If the call did not work out the escort had added a cost to her phone bill. Not to mention the cost of using a pay phone; which entailed collecting enough change to dump in the phone just to make the call and if it did not work out, the escort was mad.

Which was reasonable to be angry; I had to use a payphone many times and aside from the various smells of urine and feces the cost was there and danger. I was once mugged at a payphone and all my change taken, which had been in clear site for the juvenile muggers to see.

Many of my escorts had pagers, but they still had to find a phone to use to find out if it was a call they wanted to take. And the pagers could go off in the worst set of circumstances, from being at a family meal to a passionate moment in bed with boyfriend or lover. Eventually, I was lucky enough to have enough regular clients that my advertising costs became minimal. The phone company had, in those days, a rate dialing for all the neighboring prefixes in the San Francisco Bay area and I began to recognize all or most of them. A client would phone from such and such prefix and if a girl was in that area, she had the call.

Then the phone company came out with the call-waiting feature, which did drive me crazy. My fingers would go from one line and switch back and forth with a client and an escort on one of the lines; I was the relay.

Many girls only wanted to stay within their prefix area, because of the cost in driving or paying a babysitter. If the girl only had one call in a night and had to pay other expenses, it did not benefit her to drive a long distance, unless the customer wanted to keep her for a long time. Which did happen, but for the most part, the escort may take the call just because she needed the money. All the escorts were greedy, just some were greedier and all of the women were needy in some way.

I was an unlicensed psychiatrist for many of the women. The many stories I heard about their lives was a glimpse at the reasons for "why" the women wanted to be escorts.

There were instances of me accepting or that is hiring a girl at face-value (really phone-value), if she lived a long way and only wanted to work in her area. The clients would tell me what she looked like and if she was up to my standards. But those interviews and subsequent hiring's were rare and I tried to avoid hiring someone just because of distance.

My advice to the new escort with children was, "Always keep your children out of the customer's fantasy. Do not speak of your children or husband. Any intimate relationship could backfire on you". Telling her, "The client wants to believe you are single and free from attachments." I told this to my escorts over and over again. "You can never make money from a client, who thinks he is supporting a household." Continuing with more lectures from me; "He wants to buy you gifts. He believes that the money will go for frivolous items to please you. Not to support your family or to pay the rent for yourself, rather gifts, such as jewelry and clothes. He wishes to imagine whatever was going through his mind at the time." The escort needed to know, that what she was dishing out was a "fantasy life". If the client wanted to hear she was a student, then she should be a student. Some escorts even had cheerleading outfits. What can I say, if it made them money, well it was between the client and the lady. I had a woman who brought her snake with her if a client wanted to see the thing slither all over her. Some of the women that had worked for me, actually, had been cheerleaders when they were in high school or college, so it did work out well for them, they did not have to purchase a new outfit.

Before I moved the business out of mom's house, some of the statements she said to the girls were really funny. She would have an escort in her living room, waiting for a call and, began asking the girl things like: "You look like a nice girl. Does your mother know you are doing this? Do you have kids? What would they think if they knew about it? Next time you come, bring your own food. I work all day and am too tired to cook for you". (To top it off, mom would spray disinfectant at the exact spot the girl was sitting or the toilet seat, after she left.)

Yes, mom had a way with words. Some girls would prefer to stay at home to receive phone calls, rather than wait at mom's place. One time mom wanted to charge everyone in her living room for watching television. This never happened, but the thought of her trying to collect for using the bathroom was humorous. Nobody liked being interrogated, because they just wanted to do their job and get back to their own life.

The escort business was a "fantasy life" for them too and a unique lifestyle that mirrored what they may have dreamed about, from watching old movies. The strutting around the room after a first time with a client; the girl waving her money in hand, was unbelievable and, fun stuff to watch. Each girl, at first, believed the crap the clients told her. Like men saying, "You are the best escort ever" and "No one does that for me like you do". After a few calls the looks on the women's faces changed. Reality begins to set in and money becomes the only factor and dominates the conversations. No more thinking to herself that she is the best. The escort finds the perfect face and smile as the client is saying his bullshit to her. A simple nod up and down, convinces the client that she believes what he is saying to her.

They were meeting men from many areas of society, that may have never have crossed their paths, in their 'real' world. That was the excitement for them. Going to homes that were very expensive and some horrible homes, that looked like they had never been cleaned, and there were those living spaces that appeared to never be lived in at all. An escort had to have a sense of adventure.

Mystery surrounded each call.

Many of the escorts made up tales to tell their clients; stories that they felt comfortable to tell, over and over again, and even many times in the same 24 hour period. One escort always had a birthday within a week of meeting a new client that liked her. She collected many gifts to bring home with her fee. Another escort told how she liked to be chained up and, the next time she would tell the client, "You can do that to me." She would tell him, "I have to trust you first." That was a dangerous game to play, but she was able to have many more calls with that dangerous ploy, just to have more calls from the guy.

One girl, who was new, actually burst out in tears with a client. She told him, "I could never do this type of work and I feel horrible." She cried all the way to his door, as she was leaving, with her fee in hand and never did whatever she had promised to do with him. He was on the telephone to me after she left asking me why I would put such a nice girl like that to work. I explained that he should never have given her the complete fee, except for some gas money.

Later, because I knew him very well, I told him what she was up to and that I had to get rid of her. I fired her, because that type of lying was just not accepted. She was a professional "hooker" who had worked for other services and if she did not like the man, she should have just asked for some gas money and left. I heard it through the grapevine that she enjoyed pulling the little girl act with customers. It empowered her, but it was not honest. You don't promise something (or imply something will happen) without delivering. I felt she was just a common thief. Stealing a man's money from right under his nose, with a few tears that completed the act of lying ... it was not acceptable behavior for my escorts at *Professional Escorts* to do; it was lying and manipulation of a situation. This put the next girl in a situation of trying to make up for the last escort, the one playing tricks. It was pressure on me and the women that followed.

Chapter Thirteen
Case Studies

Now, I would like to present many of the women that I documented during my numerous years of running *Professional Escorts* of Marin County, California. I call these "case studies" for one very good reason. These are not stories taken out of context about the escorts. I was not part of their private lives with their family members. All the women are depicted as people I studied. No, I am not a psychologist. What I would call myself is a person who observes human behavior. I had a front row seat to see why women and men do what they do when it came to dating.

The changes, in society, that brought women into a business they would never think of being a part of … ten years before 1977. Why women would want to work for an escort or massage service. I saw few differences and in the following "case studies", I try to point out some of the differences. My watchful eye was not perfect, because I was so busy managing the business; some of my views did become slanted toward those women who made me money. In reading about some of these women you, the reader, are able to point out the women I favored.

Virtually, the same questions were answered, by me, about the escorts I sent out on escort calls. For the purpose of keeping identities private, the women all have been given numbers or an alpha listing. I call them case studies because they all were studied by me. They will not be presented in chronological form. The numbers, to, do not relate in any way as to when the woman worked for *Professional Escorts*, but I may give some dialogue to many of them, rather than only present the questions. Please enjoy reading about them.

These women were very special and made my service a wonderful business for people to phone and have companionship with, for at least an hour of time.

No matter what age, I put on paper in this writing, about these women; they always lied about their age, to the clients; and, sometimes me. There may have been a few exceptions, but not many. In fact, I encouraged them to lie about their ages. If a man wanted a woman 30 years old and I had an escort ready to go see him and she was 25 years of age; I told her to tell him she was 30 years of age, instead of her real age. That ruse was only done with escorts, able to pass for the ages requested. But I always kept the hiring of escorts at 18 years of age and above. The girls had to show me proof of their age.

The older women did not have to show me their identification; but provided the person looked younger, I encouraged her to say, that she was whatever age we both felt she appeared to look. And the age would seem reasonable to the client. The men did not question the facts, for the most part. But when they did doubt an age, I would say, "Well she has had a hard life." If the person was saying she was younger than her real age. For the girls who were younger and saying they were older I would say, "She just has taken very good care of herself and isn't she lucky to look so young?"

My opinion of age was that it did not matter as long as the person was of legal age. No one should even ask a lady her age. It is impolite. As soon as a man would know a woman's real age he may turn away from her. I never understood the reasoning. Get a life guy, it is only a number and that is how I felt then and now. If you are happy with a person, then why make a big deal over age? It does not make sense. A woman dates a younger man and people want to hang the woman from the nearest tree. Men date a younger woman and other men want to send him a cigar, surrounded with big grins all around the cigar. Women have been denied equal rights in the area of dating for too many years. I object to men being able to date younger women without much scandal. As a woman, even I have been subjected to complaints from my family and the young man's family about dating someone who was right between the ages of my two sons. My sons were in their twenties at the time. I was at the end of my thirties. My oldest son said to me, "Mom, don't sleep with him. He could be your son." Woops. I had already slept with the man and, it never, ever, even crossed my mind that he could be my son. Eck! Get out of here with that statement son.

This person, I dated, was a nice looking guy, who liked me and that is all that mattered. He had just been discharged from military service and was a Marine. I mean a Marine and in top shape. Wow. I was one lucky woman to be with him and to have the fun we shared.

Oh. Let me say it again. He was a Marine, who was tender and loving and a friend when I needed one. So what if he was near my son's age? He was well over 21 years of age and we got along very well.

His parents where mortified.

My one son was beside himself.

My mom actually thought it was funny. I know she did, because she smiled at me and we had a few good laughs about it.

COMPILATION OF ESCORTS AND CLIENTS

Private talk with mom and that was actually a fun conversation. I think she even blushed.

Victorian up-tight values voiced at their finest.

Put the woman in her place, have no place in the 21st century. Ladies let me preach to you. If the man is younger than you, go for it. Especially, if you are able to say he is a man. With so many men wondering if they like men or women, you are lucky to find a man. So have the fun that goes along with a younger man who is not too tired to take you out, meaning movies and dancing. He can still show you a good time. Enjoy. He will worship you just like an older man would do. Except, this younger man will allow you to have some fun between the sheets and he won't fall asleep snoring. The younger guy wants the experience of being with an older woman. So don't be turned off by it – rather – take the high road and, be turned on by it. Love the attention and have some fun.

Life is way too short for thinking a man is too young for you, just because he may be your adult children's age. Get on with life and quit making it difficult. Find a Marine, Navy, Coast Guard, Air Force, Army man and have a great time.

These guys have been trained.

I always enjoyed being with a man that had been in one of the military services, because they know how to handle a 'real' woman. Even better, if he is fresh out of basic training, because the man will be also in the best shape you may ever find a man in. Good luck ladies, and, take my advice.

Here is the numbered list of questions I asked myself. Questions, I thought, people would want to know, at the time when I first began my business. Some of the numbered ladies do not have the typed out questions before the answers, so here is the list and you may refer to it if you want to know what I am speaking to or about, in the answer for that number or, letter used to identify the escorts.

Questions for female escorts:

1. A brief physical description.
2. What line of work preceded this endeavor?
3. Do her friends and family know about her escort employment?
4. Does she have a boyfriend?
5. Does she have children?
6. Where does she live?

7. How long did she last doing escort work?
8. Was she any good at being an escort?
9. Did she make money as an escort?
10. What did she do with her money?
11. Why was she no longer working with the escort service?
12. What habits did she have?
13. Intelligence of the girl as seen by me?
14. What type customer she appealed too?
15. Any mental problems?
16. Any problems in regard to everyday living?
17. Any sexual differences she may have exhibited, which were perhaps different than the typical housewife?
18. Guilt feelings/did she have any?
19. Honesty and any other social/criminal activities/do they go hand in hand with escort work?
20. My feelings about the girl while she was working with me.

Female Escorts

My observations and, also, my take on how each person performed as an escort. That is what you will find with each case study or person I had studied, well enough to give opinions about. Hardly, can all my escorts be featured, because this writing would turn into a very large accounting of people, close to a dictionary. By the time I ended my service; there had been hundreds of women and men who wanted to work as an escort. Not all the people, who came to me, worked, but there were many who did. What I have put together, are a few of the escorts that show variety. Even though, with some escorts it may seem as though the person sounds similar to the last one featured; rest assured, they were all very different. From mannerisms to the affect and effect they had on clients, me, and the business.

Each one an individual and a character worth speaking about, and, I must say, some of what I would like to have said, about the person is left out, because of time and distance I do not wish to disparage the fragile minds that may now read this book.

(Those people who may have been my escorts.)

They are not sugar-coated statements, which remain for the reader, but are accurate representations of those people selected and spoken about. I speak my mind about them and, all are written about, while focusing on how they were or how I encountered them at that time. They have gone on to many aspirations and this is not an account of what they are doing now or in the 21st century. But the above listed 20 questions, with a few exceptions are answered.

Number 38

A friendly girl. Because of her and, some other escorts, I adjusted my thinking of how to run *Professional Escorts*, which was first and foremost, not to allow women to work at other escort or massage services, while they were working with me.

This girl was around 5'6" tall. She had longish brown hair, and pretty face with large dark eyes. She looked like a gypsy girl, probably, because her clothing was long and flowing … representative of the old hippie girls and those days that are now, past. Number 38 was around 23 years of age and had a good figure. She would tease a client and, thoroughly enjoyed sex and the fun that went along with the act, she delivered to the customer. Whatever that act was, and it usually was sex. First and foremost she was a student. What I did not like was that she worked for several other escort services. Her academic studies came first but money was a close second for her. Some of her friends and family knew how money was getting into her bank account. She was selective as to who knew, what, about her. Number 38 kept her distance from me.

There were her many boyfriends and all the attention she enjoyed men to give her but, luckily, she did not have children. Thirty-eight lived in a shared apartment situation in San Francisco. I know that everything in the world was to evolve around her. That is what she wanted, because she was extremely self-centered. She lasted off and on, around three months. She was good at the business of escorting and could have been great, if she had wanted to put some time into the work. I would say that had she given up school work and friends, the opportunities were there to have made a great living from the business. Some money was made while she worked, but she could have made more. She blew it, mostly on her high living and drugs. The preference for this person was to use drugs and, to be "high" rather than, not to use drugs and be "straight". She wanted to work for an escort service in the city that was close to her location. "Convenience", meant everything to her. This was not a person, who would go out of her way to, even pay me. I had to chase her down for my fees.

Plus, in all reality, she did not want to work and used getting hired at another escort service, as an excuse to leave my service. Only did she tell me, when she found out I knew that she was working with one or two other escort services. She had a lot of bad habits and they consisted of drugs, liquor, clothes and spending money on her for whatever she wanted, a lot of selfish buying.

This was a "me first" girl, who was very able in throwing people off the track as to what she really was. Mostly because of how they looked at her … she dressed as a "want to-be" hippie. Real hippies were not as selfish as her. I found her to be a clever girl, with above average intelligence. Someone that could think on their feet or back, as the case may be and, still is thought of as sweet. A born actress and deceiver. She appealed to most men, because she was young and pretty and had a pleasing personality, even though it was phony, it was pleasing.

No doubt she had problems, but I did not know what they were. If I had to guess it would be self-esteem, which she compensated by escorting, to pump up her confidence in social situations. She had trouble keeping her expenses in check. She liked being with other girls on escort calls and I would say those calls appealed to her bisexuality. Possible guilt feelings when it came to her family finding out what she was doing or if they did, the disappointment they would feel toward her. She had misplaced values, but I found her to be a fairly honest girl. Twenty-eight, also, sold drugs when she needed extra cash. I liked her. She could have come back to work for me anytime, when she wished to really put an effort into working and not work for another service, and if she wanted to actually take all the clients I had ready, willing, and able to see her. It was a shame we were off track together, because we could have benefited each other with lots of work and money. I saw a lot of potential in her.

Number 66

Unfortunately, this woman had to be fired and, could have really been a great escort if she screwed her head on straight. This does become a familiar statement, because most of the women were scattered. Their brains just did not keep them on one track for very long. She was a slender blonde, with hazel eyes, lots of potential, even though her hair was stringy and shoulder length. She had pale white skin and a young face for actually being around 35 years of age. She had been a drug dealer and remained on Welfare, while working for my escort service. Her friends and family knew she was working as an escort. Her boyfriend was a white man and a wimp. She did have children. Number 66 lived in Petaluma, California. She was with the service around one and a half months. And she was good at escorting and, she did make money, I am sure she made much more than she told me. The money went for living expenses and drugs. She had been caught, by me, for lying, cheating, and stealing, so she was fired. She had multiple drug habits and was using, primarily, heroin and methadone. This girl enjoyed having lots of clothes and much of her money that was not used on drugs went to fill her clothes closet. I would say she was cleaver but of average intelligence.

Most men would have liked her. Yes, to mental problems, because she had a drug habit. She really needed someone to take care of her and her finances. There were no guilt feelings from her enjoyment of other women. Not an honest person with herself or anyone else. I liked her, in a feel sorry for her, way. Some of the women had a manner about them that you just wanted to show compassion for them. This escort was doing her best to take clients, from the service; she saw them and tried to turn the clients to be just her clients. It is called stealing in the business. But any business that has employees stealing clients, would take issue with her. The clients told me and that is why I had to drop her as an escort. If ever there was a client that wanted a sleazy female, this girl was cleverly maladjusted, whereby, and she was willing to lay down with any man or woman. I was surprised she did not have more children to feed.

Number 44

Number 44 wanted to work from Concord to San Mateo, California. She was a slender brunette, around 5'6" tall with hair worn short and she had dark eyes surrounded by very white skin. This woman had been a waitress and also worked as a topless dancer. Some of each group, family, and friends knew what she was doing. Fortunately, for her, she met the current boyfriend, at the time, through my service and, started living with him. Number 44 did not have children. She began existing in a shared apartment with her new boyfriend, a former client of my escort service. Living with a and ex-client was stupid.

Once a "trick", always a "trick" and everyone knew that fact in the escort and dating business. Men did not change and, wish to be loyal to just one woman. They would justify dating outside of the relationship, with all the facts in front of them and, the main fact was, that the girl had been paid to be with men. No other way to say it. The relationship was doomed from the very beginning. She was with *Professional Escorts* on and off about two months and was all right when working. But she was not dependable.

Her earning could have been better, she did make much money and definitely not as much as she could have made. Her style was to turn down more work than she should have. She was a little rough with her language, from being a waitress and spoke as if the person she was going to see was a ham sandwich and sometimes worse. She spoke about a person, as if that person did not leave a tip on the table; just a little crude here, in manners and suggestions about her employment choice. The comments she made about clients were funny but very crude.

The money she made went for her bills. When she had the audacity to start living with a customer (male) who she had turned into a boyfriend … he did not want her to work, anymore. This was it for me with her. The habits noticeable were, and obsession with makeup, nails, and clothes. She seemed to be very average in intelligence. Her appeal was to guys infatuated with dumb brunettes.

Relationships were more than a challenge for her. Lying was a first on her list of problems and she excelled in this area. She had trouble keeping up with her expenses. This was another escort preferring to be with women. The idea of her making love to other women, no doubt, turned her boyfriend on. She had a lot of guilt feelings over those urges. She liked doing things she shouldn't do, and then felt guilty about what she had done. She made a perfect Catholic girl; always wanting to go to confession. I was the person always hearing her confessions, because of her inability to realize that she worked for me.

She was pretty honest in some areas of her life and I liked her. Though I thought she was lousy for escort of work, because she wanted to make every client her boyfriend and not keep the men at a distance, which was better for her mental health and her finances. I sometimes wondered where this girl ended up and who she ended up staying with on a more permanent basis.

This person could be someone that ended up, dead. Her lies were bound to catch up with her in any relationship she found herself tied too.

Number 63

This girl felt or believed she was a witch. I don't remember if she thought herself to be a black witch or a white witch. She had a lot of unusual ideas. The woman was about 5'6" tall with a good figure but she had a dog face. Meaning she was not very attractive. She had brown shoulder length hair and brown eyes with the hair being her best visual feature. Surprisingly, she did dress well and had a friendly disposition. Other employment had her working for a newspaper and in advertising and public relations related work. This one did not have a boyfriend and her friends and family did not know she was working as an escort.

Number 63 did not have children. She lived in Marin County, California in an apartment. She was with me two months. She was fantastic and did make money for the both of us. She paid living expenses and was really into saving her money. She and I had a disagreement about some time and money. I felt she had cheated me on some time. I was correct, but she held onto her belief that she was telling me the truth. Rarely (the truth), did that ever happen with the escorts. Truth was not the first sentence out of any escorts mouth when the escort was cheating me out of my fee. Most escorts would cave in, when I confronted them with the news that I found out about the lie as to how much time was spent with a client. Not this one, though, she was intent on lying forever.

Primarily she had a clothes addiction and was caught up on her own grooming needs. She was an intelligent person. Most men liked her after they saw her body. Men wanted a perfect shaped escort or a beautiful face and she had what they wanted. Definitely, had the figure. Also, a lot of "spacey" ideas.

Not very down-to-earth thinking, but she had her act pretty well together on how to get men to like her, only she kept having all the wrong people around her as friends. She loved sex and would do anything sexual. No guilt feelings at all. But not an honest person. If she could get away with something she would try. I liked the girl, and, felt if her honesty was always in question. Had she remained with me, and adjusted her lying ways, to telling the truth, I really believe she would have been a great escort for the service.

This girl was probably a borderline sociopath. If there is anything as a borderline sociopath. Granted, I am no psychologist or psychiatrist but she had a warm-coldness about her. A personality that was only evident, when you were speaking to her for a long period of time. And I spoke to her a lot. I think she was always trying to either learn from me or test out her lies. I was more of a mother figure to her. The mother she could never have and, told her 'mother' what she really wanted to do with men. Scary, but true.

Number 68

Number 68: This person was a very disturbed young woman. She was around 26 years old and looked to be 17 years of age and was 5'4" tall, with scars running up and down both arms, from her pervious times of trying to commit suicide. She was from Nicaragua and in the country illegally. Why I had to know this information I don't know. But for each girl, I was the person to confess too, all their dirty little secrets. Many of the clients felt at ease with me to, so confessions were part of my job. I heard many confessions.

Sixty-eight had long kinky black hair, that looked more like it should be worn on the head of an African woman instead and she had coal black eyes. Her skin was smooth brown and her weight was at 105 lbs. and sometimes less due to the continuing drug use. A cute shape and a pretty face in an unusual way and she had tried working the streets in San Francisco. The city is also where she worked as a waitress. Her friends and family knew she was working as an escort.

Her boyfriend was white and old. Way too old for her. She did have children. She lived in San Francisco with her boyfriend, in an apartment. It was a large flat and decorated with a lot of art work. She was with me for about three to six months and it could have been longer, but my memory thinks it was along eight months that she would call in to work. Not really working the entire eight months.

This woman was good at what she did and did make a lot of money. The money was spent on her boyfriend for what he wanted and, also, it went for drugs for him and his friends. She was the person paying the bills for the quasi-family. She did not drive and it was a hassle for her to come to Marin County from the city, so I ended up going to her, for my fees. She also wanted to try keeping the customers that really liked her as her own clients, and have them come to her place. This was done without my knowledge and, when I found out about her double dealing with me that was the end of her.

Her main habits were drugs, liquor, and her boyfriend. She should have bought more for herself. I found her to be very smart, but unaware of her intelligence, she could have done very well in school if she just tried to go back to school.

Those clients that liked the little girl look, and many customers wanted such an appearance, so she could have been very busy working, day and night.

She still needed (and was seeing) to see a psychiatrist and, also, she was still showing signs of being suicidal. There were some abuse issues in her past and the older boyfriend was a by-product of that abuse. Without her boyfriend she felt lost and, she would always need some sort of guidance in order to maintain a living standard. What I mean here, is that, she needed someone to make sure the bills were paid. Her preferences were being with old men, due to something that had happened with her father, when she was a child. Her father really hurt her mind and no doubt her body. She felt guilty about everything and every person, which is why she needed the drugs or the boyfriend, because those things distracted her from what she was doing. She could have been a very honest person, but her boyfriend was training her to be dishonest with everyone but him. He was no good for her and appeared to counter what the psychiatrist was doing for her. He was an evil person and, just was totally using the girl and she could not see that she was being used, or if she did know, that may be why she kept attempting suicide.

When I first met him, the evil drizzled out of him and, I would have bought her a ticket back to her home, if that would have helped her to get away from him. But there are some relationships that just have to work through their own destiny. Perhaps she liked the abuse from him, as long as it was not coming from her father. I liked the girl, but was afraid to voice any of my opinions, because the girl was very protective of people, when she loved them and she thought she loved this old man. She had streetwise, animal instincts for survival, built into her, from a very early age. She would kill for those people she loved and trusted. She was fierce and headed for an early grave or prison. I actually was happy when she no longer was working for me.

The responsibility, I felt, of having her fragile life working for me, was more then I needed to do, at the time. And, I was always asked by clients, the status of her arms. The girl had those horrible scars, from attempting suicide, on both arms. My clients felt uncomfortable seeing her. They would tell me she was not up to the standards that the other women working for me had, and, what I wanted the women to look like and be. When the clients know the difference, it is when I was ready to fire the escort. Luckily, she moved on to some other escort service.

Number 69

This was a very unusual girl. She ended up leaving to work with nuns in Southern California. And, most interestingly, she had thoughts about becoming a nun or doing missionary work. One of the most honest women to come my way and told me all this information, about going to a nunnery, at the initial interview. My mind was blown. I could not understand why she wanted to work for an escort service. But who was I to wonder?

The girl was around 5'6" tall with brown hair, which she wore touching her shoulders. She had brown eyes and had an average figure and a wholesome face ... a face that had little makeup spread upon it. A very nice smile and she was around 25 years old and was a student.

She also worked as some sort of company representative. Some of her friends in the area knew she worked as an escort, but not her family. She had a white boyfriend. She did not have children. She lived near Fresno, California and was with me for about two months. She was good, but did not make a great deal of money. And this was due to her living many miles away from most of the clients. She paid her bills with the money that she made. Eventually, she moved to the Los Angeles area, where she was to become part of some religious order of nuns. Not really any bad habits that I knew of and possibly the only habit she had may have been praying. Her bad habit could have been her choice to be an escort. This was a very smart girl. Maybe she was putting me on about going off to a nunnery. Her own joke.

She appealed to clients that liked a nice girl who could speak well and, the client would have an intelligent conversation with her. This escort was a lovely companion, one they (the clients) could take to any dinner party with friends or business associates.

No problems surfaced while I knew her. She could not keep up with her spending and bills before leaving the service. She needed to experience a lot of sex, because she had been told all her life sex was bad. From all of her experiences with the escort service, she now felt more comfortable having sex with a partner and she preferred to be with only one man. I know this all sounds odd, but this woman was a very nice person. There were some guilt feelings associated with being an escort and the biggest mistake she could make would be to tell her husband when she marries. I explained that she should not confess this work to him. But she was the type of person to feel compelled to tell. I often wonder what happened to her, because she was conflicted about getting married or being a nun. She was a very honest girl. I liked her a lot. One of the nicest girls I ever had worked with me. If she went to work with the nuns, I can only imagine what her confessions were, to the priest servicing the order. Her Catholic upbringing must have been intense, because she always told me what went on with her clients. Word for word and action with reactions by the clients, these were very interesting tell-all ... spat-talk.

Catholic confessionals must have been invented, with girls such as her in mind. I heard from her about twice after she moved to be with the nuns. And I always felt she may have been a nun on vacation. And this may have been her only lie to me, in not telling me the truth about herself. Not necessarily the truth, but a comical thought I had when thinking about her. I even used that line when going out or meeting a guy at a bar for the first time. "Yep, just a nun on vacation." There always a great reaction to whomever I told that line to.

Number 30

This was not a person that made a huge impact on my business or me. She was a tall brunette around 5'9" and she was slender with models figure. She had a foreign look about herself from the way she dressed, to the way she carried herself. I admired her shoulder length hair that was gorgeous and she was around 36 years of age. She had been a free-lancer (sex) and also as a model.

Some friends and some family knew what she was doing. She did have a boyfriend and he was white, but she seemed not to care if she had him around or not. No children, too selfish to want any children to share her life with or spoil her figure by becoming pregnant. This person lived in Contra Costa County. About three months she lasted with me, till I found out what she was doing. She was taking clients from my service and leaving me out of the money circle. She was just all right with the clients and, was not missed when, finally, I fired her. She could have made more than what she did. She spent what she did make on things she felt she needed to attract men; clothes, shoes, jewelry, makeup, etc.

I did not want her to work for my service. Especially, after the girl tried to begin her own service, it failed, then she tried to come back to work for me.

Never would I allow her back. The only reason why I had her around was because I needed an escort in her area at the time. The biggest "no" in the escort business was a person using your escort service to steal clients. Her habits were men, herself, clothes, and travel. She was a clever and conniving person, but still only average intelligence and her IQ was in the neighborhood of possibly 110. She appealed to men who liked older women with an unusual appearance and foreign look. Actually, she did have a very nice foreign look about her. Meaning, she dressed like she had just dropped in from some other country. Yes, she had problems, mostly; she had trouble functioning in the "real" world.

The world of the escort is a "make believe world" and that is why many of the escorts had issues coming to grips with going in and out of homes. A world of "make believe" was at the next home and client. Then after leaving the home it was back to problems and the "real" world.

Yes, she could not keep up with her own exaggerated lifestyle. She would do anything for money. Some guilt feelings, but they would only last a few seconds on her part and in her mind. I got the idea that her idea of concentration was thinking about where she would spend what money she made. Not an honest person and she had trouble facing and telling the truth. I felt she would steal from anyone and of course me.

On a personal level, I thought she was all right and I still do. But I felt sorry for her as a woman, who was in a major transition in her life, knowing that she was not equipped to handle losing her beauty and she did not know what to do with that loss, in the life she had made for herself. The life she had, up to that point and time, was all about her and the appearance she was able to sustain. A very shallow person when speaking to me. Her thoughts were only about the exterior of a person, and that meant everything to her, I assumed the clients saw this too. She did not care about furthering her education. She ripped me off for a lot of money by stealing clients and not paying me.

There was one client that she liked and he was in a wheel chair. I have to admit this person must have appealed to her, because he had his own problems and in some way her aging was minimized, when she was with him, because he was lucky to have her. She continued to see him after leaving my service and I was surprised this relationship went on for over a year.

Number 31

This person was a tall blonde girl with blue eyes and long blonde hair, who was not slender, but not too many pounds overweight. I think she was around 25 years of age and she did have a pretty face. Possibly, she was 5'8" tall and she was leggy, with a fresh look about her manner of dress. You needed to be around her for a longer time to know that there was nothing fresh or wholesome about her.

Number 31 had been a waitress, just prior to working with me. A little of each group knew she was working for me. A white boyfriend was in the background. She did not have children. She lived in motel rooms and she worked for me about two months. At times she worked well and did make some money, but it all went for living expenses and drugs. She went out of town for a while and told me she was also losing interest in doing escort work.

This losing interest happened when a need was filled for her, such as her need for those drugs. She was leaning more and more on drugs. Heroin was her drug of choice and her dependency increased for cocaine, along with the heroin. She had below average intelligence, with an IQ possibly of 100. Drugs were taking a toll on her mind.

Most men liked her. She had mental problems and told me about a few issues in her background that bothered her. She was unable to deal with life in a structured or restrictive environment, she always wanted freedom. Yes, she had problems living and it was the way she handled her life that caused those very problems. She was still acting as though she was a little girl and totally unable to act her age. Many of the women, such as her, who had been abused as a child, did not grow up. They were still acting out for approval as children.

She liked being sexual with women. Lots of guilt feelings about the work. But she felt she had to do this type of work, in order to have the drugs. The work and drugs went hand in hand; they both were excuses for how her life was handled. She was fairly honest, but I doubt if I would have let her be in my home for any length of time, without someone being there. I liked her, but wanted to keep her away from my home and at a distance. Something was scary about this person.

My personal wish was not to be involved with her problems and, she brought them to work with her. Actually, I was filled with many mixed feelings about her and was worried that she may get herself into trouble. She needed a guidance counselor or intense re-upbringing, if there is such a program in society. At this time, the 21st century, I doubt if she is even alive.

The distance between her and the grave was short.

Number 25

Surprisingly, she was a very nice girl attending college.

This girl was around 5'6" tall with longish brown hair and brown eyes. She had a childlike figure and looked like she was still going through puberty. Number 25 had very pretty eyes and was around 20 years of age and along with being a student, she worked for a restaurant. Some of her family knew and some of friends. Yes, she did have a boyfriend and no children.

She lived in an apartment and lasted on and off for around two years. That was more off, then on. Sort of made money, only when she was working full-time; the men liked her. Not the money she should have made, if she would have put her heart into what she was doing. Money went for her living and school expenses. I would let her work when she asked to work and, this meant she could call me whenever the mood struck, her mind to work. I actually thought she forgot she was working for an escort service.

Eventually, she just lost interest in working, because she graduated from college and went on to other things. She liked weed (marijuana) and her main habits were her addiction to education. She was hooked on educating herself and doing better in life. An intelligent and well-read person with an IQ over 135.

(When I give a thought about IQs, it is because I think that is what the IQ was for the person. Right or wrong, it is strictly my opinion.)

Most men that liked young girls were her clients.

No doubt there were mental problems, but they were not very obvious and I did not see any display of abnormal behavior. She had trouble supporting herself; because she was attending higher education. She enjoyed being with women. There were some guilt feelings in regard to others finding out what she was doing. Escorting was not totally her thing. An honest girl and I liked her. My feelings were that she needed guidance in the "real world". She was an idealistic person. She had a lot of great opinions about the political state of America. I often wondered if she married and had children.

Many women that liked other women and played out their individual fanaticizes, through escorting, were similar to her. Educated and in fear of others remarks, if her friends knew she liked escorting for the boundaries she was able to cross with women. This woman was an explorer of her sexuality.

Number 26

Recently out of prison when she came to me, and, she was trying to go "straight". I know that may sound odd to a person reading this, because if you are going "straight", working for an escort service may seem funny. But she really wanted to stay away from crime that hurt others. Escorting was consensual and had its appeal for her.

This girl was a very classy blonde. She was an excellent dresser; 5'8" tall with blue eyes and a good figure. Number 26 was good looking, in a straight sort of "way". The "way", that means she could enter an office building and blend in with all the other well-dressed office workers.

The downfall for her was that she was a thief, a professional thief. She was trying to work at some straight jobs, in offices and such. Perhaps a new white collar criminal, and the way she looked would have allowed her to pull off any white collar crime, in any office setting. I wonder if she worked for Enron? She was a private person. She sometimes had a boyfriend.

The boyfriends or men would come and go with her. No children were part of this person's life. She was another strange one. I had trouble finding a slot to put her in. Her home was in Concord and she lived in an apartment. She lasted a couple of months and was good at escort work and could have made a lot more than she did, but, as usual, this escort loved to spend the money.

I had no idea how she spent her money because she was a very secretive person. There was always the need for more money with her. Every phone call to me was about how she had to make money. She told me she was trying to go 'straight' and stay away from the fast life. That is the reason she gave me for no longer working as an escort, when she decided to leave my business.

Guys younger than herself and some drugs were her habits. Clothes could have been considered her main habits. She was a very smart and street-wise girl. Her IQ was very high and she was adaptable to most clients needs and appealed to all the men.

No doubt, quite a few mental issues. But she was very adept at keeping them to herself. Did not like talking about her life outside of escort work, when we were talking. And, this beautiful woman found it difficult to keep up with the old life style, she once had, that included a 'straight' job and the low wages it brought. She liked women sexually, better than men, and with those feelings came the guilt.

The reasons were not clear and she would not talk about those issues in her life. She was fairly honest. Although, I would not have turned my back on her and, my meaning here is, that if I did not keep a close watch on her – she would have cheated me out of my fee. I mean stealing had been her job before going to prison. I liked her because I knew where this girl stood. She was not a chronic liar but definitely out for herself. She came first and everyone else did not come close to the high opinion she projected of herself. This must have been a personal security issue with her, to keep people at a distance. The movie, *Basic Instinct* comes to mind when thinking of her. There was this undeniable coldness about her, that I could not penetrate, to find warmth in her, if there was any warmth to find.

Maybe this escort was a sociopath.

Number 85

Now, let me introduce two girls from Chicago that were sisters and wanted to work for my escort service. I lump them together for one number, because they were not worth two separate numbers. This girl and her sister were two blondes, and both stood around 5'3" tall and had very cheap looking total appearance.

Pimples on their faces and both had blue eyes and stringy hair.

They were hustlers from Chicago.

They looked like cocktail waitresses from harbor wharf bars, which catered to longshoremen, and, finally, they both got smart and did not just want tips for the favors they were putting on the table.

Each one wanted to make money.

No one knew what they were up too. They both had boyfriends and those males were white. One had a child and the other one did not. Very secretive women. Usually women enjoyed speaking to me. Not them. That is how I knew that my eyes were going to watch them.

They lived together in an apartment in Marin County and were able to last one night and one calls each for them. Both were good, the only night they worked. Yes, for one call each, they did very well. They looked like they were on drugs and that is where the money would be spent.

These were independent women, who would sit on a bar stool to pick up men, to charge them for their favors. In good conscience, they told me that they were more accustomed to keeping all their money and felt they could find their own work. They looked like they were just into each other. Both were street smart and of average IQ.

They appealed to most men.

More kinky issues in their bags of tricks and they seemed to have their shit together. They liked each other and were lesbians. But they did tell me they were sisters and they looked like sisters. No guilt feelings at all. Not honest with me at first, but after the only call they did; then they were honest with me. I did not like them. They were too cheap looking to work for me.

The honesty given me was that they preferred to work the bars. I told them how dangerous that work was, but they had their minds made up. For them I was an outsider and not privy to their inner goals in life. I was glad they made the choice not to work for an escort service, especially mine. If they had remained with me, they would have been trouble and my service may have suffered.

Number 32

This number was "brainless" to ways of the world - real estate agent who wanted to walk on the wild side of life, for a moment, and decided to work with my escort business. Lucky me, and believe me I am being sarcastic here. She was around 5'3" tall with average features for a Philippine girl and a pretty good figure.

Number 32 had medium length hair and a bad looking complexion. Her face was accented with a protruding mouth or teeth that pushed her mouth outward and distracted from her overall appearance. She continued to work in real estate while being an escort. None of her family knew, but maybe some friends. No boyfriend and no children. She lived in Contra Costa County. Her working schedule for me was, off and on for six months. Mostly off.

She was not really any good and did not make any money for the business. But there could have been money given to her, whom I did not know about, and money she was able to make went for the many bills she had. This was another woman not really into working at all and, only did it as a means to an end. She paid bills. Her habits, well there was not anything noticeable such as drugs. Here was a person smart from books, but without common sense. Dumb in the ways of the real world. Not too many clients wanted to see her. Probably because there was, absolutely, no sex appeal in her and to top it off, no doubt, she had mental problems. She had trouble keeping up with her living expenses and another escort who liked women.

There were lots of guilt feelings about what she was doing. She really felt guilty and it showed on her face and with her demeanor. A sneakily – honest person and I felt she was a nice girl. She didn't belong with an escort service. Her head was not really into what she was doing. This woman needed to be married. And I rarely would make a comment in favor of a lifetime servitude and commitment such as marriage, unless the insult fit the person.

Number 21

Remembering the girls is fun and a pleasure, emphasizing with number 21, a pleasure, she was most enjoyable. Always a smile on her face and something positive and welcoming to add to a conversation. This person brought to my escort service, something, I wish all the girls could have had. She was able to make a room light up. Sex appeal and charm were not put on by her, but just a part of the way she would take a breath of air. A fascinating person.

Highlighting what happened with her as an escort, I am pleased to say, "Mostly" is positive. The day I met her, I knew that she was everything I was always looking for in my escorts. She had another job, which was more to her than a job; it was her career and she was dedicated to it.

I always found that girls, who had other employment, were much more receptive to my guiding them in the escort business. This girl was no different. She listened to my every word, intently, as I gave her my interviewing speech. All her questions after my speech were intelligent and well thought out. It appeared as though she would be able to accept the program as I laid it out. Because it had taken her about three months since her initial phone call to me – to actually come in for the interview; I knew that she was more interested than most women, because she took her time in applying. She had thought over the work for a long time and adjusted her mind to what she wanted to do.

The girl was about 5'5" tall with good figure and the fake saline purchased breasts. She had long brown hair and blue eyes with a clear complexion and a prominent nose and an average angelic looking face. This person was a nurse and continued with her day job. Some of her friends and some family members knew that she was working as an escort. There was more than one boyfriend in her life. She did not have children and lived in Richmond, in a home she owned. Her time spent with my escort service was at least one and a half years or maybe it was two years. Hard telling, because I did not have problems with her that had me counting when she would give escorting up.

Yes she was good and yes she made money. She had expensive habits and purchased mostly clothes and furniture. She felt like devoting more time to nursing and mentally withdrew herself away from the business and me. Perhaps she kept some clients on the side for awhile. It would have been difficult for her to tell me face to face that she was taking clients, if I asked her; she would have been honest with me. So our working relationship just drifted away. She was turning to drugs and most definitely had a clothes habit. She was smart and personable. Her appeal was mostly to men of means and just about all men liked her. There were mental problems and she alluded to them with me but kept them to herself. I was never privy to what the problems were, but one day I read her palm and saw a definite split personality, which I expressed to her and she told me I was correct. I never pursued the conversation. She kept her problems to herself very well; but those very problems were deep inside her heart and mind. She had trouble keeping ahead of her expenses.

This was due to her wanting nice expensive items to decorate her home with and for her; the list was endless to buy jewelry. She was working as an escort mostly to pay her bills. After working for a while she had some relationships with other escorts (women) and I feel this surprised her and also bothered her that she did not object to seeing one of those escorts frequently on calls. They enjoyed going out on calls together. Just doing little sex romps for the men who wanted to pay to see them going after each other in bed.

Number 21 liked women and also loved sex. I believe she did have guilt feelings in regard to her family finding out that her escorting dates were just not going to dinner with clients. But true guilt about the work was not something I saw. I don't remember her ever mentioning a fear of the work or yelling at me saying that she can't do this anymore. Some women would yell when they had enough of dating men for money, but she did not fall into this category. She always gave the impression of having high morals and I think she would not have wanted her family to think unfavorably of her, if they found out she was doing more than she told them she was doing.

Plus, I know she felt guilty about the drug use. Part of her turning to other women gave her strong guilt feelings, more so than seeing the men for money. So I have to say she did have guilt feelings. She wanted to be honest, but could be very secretive. This girl would have made a great spy.

Not actually lying, but just not telling everything, would be her way of going about or around the truth. She would sell drugs, but she did try to be honest with me when I asked her about it. I was actually surprised that selling drugs had come about from her escorting. It had to have been one of the drug dealers that got her started doing such a thing. Because of her honesty I knew which client got her started on a habit. But if we had not drifted apart, I would have had to fire her. I could not have a girl dealing drugs to clients.

When I found out about the drugs, toward the end of our working relationship it was not just the surprise I felt, but there was disappointment too.   She really needed large sums of money for some reason. I never found out why. It was probably to pay off the drug dealers that had a grip on her. I liked her, although I always felt as though the girl kept a distance between herself and others. It was as though a picket fence was between us and extended to all areas of her life. I know she trusted me because I was able to come to her home.

This following was a telephone conversation for an outcall I was trying to give her (#21) one night. It went like this:

Number 21 said, "Dian?"

"Yes, may I help you?"

"It's me #21."

"Oh, I didn't recognize your voice. Where the hell have you been? I've had a lot of work for you and #21. How the hell do you think you're going to pay your mortgage and my rent?"

"I know Dian, but it's been a mess at the hospital. Is there anything right now? I can work till 2am, but then I just have to sign off and get some rest."

"It's 1am now. Maybe you'll get lucky. I don't understand you. You say you like money and need money, but you're never around anymore. People are calling for you, such as Sam and Charlie goes to bed early. You keep missing them. Here I sit all night with calls up my ass and no one around. Then when you are around, all I hear is you want me to produce a miracle for you in one hour."

"Dian, I know, I have next week off and I can devote more time to this but right now my family is getting suspicious, because I wasn't going to my straight job for a while."

"I understand #21 but shit, look at it from my stand point. When you do work everyone loves you and then when you're not working they keep calling for you and I don't have you to send to them. They won't be talked into taking anyone else, so here I sit losing money. I don't like to lose money."

Phone: Ring, Ring, Ring, Ring, Ring.

"Hey, this one is for you. What have you been doing? Sending out smoke signals? I told him you would call him right back."

"Dian, he is a pain in the ass. You know he can't get it up. He does all that coke and then expects me to get him off. The only thing I like about him is his good coke. But I think I can get a couple of hours out of him and I really need the money. Shit, there I go again talking myself into it. Okay. I'll call you when I get there."

Thirty minutes later.

Phoning #21 and leaving a message.

"Hello, it's Dian. Hello, it's Dian."

"I guess she's asleep Charlie. What about someone else?"

"No, I will try another time. I really wanted to see her."

"Okay, bye."

This was another lost call and for her, it was the end of our working relationship. When she was working a lot she was very dependable. I was sad that drugs had finally taken hold of her life and were more prominent and dominant than any work. Even now I wish that she had never begun escort work because the change in her was not a good one.

Plus, I think her family found out and may have stopped her from working.

That last phone call was the "cherry on the cake" for me. I had enough of her putting off working until it suited her to work. I could not run the business well if girls could not or would not do the calls.

Number 3

This girl knew what she wanted from the moment she stepped into my bedroom for the interview. Why my bedroom? I answered the phones in my bedroom usually, so I could keep a keen eye on my valuables.

The living room, also, was my sons' space for doing what they wanted to do. With the living room looking so stark – the girls did not feel I had anything of value until they entered my bedroom, where I kept all my things. That was when I lived in Novato. The house had three bedrooms and my bedroom had a bathroom attached to the room.

My sons had their own rooms and I did not want the boys to hear our conversations. So my huge waterbed became my interview location. The girls were able to congregate in my room and we all talked about everything that drifted through our minds in those days.

When I moved and went to the Graceland address in San Rafael, after living in Novato; the interviews were then in the living room, unless I was sick, which happened a great deal from all the stress I was under.

One escort had an interview with me at the Graceland address on one of my many stressed-out days. She worked at the hospital and thought I should go in because I looked awful. After awhile of working for me, I enjoyed one statement by her, "I did not think this work would be long-term." That was funny and she told me that, several years after she had begun working for me.

When I moved to my 2 Upper Road, Ross address, all interviews were done in the huge living room or dining area. Never in my bedroom. The interviews could be in my office there. I didn't like walking women or men up to my office for interviews because the bedrooms were situated on the third floor in Ross, so it was necessary to have interviews downstairs for the convenience and to keep some areas of the home private.

The upstairs was my living area. Off limits! My living room was circular and had been a new design for an aspiring architect when he built the home, many years before I ever moved in. And this living room was semi-circular and large. The woman I rented from had been the babysitter or nanny for the family who had the home built for themselves. This woman ended up with the owner and eventually the house. She was a very devious person.

When I moved in she never told me all the rent money I paid her was not going toward the mortgage. The lady felt all the women in Ross were whores in one way or another and that is why she rented to me. I never gave it a second thought. But if truth be known – they probably gave her a difficult time for taking someone else's husband.

The business I was running - did not take husbands unless they were ready and willing to go somewhere. Ladies – when your figures and faces go and you do not keep up the romance – where do you think your husband is going to find what he wants in a woman?

Most women think that if they are cleaning house and taking care of the hubby's kids that they are doing a perfect job. Yeah. Well women in America need to ask themselves one question. Do you really think your husband wants to be married to his mother? No. He wants you to do all the work and then be ready, willing, and able in bed. Entice him every night or at least three times a week or lose him. Fact not fiction, and keep your figures intact. He might say that the weight is no problem – but why risk your health by gaining weight or the loss of your hubby.

Make it a game to get him to lose weight with you and stay in shape. Sex is far better with a limber body instead of a flabby body that does not move and makes one partner work harder than the other.

Back to number 35, who had very wide eyes and she was bright and would hang on every word I said. She had been working for, mostly, minimum wages, and my telling her that she would be making $100 per hour ... just, was more than a dream to her. She wanted very much to have everything life sold and her way, only, she was out to get her part of the "American pie". This girl was a beautiful manipulator of people. She was the best girl I had up to that point, working for me and could turn a $50 dollar call into a $500 dollar call. Incredible, those men dug into their savings for her company. She could have had the world and in the end found only a cocaine habit for all her trouble.

Number 35 was young, not even 21 years old when she started working for me. But for 19 years old (almost 20) she had the poise and intelligence of a woman married to a diplomat. I really can't give the girl enough accolades.

Unfortunately, my opinion of her did turn, badly, toward the end. The government should have recruited her as a spy. She was so adept at having men do anything for her. She twisted them around not only her fingers but her entire hands. I even believed her and at the time she was working with me; I was already pretty jaded.

Number 35 was very pretty at first. This girl was around 5'6" tall and had a slender figure with dark or almost black hair and dark eyes and wore her hair very short. She had big eyes that complimented her very pretty face. Her figure was good, as well as her overall appearance. She had been a student, waitress, sales clerk. At first only a couple of her friends knew and then all her family and friends ended up knowing. But, at first, she kept her escort work a secret. She did have a black boyfriend in the beginning and he was soon dropped. He came into her world later and toward the end of working for me. She did not have children. She lived in her own apartment.

The apartment she had when I met her was not a nice apartment, but when the money came rolling in, she moved to a very expensive and upscale apartment near the College of Marin in Kentfield, California. She was able to last almost a year. Yes, she was very good at what she did. Yes, she made a great deal of money. Thousands of dollars a week went to her bank account. At first all that money went for her living expenses and then later she developed a drug habit. I found her lying, cheating, and just plain stealing to support her habit. Her sense of responsible behavior left her when the drug habit kicked in.

Drugs were a habit for her and her preference was cocaine. She also liked expensive clothes and living quarters. She was too educated for her age to cope with some of the client's that were uneducated and on drugs; so she ended up joining in with their drug use. This was to party on the cocaine and stay up all night. An all night call went from $500 a night to $1,000 a night. When she was working for me it was $1,000 a night and she wanted that money. For all I know she was getting $2,000 a night. Keeping the other thousand as a tip. Money became her "God".

This brunette appealed to almost everyone, but the drug dealers got a strong hold on her. I covered her in my book on clients and some of her adventures. Actually, this is the first part of the compilation, so look for her in that book. Yes, she was developing mental problems and this was primarily caused by doing drugs. Not at first did she have problems with expenses, but after her drug addiction set in, she could not meet her living expenses nor cope with paying her bills. She loved women and having sex with them; I believe preferred them to men. She did not feel guilty about anything. I think she was just sorry she could not continue to use me, anymore. I have to admit that she was able to hide her addiction for a long time. Maybe at first she was honest; then the drugs changed her personality and moral compass and she still owes me money from a bad check she gave me for my last fee, on a call she did. I liked her at first and trusted her a lot. But after six months I did not trust her anymore or feel comfortable with her around my home.

When a girl became addicted to drugs, the life, or whatever, it was more than obvious and I could not speak to them anymore. They did not want to hear my advice, let alone take the advice. No different with this girl,; I am sure she needed to talk but was unwilling or unable to speak to me, because she must have felt I would see through her lies and recognize the drug issue. We mostly spoke on the phone after the first six months. I actually drove past a known drug dealer client's house and saw her vehicle there … when she was not supposed to be there and had phoned in sick that night. All trust was over after that little trip I made to the client's location. Yes, I drove past the house, but I did not believe her when she turned down a call and the old investigator in me had to know what the truth was and I found out, she was lying to me.

The last time I saw her … she was working at Pier 39 in San Francisco and was horribly overweight. I say "horribly" overweight because the extra 100 lbs. did not do anything for her appearance. She looked much older than her years and she was trying to stay with a retail job.

I confronted her for my money and she was not going to pay me and make good on the bad check she had given me. The way she looked gave me a feeling of repulsion. It was as if her soul had come to the forefront of her face and was there for everyone to see. Something had gone extremely wrong inside of her and all efforts to help her … fell on deaf ears. We were done and I was very disappointed with her. I had given her respect and taught her how to make some needed cash that she once told me would go for her education. That ship passed. A very sad outcome, to once, would have been a woman with a bright future. This happened over 20 years ago and I still want to kick her ass. Lol lol

Number 37

This was a dumb blonde who lived in Tiburon and gave me nothing but grief. I hated to phone her and give her calls. This girl had a good figure and was around 5'2" tall and had blonde hair with blue eyes. She had a cute face and looked younger than her actual age of 26 years. She had worked for other escort services and also had done massage. She was also working as a waitress, while working for me. Some of each group (family and friends) did know that she was doing escort work. Yes, she had a white boyfriend. She did not have children. Lived in Marin County and the location was Tiburon, at an apartment complex, and was with me off and on two months. Sort of good at what she did, when she wanted to work and was able to connect with the clients, but never really connected with me and could have made a lot more.

Basically, she wasted my time in ever hiring her. Spent most of her money, if not all of her money, on self and the needs she perceived were required, by her lifestyle. Her boyfriend did not want her working and she had just moved in with him. (He was a user and I doubt that he did not want her to work.) I believe she made the right choice – not to work. The habits I was aware of included drugs, liquor, clothes, and having a good time, she was a real party girl. Her habits just listed … were in the proper order. She was a typical dumb blonde and was not faking. The appeal she held inside was for almost any man, because she liked getting her hands on his life and her hands in his pocket book.

The usual, meeting bills were her problems in life. No doubt had mental problems which were well hidden, except for her obvious lack of attention to details. She was scattered and would do just about anything sexual … was creative with sex and men. I believe she gave "art" to her sexual antics in bed.

All she wanted was sex; probably to make up for her lack of topics to speak on. Not really a guilty feeling girl. She felt that anything she did was her business and projected that attitude to me, a lot. I was not able to guide her into other directions that could help her reach a potential in life that did not have sex as the primary goal. She would never want to show the town of San Francisco to anyone or any tourist … as a real escort. She really should have went to Nevada and worked in a brothel. This woman had the "brothel mind". The "brothel mind" of "next", "oh next", "no money, no service", "time to get out of here", "next".

Not a particularly honest person. Would sell drugs and do anything for money; and this was even after I told her not to sell drugs when seeing my clients. I thought if she had any brains they were all in her ass. She was an inconsiderate person and wasting her young life. As the escort owner I was very happy when she decided not to work. But that was probably a lie, her deciding not to work. The truth was more real ... that she had wanted to be worked by her boyfriend. This person loved variety and one man would never have satisfied her. I would not be surprised if she had died before the age of 30.

Number 40

Okay, crazy girl. This girl was around 5'6" tall, overweight, and brown hair and glasses. She also sported a complexion problem that could have been corrected with plastic surgery. Her face was pretty but she really didn't know it. She could have made herself more appealing if she would have only tried.

The most god awful trendy clothes were what she wore and liked to wear; but she was about 22 years old and maybe those were the clothes of the day and I was the one out of step. She was an artist and also worked as a sales clerk when necessary. Some of her friends knew about her extracurricular activities as an escort, but not her family. She had a white boyfriend and did not have children. She lived with a roommate as a sharing situation in an apartment in San Francisco.

This one lasted around three months and that was working off and on. Not really good at the work. Hardly any money was made by her and what she did make, she spent it on drugs. Eventually, she went home to live with her parents; probably because she had a very bad speed and heroin habit. A smart and very creative girl and it was too bad that she was not making a living from her art work. She did not appeal to many clients. Yes, she had mental problems and was seeing a psychiatrist. Yes, she just could not hold herself together. She was too creative for what it took in common sense to meet her everyday living needs. What I mean here is that her mind was always in the clouds, and the skills needed to pay her bills and take care of her, properly, were not there.

If she did not have her parents to fall back on, then being taken care of by "the system" would have worked out for her. Plus, she was awakening to her desire for women in a sexual manner. Not necessarily any lasting relationship, just sex. On top of her "awakening" was filled with endless guilt feelings and those "feelings" were in regard to everything she did. If she was not doing her art work; she felt as though she was cheating on herself or messing up her life more than it already was. Confusion about life had to be a direct response from no preparation given to her from anyone, least of all her parents.

An honest girl and I liked her and still would have let her work for me if she had wanted too. Although, I did not believe the girl should have been doing escort work, due to her mental problems. If those issues of hers could ever be resolved, escorting may have been a great way for her to survive in the world.

Number 40 had a quirky personality and while listening to her you never knew what would come out of her mouth. Maybe comedy could have given her a way to relate to the world.

Number 22

This was a very pretty young black girl with exceptional qualities of grace and charm. She was very eager to work for me and had been brought to me by some other girls that were working for me at the time. They had all gone to high school together and working for an escort service was enticing to them. It was an experience they all agreed to and wanted. She had interviewed with at least one other escort service and was concerned about working for a man. I assured her that there was no man running my business. That was fine with her, because the other girls were very happy making all the money that came from being part of *Professional Escorts*. She was very sure that the work was what she wanted to do. I made sure she was over 18 years of age and put her to work.

Over the course of time she worked for me there were many times I picked her up in a limousine to take her to parties with some of the other girls. She was very happy for awhile. But one day her mother phoned me. Number 22 was living directly across from her parent's house in Novato. Her mother had seen the limousines come to pick her girl up, too many times, and this mother questioned how her little girl was making her money. I was very blunt with her mother.

Blunt, mainly because she wanted to phone the police on me, so I needed to explain everything to her. She was the mother of this girl and I felt that she should take some comfort in a few facts, so I proceeded to tell her, "Your daughter came to me. I did not pick her up walking down the street. You are very lucky she did come to me because I have made sure that the experience is something that would not hurt her. She has only gone out with people I know and she may quit whenever she wants. But I will tell you one thing – she wanted to do this type of work and if she had gone anywhere else – she may have ended up on drugs or a lot worse."

Her mother was not thrilled with what I said, but she did not go to the police. What could she do? Her daughter was not living at home and was of a legal age according to the laws of California and could make her own decisions.
I tried to mentor this girl and hoped she would just attend college or get married to her long time white boyfriend. I really liked her and wanted the best for her. Not working for me was okay. I did the right thing by allowing her to test the waters but she did not drown while working for me.

This girl was around 18 to 19 years of age. Black or should I say a very light-skinned African American girl. She was 5'4" tall and a very pretty girl both inside and out. She had a very good figure and was slender.

Number 22 did not have a large chest but she did have long legs and was in great shape. She had been a waitress. Some of her friends and her family knew. She had a blonde Lilly-white boyfriend and a few months after working with me, she had a baby with her boyfriend. They lived in an apartment and she lasted about four to six months with my escort service. Yes, she was good and loved being with men. Yes, she made money, a great deal. She went wild with her money. Mostly supported her living needs and bought gifts for her boyfriend and many clothes for herself, and she loved clothes.

After her parents found out – I discouraged her and she finally quit.

Just clothes were her habits and she looked great in them, she had a beautiful sense of style and a lot of class. Her boyfriend was also a habit of hers and doing things for him. She had average intelligence and was developing street-smarts. Most men liked her after they saw her. I was able to talk a blonde loving man into seeing her and then he was just fine with seeing this lovely girl. No mental problems that I was aware of at the time. She was very well-adjusted. I would attribute that to a strong family connection. Once there was a confession about a family member who had come on to her. I actually forget if he raped her, but it was one issue she dealt with and shared with me.

This work was just a "fling" for her. Something to say she did.

Plus, she was not working long enough and seeing any weirdo's for it to be a problem for her mind. I made sure she was as protected as I could give her protection. I sent her to a lot of parties instead of sending her to private homes, all the time. Some women only liked going to private homes and not doing parties.

There were other women with her to protect her at these parties and I felt it kept her safe. She spent a little too much for what she was earning and she was earning a lot. She liked women and loved lots of sex. She had a healthy appetite for men, mostly. She felt guilty over her sexual feelings toward women. This woman was pretty honest with me. This girl would not know how to steal or do criminal activities when I knew her. Doing any criminal activities did not interest her. Some people, whether escorts or not, you just knew when you met them that they could not be trusted. This girl had "trust" written all over her. I liked her a lot. I found her to be trustworthy and one of the nicest girls I ever had worked with me. She was just a damn nice girl who wanted to walk on the wild side of life, to see how it was. I was very happy that she did not remain in escort work.

Dating and going to parties were okay, but she may have changed if she stayed too long working for an escort service. The last time I saw her … she had an African American boyfriend and he had her working out at his gym, so she could possibly be in competitions with other body-builders. I thought it was very nice of her to bring him by to meet me. I always wish her well.

Number 39

This woman came to work for me to learn the escort business. She was a woman around 34 years of age and stood about 5'4" tall with short dark hair and light eyes. She had a very average face. Her body needed a lot of work. She had a tendency to gain weight, but otherwise her appearance was neat and clean and straight looking. She had been a secretary. One day she told me that she had owned her own escort service in San Diego. Her friends knew but not her family. Yes, she had a husband and he was white. She did have children. She lived in Richmond, California. She was with me for about three months. She was pretty good at what she did. Yes, she did make money. As many of the girls did, she spent it on living expenses and saved it, so she could start her own escort service in the Bay Area.

After she learned all she could from me, she did start her own escort service. Her habits were drugs, liquor, and clothes. Slightly above average intelligence, but definitely she over estimated her own abilities and intelligence. If she got started talking, most men liked her. But her appearance did not appeal to all men. So many men did not like the straight look. Those men were calling me for the sexy women, not women who did escorting as a sideline from their "real" job.

I would say, "Yes to mental problems and those issues were she could not tell the truth." She just had problems keeping her lies straight. She liked women.

Possibly she felt or had guilt feelings, but those feelings were well-hidden and part of her mental problems. I felt she could never be an honest person in this line of work. She was a born liar. I liked her as a person; but felt a lot of distain for her, after I learned that the girl would steal and lie as a matter of course. I mean the lies just flowed from her and were as natural as breathing. By stealing clients for her own business, she was stealing from me. The lies were not necessary. I may have developed her into an asset to open another office for me if she had been honest about what she wanted to do.

The common theme of girls lying is throughout this writing, but so many of the women did lie and so many of them had personal problems they were working out by taking money from men for sexual favors. She was intent on proving something to herself. I could see how she manipulated people, but, in reality, she was "manipulating" herself into believing she controlled all situations.

Number 28

This girl had worked for the *Mitchell Brothers* in San Francisco. *Mitchell Brothers* was a location where men or women could come and see nude dancers; many years later one of the Mitchell brothers killed the other brother at one of their homes in Marin County and that was not the end of their business. It is still being operated in San Francisco at the time of this writing. Some other women that worked for me had worked for these two brothers.

Also, a male friend of mine worked for them. Everyone in the business was aware of everyone else. I did not like or dislike these men. I knew of them, but don't remember every meeting them face to face.

Number 28 stood 5'9" tall and was a natural redhead. She had some freckles and blue or green eyes with pale white skin. She had long legs and a really nice figure and weighed around 125 lbs. This girl was into pornography filming and wanted to be a porn star. Also, she was working as an adult teaser-dancer at one of the local clubs in San Francisco. Just about everyone she knew, did know what she was doing. She had a boyfriend off and on. Luckily, she did not have children. She lived in an apartment in San Francisco. She was with me about a month or two and her availability was sporadic. When working she was good. No, to did she make money, because there wasn't any consistency with her. She really did not know how to do this kind of work and was more an exhibitionist. She preferred to screw all day in a porno film; that was for not as much money as if she had worked all day for the escort service. She bought clothes and paid her living expenses, plus, she paid for her drugs. She told me her boyfriend did not want her working. Yet he was okay with her working in porno films. Go figure how he rationalized that work over working at an escort service. Her habits were drugs, doing porno films, and modeling when ever and where ever she could find work.

This was her cycle and her life had turned into a habit. She had just barely enough brains to function in the world. She appealed to those clients that liked an exhibitionist and someone that was more into showing them what they could do with her, rather than in doing it. No doubt mental problems and also this must be why she liked screwing in front of a lot of people; she was a very unusual woman with no inhibitions.

Most of the time she had problems keeping up with her expenses that were required for her to live, such as rent and drugs. She preferred women to men. In fact, I suspected she only takes a boyfriend, so that boyfriend can take care of her expenses. Some guilt feelings, but not enough to stop her from working, not ever, if she had her way. There were moments when I felt her to be sort of honest, but there was that attitude that she would do anything for money; similar to being sort of pregnant. I thought she was nice, but stupid for not devoting her time to really making some money escorting.

Now, so many years after the fact; it would be interesting to know how her life went. Possibly she married, out of necessity.

Chapter Fourteen
More Case Studies

Before I began to number the girls, they had been catalogued with my using letters. Letter A was Stony, and I spoke about her in the <u>Making of a Madam, a Twentieth Century Woman</u>. The letter B was also spoken about in the same book. Letter C was not spoken about before and I would like to introduce her and others through the same format as the numbered women.

In fact, there are some numbered case studies in this chapter just because those studies fit well in this area.

Letter C

This lady was 5'8" tall with a slender and a very good figure. She was a black girl around 20 years old, who was complimented by a pretty face. C had been a prostitute for some pimp out of Marin City, a town in Marin County that is across from Sausalito. C also sat at the bar in a cocktail lounge on 4th Street in San Rafael, California, while she was looking for clients, surprisingly, as she adjusts her bar stool, continually. I watched her do this little show to draw attention to her at the bar. Yes, she got the needed attention. I just rolled my eyes and distanced myself from her. I did get a few laughs with her later over how trivial the entire evening was, and she let me know it was as easy as making a pie to pick up men who would pay her from the bar. The bartender knew her and she pushed extra cash his way so she would not be thrown out.

There was a strong dependence upon cocaine and she needed a doctor for her mental health and of course she was unable to handle her child or cat; unable to keep food in her apartment. She did not have a sense of responsibility. This was a sad time for her child. C would lay down for anyone – whether male or female. She liked orgies. Her views of raising children and her child were straight out of the insanity book 101. C did not even know how to spell honesty. Everything that came out of her mouth was a lie. C sold cocaine to support her own habit. She also was an on again/off again heroin user.

C would take any opportunity to rip off a client.

If she was seeing someone for awhile - she knew how to get to him for money and then she would strike by taking him for as much money as she could.

When not at the previously mentioned locations she visited other trick's (a location known to men where they can pick up women) spots, as she called them, in the Marin County area. But most spots were limited to her, because   she had no transportation. Street-walking, anywhere, when she could not find a place to pick up men. With her, everyone knew what she was doing; both friends and family. No doubt even the mailman knew what she was doing. C was an instinctive liar. If she had a husband – he didn't know about it. Lol lol

The same went for any potential bedfellows. She told lots of stories. I found her stories amusing, as I listened not believing a word she said. She had an adorable little boy. C lived in low-income housing apartments in San Rafael. She lasted with me, maybe a month. She couldn't be trusted and I got rid of her with a butcher knife threat the last time she tried to come over and into my apartment without being invited. C had been seen stealing, out of my purse, by my youngest son, Thomas. He could barely say the words, but I got the message as he pointed to my purse. He knew my purse was off limits and had sense this snake go into my purse as I slept.

I found that my money was gone and he pointed to who did it. I believed a four year old over Miss C. She never denied that she took my money. Maybe she could have made money, but there were complaints of her not being clean by my clients. Someone phoned and said she gave him a venereal disease.

If she did make any money; I did not see any of it. What I saw was that all her money went for drugs. She worked for me when I had "Fingers" outcall massage. I never was able to collect a fee from her.

She was no longer working with me because of stealing from my purse while I was sleeping. I fired her. The easy to recognize habits were liquor, cocaine, and lying. Most of what she got away with was due to her being clever and stupid at the same time. When it came to money, the brain cells were not there. Never there for saving her money or knowing that she had to buy food for her child.

No way, no how did she have a logical mind; meaning nothing was done logically or in a sequential order. The appeal she had was for the sleazy customer. One of C's failings was her inability to tell the truth. She did not have a sense of the difference between right and wrong. On the few occasions that she was able to hustle a client out of me – I only heard after the deed of taking the man for a lot of money. The reason was simple – she saw him without using me, so the client did not want to tell me, but she ended up explaining everything to me. I would joke with the guy after that – and he had better not cheat on me again or the same thing may happen. I doubt if any employment situation would find her honest on the job. Not any job.

Usually, the men knew I was right. If the girl was not with me anymore or on my clock, than he better be careful. That went for the girls too. I was doing the monitoring of bad behavior, but if not for someone doing that monitoring than the people would be very unhappy. A person such as me was a necessary for both parties to play nice and make sure they went through me to see each other. At first I liked C, because C had a friendly demeanor. But as I caught onto her "no scruples life style", there was no room with my service for her antics. Easily, I could visualize her going to prison for years. I actually do not know what happened to her.

Letter D

This girl was a model. She was around 30 years of age and about 5'7" tall with longish brown hair. D had big eyes, protruding teeth and a slender good figure. She was pretty and Caucasian. She was a secretary and occasionally a model. Some of her friends knew – not her family. Or that is what she told me.

Her husband, from Iran had died, and it appeared she might have a boyfriend and she kept him secret. Possibly he was the one who supplied her with her drugs and when he died – she had to fend for herself. Her husband had been hit by a car in front of the apartment building where she lived. She told me that she thought people may have killed him because of the drug dealing he was doing. This woman was so beautiful that possibly the new boyfriend, who was from the same country as the husband, had killed the husband. There was a mystery there.

Yes, to having a daughter. She lived in a San Francisco apartment. D lasted about three or four months. Yes, she was good and made money.

Unfortunately, her money went for heroin. I saw her spend what was supposed to be her last fifty dollars on a "fix" from a guy she didn't even know, for sure, what kind of dope it was.

The heroin could have been bogus. (Meaning: bad drug or not heroin at all.) I was amazed that anyone would buy drugs from some person virtually off the street and she was not familiar with the dope he was selling. She resented me knowing about her heroin habit and the heroin made her lazy. She was rude to me once and that was the last time I wanted to have anything to do with the "junkie" personality she displayed to me. Heroin was her main habit. Vanity took a close second.

Also, she was an accomplished liar – able to cover up her habit, so her habit of lying was also a habit to cover up the main habit – heroin. She was college educated but weak of mind. Not able to utilize her schooling for the best possible life for herself and her daughter.

Yes, many mental problems from her dependence on drugs. She appealed to the drug user and seller. She was unable to keep her bills paid and clean her house. All signs of the drug problem. D liked garter belts and very sleazy-sexy outfits. She looked as though she could stand on any street corner. D liked using her sexual gifts for anything she wanted. Because I was a girl, she must have felt frustrated that she could not get to me with her posturing of sexual favors my way. No doubt this was the reason for the conflict we had.

Many guilt feelings were expressed by her, to me. I suspect that is why she lied and took drugs. But in reality she was working to support her habit. She did not begin her drug habit by working with me. From what I remember telling me her husband had gotten her hooked and after he died she was stuck trying to "score" from his friend. She was not honest and she sold drugs to maintain her habit. I felt she was open to stealing when the opportunity presented itself. I liked her one personality, but the bad side of her was too likely to rear-up and show at any time.

I felt there was too much instability within this girls' personality.

After the break – I never wanted to see her again. She was not welcome at my home or to work for me; but speaking with me from a distance and only phoning into my phone number was alright. Eventually, something horrible did happen to her. She had fallen into a drug stupor with a cigarette hanging out of her mouth and the cigarette clinging to the side of her face.

The cigarette dropped onto her clothes and couch resulting in one side of her becoming burned and her face disfigured from the flames that filled the very location she was asleep at in her living room.

When the firemen got there they had to wake her up.

Only heroin could have done that to her … kept her from waking.

Thankfully, her child survived without any harm.

Her beautiful face was ruined and only continuing plastic surgery helped her appearance. One of my other escorts saw her and told me that she did not look the same. This was a miserable way to have her kick the habit and I only wished for her to have a productive and worthwhile life after such an experience. We did speak on the phone after this escort saw her and I thought she was much more humble. I would have liked to visit her, but she did not want anyone to come over, or, at least, not me. I wasn't interested in the scars, but I did want to be her friend.

This girl was being taken care of by her mother, after the fire. I think that was the best place for her.

Letter O

The escort O was a very unusual person.

I have no idea why she wanted to work as an escort. She was 5'2" tall and a pretty oriental girl with long black hair and a good figure. She was a counselor for a well-known meditation center based in San Francisco. O also worked as a "display dancer" at one of the clubs in San Francisco. I think this had to do with some Zen type of dancing.

No friends or family knew what she was doing. I did not know if she had a boyfriend or husband. She did not have children. She lived at the *Meditation Center*. She was only with me about two weeks and that was mostly off – rather than on. O was really well-liked by those who saw her for that short time. She made a little money and, no doubt, was the reason for not working with me, because it interfered with her meditation.

There were no habits that I could see, other than a heavy sexual need that was within her being. Here was a smart girl but scattering her potential in life and the *Center* was not really a good choice for her. Even the meditation was not keeping her on the right road.

O appealed to men who liked oriental women or small girls. No doubt a split personality was manifesting in her when she came to work for me. She liked having money - for what reason – I did not know. She loved sex and was vocal about that to me. By all appearances she was honest. Perhaps she felt guilt in regard to her family finding out some day. This could also be her "family" at the *Center*. But otherwise I believe she had no feelings of guilt. I thought she was nice. O did not work long enough for me to have many opinions about her.

I do think she is a person, who should have continued working longer, in order to work out some problems she had, and was trying to mask them, by being someone she was not. That means – the meditation was not working on her, because she really did not like it as much as she liked working and receiving money for sex. My thoughts here were that the *Center* was hustling her for a lot of money to stay there, even though she told me it was free, because she worked for them. There was some sexual activity happening at the *Center* that she would not go into, but I felt some negative influences were at the *Center* and targeting her.

Letter Q

The girl Q was a bartender in San Francisco at a popular spot. I know she confided in me, that she had worked at the bar, before she ever came to work with me, and continued her employment there even while an escort. I remember picking up me fee from her there one night and the bar was not a 'dive' joint it was really very nice. Q was 5'6" tall and heavy set, brown eyes, brown hair wearing it at shoulder length. She was a pretty girl around 23 years of age. She had been a secretary, who then went on to become a bartender, in a lesbian bar after attending bartender school. Her friends knew about the escort job but her family probably did not know that she worked as an escort. She did not have a boyfriend and did not have a girlfriend, nor did she have any children. She lived in an apartment within the area of San Rafael known as the Canal area.

This area was and is a primarily low-income location in Marin County, which enjoys boasting that it is very affluent (Marin county boasts of being affluent, and tries to entice people with money to live there.) Now, in the 21st century many of the legal and illegal immigrants live there, (in the Canal area).

The area also has a huge crime rate.

Q lasted with me only two weeks to a month. She was an independent call-girl trying to get out of the business of being an independent call- girl and was very good as a worker for my service. Many lesbians I found were very good doing this work. She made money for herself but not necessarily me. Her money went for drugs. Q wanted to quit the business or have just a few clients of her own and it was difficult to tell which was more important to her. I figure she took clients from me for a while, and used them when she stopped working for me. I think her being a bartender was to have a private life, a life that was the "real" her.

There was, also, her liquor and drug habit. I believed her to have average intelligence and even with lower intelligence she would appeal to most men.

Yes, Letter O liked women and did not want to and this led to her conflict within her soul, because she found out the attraction to women was very strong. But then again if she really was so disturbed by the attraction to other women, then she should not have had a job at a lesbian bar, which fortifies the fact that she had average to below average intelligence. Even my reading this allows for me to say, "She was messed up". Yes, she felt guilty about doing escort work and her sexual preferences. The opposite sex, or men, were becoming less attractive to her. She just preferred women. Not really a split personality, just a woman finding herself in a changing world in San Francisco. A world where she could be who she thought she was.

It was difficult for her to be honest and this carried over into all her personal relationships. I felt she was a nice person, but I did not want her working for me, because the change was so significant that I felt the work was pushing her more toward women and she seemed to be headed for instability in her personae. Men's attitudes were not or are not always friendly to the woman who chooses to charge for her time.

Especially, if her body is not perfect and this woman's body was not close to perfect. So she was caught, knowing about a skewed counter-likeable personality that many men paying have, and take great pleasure in lamenting toward the woman that is in front of them, with hand out for money. Basically she was interested in the wrong business. Although, some lesbian women were centered on only having sex with women that were in shape. This girl had to change her body shape to be happy in which ever world she was going to ultimately find herself. Either as a lesbian or a heterosexual person.

Letter F

The Lady F was a language major at a university in San Francisco, and she traveled to Italy, so she might learn the language well. This lady was around 5'2" tall with very short brown-black hair. If she had a bathing suit on you could easily see that her arm pits were not shaved nor her legs. I was constantly hinting and then just coming right out and began questioning her about the hair she had on those legs. I know she wanted to be European, but hell, she was in the states and had to conform in order to make the money she wanted and needed to return to Italy and her studies.

Finally, I resorted to asking her to shave the hair in certain areas of her body. She liked the European custom of not shaving. But her need for money was more important to her, so she shaved. Underarm hair is a turnoff to most American men. The leg hair was very bushy and men did not like snuggling up to what felt like … another man.

F was around 25 years of age and had olive toned skin. She was what I called 'cute'. Not beautiful or pretty, but just cute face and a very clean look about herself. F's clothes were the San Francisco 'in' look of the time.

This look was not always part of the feminine curvy line of clothes; these clothes were baggier rather than close fitting. Cheap jewelry adorned her. Usually, those times when she wanted to have a more feminine look. The jewelry and tight jeans or slacks she would wear and did give her that feminine appearance. She had been a housekeeper. But her main course of study had been languages and this is where her degree was in. Italian was the primary language that she liked to speak.

F did leave the country to teach foreign students English. After being a housekeeper, again, she traveled to Italy to become a school teacher and follow her dreams of seeing that country. Along with her teaching, she became a waitress in Italy. She had done some student teaching in the Bay Area. Her family did not know, but most of her very close friends knew about the escorting. She was fairly open with her friends and told them what she was doing. She had a husband; this marriage was so the guy could stay in this country. The marriage was not a big love affair for her. She mostly had girlfriends. I don't know if he paid her to marry him

One year she would be gay and the next year bi-sexual. So to say boyfriend or girlfriend – was dependent upon what year it was … would apply to her relationship that year. She did not have children and no plans for getting pregnant or ever having children. She lived with roommates.

She was in San Francisco living in apartments and, usually, she lived with other women. She lasted working on and off for almost three years. But most of her work was done on a part-time basis. Yes, she was good. I have said this many times before, "Lesbians are great workers in escorting and prostitution." It must be their distancing of their hearts too far away from the men. The men for some reason really liked her. I think mostly it was because she was a person who could listen very well and reason well in conversations with men. Possibly she identified with the way men think. She made an average income for an escort. That income would have been about two to three thousand dollars a month.

F could have made more money but she preferred to develop her escort relationships into ongoing friendships, which, ultimately, would have the effect of shorting herself out of making money.

There were regular clients, but too much time was spent with them and she did not receive her pay for all the hours worked. She was able to pay for her traveling abroad and living in a foreign country for a year. F primarily saved her money. One of the few women I met who was able to save her money. She loved foreign life and all that went with living away from the United States, which gave her mental rest from the business, plus, she was more interested in her own career as a teacher and Italy was her way to achieve perfection in the Italian language.

Common sense was much a part of her character as breathing and she was definitely an intelligent human being. Other women and flirting with them was a habit of hers. She, also, did have a bout with cocaine, but overcame it quickly. The men from other countries, she liked a lot. She also appealed to the 'coke-talker'. The guy, who wanted to stay up all night doing drugs, loved her company. F also appealed to the older man in need of a friend. She gave of herself to her clients and put everything on a very personal basis. Her mental problems were not visible if she had any. She possibly had problems, but was able to conquer them all by herself without therapy; a strong mind and I was impressed that she didn't need to confide her problems or tell me if she had any.

Her downfall, that I could see, was that she was too trusting of the wrong people. Her main problems with living were her inability to 'care' (wishing) to make enough money to meet her living needs after she went onto a cocaine habit. When she rid herself of the need for drugs she was just fine. Drugs as an addiction for her, was probably just by accident from all the use with clients. After that small fall, she was okay with money because she saved it for her move to Italy. She was a lesbian. The only guilt feelings she had were if she might hurt someone's feelings. Otherwise, she felt comfortable doing what she was doing. But she did not like what she was doing. Just because a person can be very good at something, no matter what the work, does not mean that person likes the work. This made her very valuable, because she did not want to do the work forever. She was basically an honest person, once upon a time. But if she needed extra money, she was inclined to keep the money and she did not report that to me. Her idea of how to work with me was intentionally not reporting the extra money made. This justifying not telling me all the money she made, because it was practical for her to do things that way. Money had turned her into a sneaky person and a liar.

F saw no problem with doing two hours and only reporting one hour. It made sense to her not to tell the complete amount, because she was usually giving the client too much time. She also sold drugs for whatever reasons she needed, at the time for money, and again to support her habit or basic needs. I liked her. She wrote to me when in Italy and kept in touch for a very long time. I wish her well and Italy, with their system of learning, was lucky to have her as a student teacher and maybe she came back to the United States. Since moving I have not heard from her.

Letter G

Letter G came to work for me in order to have enough information to begin her own escort service. This girl was around 34 years old and about 5'4" tall with short dark hair and light eyes. She had a very average face. Her body needed a lot of work and she had a tendency to gain weight. What I mean by a lot of work is that plastic surgery and a lot of exercise would have helped her appearance. But otherwise her exterior was neat, clean, and straight looking. She had been a secretary and also had owned her own escort service in San Diego. Her friends knew but not her family. Her boyfriend was a black man and he was her husband; at first she tried to say he was only her boyfriend. Yes, she had children and lived in Richmond, California. She was with me about three months.

This girl was able to make good money. She spent her money on living expenses and saved it, so she could start her own escort service.

After she learned all she could from me, she did start her own escort service. Her habits were drugs, liquor, and clothes. G was slightly above average in intelligence. But she definitely overestimated herself, in regard to intelligence, because, I believe, she was another one of the escorts who thought she was getting over on me. The kind of woman, who, when she was with her man, told him how dumb I was, because she was able to learn so much from me and had already, taken as many customers from my business. Thinking like that was stupid. The customers I had may call her for some "freebie" time, but when that did not work out for them; they were back with someone they trusted.

When she talked a lot, most men liked her because she could keep the conversation going, and then the client would forget about her appearance which did not appeal to all men. But if the opposite were true and she had maybe a sore throat and needed to depend on her appearance; the client may have asked her to leave.

Yes, her main mental problem was she could not tell the truth, and just had problems keeping her lies straight. She liked women. Possibly she felt guilt, but those feelings were well-hidden. She could never be an honest person in escort work. She was a born liar. The people I met at the time who were born liars were so likeable. It was too bad they could not stop the damn lying. She was one of those people I wish could stop lying. I did liked her as a person, but felt a lot of dislike for her after learning the girl would steal and lie as a matter of course. (Such nerve she had to steal from me! After so many case studies, thus far, it is clear that stealing my fees were, in fact, a major problem in running the business.) She may have been friends with Number 39 because they were two different people but very much alike and had met each other. Which means they both had the same set of stories to tell me; and there were other women that came to me telling me they had services in other areas of the country, so I believed them and I should have known better because they were all liars. Women who spent so much time making up stories did not last in the business. Men were wise to them and so was I.

Number 92

This girl was overweight and looked as if she had never lost her baby fat. She was around 5'6" tall and had a baby face. Soft prettiness came with those facial features, which were framed by lovely dark hair that was healthy looking.
She wore glasses and had been a bookkeeper and also a student. Only a few friends and no family knew about her escort work. She had boyfriends off again and on again. No children. She lived alone in a San Francisco apartment. Because of her need for money she was with me about seven months. Yes, she was pretty good with the clients. Yes, she made money, but not as much as she could have made if she had lost some of her weight. She blew the money on clothes and drugs. I fired her and she also quit at the same time that I fired her. A mutual parting of the ways.

Drugs and clothes made her happy. She was a smart girl and appealed to those men that liked the wholesome look in a woman. Yes, to mental problems. Lots, she was seeing a psychiatrist. She could not keep her money in her pockets. She was always spending what she made as an escort. She liked women but found lots of trouble in admitting to that fact. Hordes of guilt feelings about what she was doing and also some 'baggage' was in her past. A thief and a two-faced person. Who, no doubt, had this behavior due, in part, to the mental problem that she was seeing her doctor about. I liked her but felt uneasy with her. I felt this girl was a borderline to go insane and may do a very violent act, someday because of her past criminal character and behavior.

This is a person who would have benefited from staying at a facility for people with mental problems. She was sometimes observably unstable.

Number 91

An escort who had other plans and she lived in Sonoma County, California. This girl was around 28 years old and stood 5'8" tall and she had a large chest. She did not wear makeup. Pale skin was framed from longish brown/red hair. She did massage work and sewing as her profession. This was before calling me for an interview to work as an escort. I believe she may have been referred by someone who worked for me at that time. The plans she had were simple. All she wanted was her own store front to sew and make clothes at.

Only a few friends knew what she was doing and no family knew.

When she did have a boyfriend, he was black and wanted her to stop working. They had children together. This must have been another woman lying to me about her relationship. The guy was probably her husband the entire time she worked for me. She lived in Sonoma County and was with me about seven months and during that time I did not really get great reviews about her worth as an escort. No to making money with me and this was mainly because she would take any amount of money the client would give her, instead of holding out for more money. This was where her insecurity of self came into play. I don't care if you are ugly from ugly patch, if you think you are great and believe in yourself, the client will too. She used her money for living expenses. She was off doing or into her own thing, whatever that was for awhile when she had no calls from me. She was a bit of a hippy-type person. I say that because her clothes were long skirts and flowing blouses.

This woman did not like tight fitting clothes. I even wondered if she wore deodorant. Many hippies gave up deodorant because of the chemicals. She was a natural living person and I think she even had a garden at her home for fresh vegetables. Nothing drug related, she was just spacing out doing her own thing all the time. Maybe she liked "weed". No doubt … a latent genius. Her smarts would show up every now and then in some conversations; she was very bright when all her lights were on inside her skull. She appealed to about fifty-percent of the men. Not anything I could see in the way of mental problems. She was pretty much together, just had a lot of abstract views. As with most of the escorts she had problems keeping enough money for what her aspirations were.

No sexual preferences that stood out or she told me about. No guilt feelings and an honest person, who I liked. Eventually, she owned her own sewing business and she seemed to prosper in that line of work, where she was able to show what she could do and create for her clients. Here is where she shined, rather than feeding into inadequacies, she may have had at that time in regard to her appearance. With her own business of sewing, there was freedom to be herself. I enjoyed her coming to my house to chat and wait for the phone to ring and bring business her way. I even paid her to sew a few things for me and make a couple of blouses. I really liked her work. Sewing was her true calling.

Number 90

This woman lived in Cotati, California. Number 90 was around 5'3" tall with long blonde hair and blue eyes. She had a good figure (with a little help from a doctor) and that included giving her a large chest. She was around 110 lbs. and was about 28 years old. Number 90 was a dancer and a singer. Her family and friends knew she was working. Yes, to a boyfriend, he was a white man. Yes, to children. She lived in Sonoma County. She was with me for about four months. Yes, she was good enough to make some money, and blew it on herself with a lot of help from her boyfriend.

All her vehicles went dead and she had a couple of bad experiences with some of the clients. Those bad experiences gave her the excuse to not continue doing this type of work. Possibly taking the broken cars as a sign she had to stay home and away from escorting. Superstitious thoughts about escorting and mostly she was a clothes hound, but her boyfriend was also a habit that she could not break. I enjoyed the way she left the business. Left escort work behind her, because it was all up to some Karmic writing in the sky.

She was smart and appealed to most men and was very attractive. Yes, about mental problems; a very insecure person. She could not keep up with her living expenses or excesses and loved sex and kinky sex. No guilt feelings and a fairly honest girl. But if she could she would try to deceive, through casual lies. Not well thought out lies. This was her way out of anything or situation she was caught in and had to tell what had happened it was a balancing act of lies or adjusting the truth a bit.

I liked her and not because of the fees, for me, she had brought into the business, but because she had an inner glow and freshness that stood out. Her lying was really no big deal, because very few of the escorts told me the truth. I was waiting for different lies to pop up from her and the other escorts. The old familiar lies became boring.

Number 89

This girl actually worked for me for over a year and it was off and on again. The following represents my first documenting of her. The last time I saw her she was living in her own apartment and was seeing clients from an ad she had put in the paper. She also wanted work or clients from my service and I allowed her to see some clients. Why? Because she was not able to keep a huge clientele for herself, she was too scattered. Keeping clients would never have worked for her, unless the man really liked her and would put up with her highs and lows.

When I wrote the following; she was as I had written, but my last encounters with Number 89, found her not holding her finances together very well, due to continuing drug and alcohol abuse problems. She had turned from a pleasant person into an argumentative person. I prefer the person that I once knew, and that is the person I wrote about here.

This girl was around 5'4" tall with short blonde hair and blue eyes. Not a very attractive nose. A cute face but not a beautiful face and she were about 28 years old. One of her degrees was in cosmetology and she was a practicing beautician, even while doing escort work; she saw clients at her home wanting their hair cut or trimmed or colored. Then the escort clients were able to come to her home. Some of her friends knew but none of her family. She had a few boyfriends and they may have been past clients. No children. She lived in the Canal District of San Rafael, California. Working for me was limited to about two-three years. Yes, she was good and possibly because of her vibrant personality. Some money was made, but she could have made a lot more if she was more available for the calls I wanted to send her way.

She saved her money and went on vacation for a couple of months (to the Mid-West) and did come back and then she worked longer for me. She liked drugs, alcohol, and clothes. She had lots of mental problems and was very talkative about them and she had the gift of gab and no doubt failed to charge the clients for the time she was talking. Yes, she let everyone know what was wrong when something was wrong. Not really full of problems living and keeping up with her situation. She was pretty well-organized, even though she was not really living in her own apartment. She just liked a lot of sex. No guilt feelings, but some doubts that her appearance was as appealing as some other escorts.

I found her to be a fairly honest person and I liked her. She attracted friends to her. You were her best buddy, just because. Her smile was infectious. But eventually she changed and the change was for the worst. I hope she got over her debts, addictions, and self-doubts.

Many times, when I went over her apartment, toward the end of our working relationship, she would be angry with me and I could not figure out why. She had wanted me to give her calls and then when I tried she was upset with me and she was reluctant to give my fees to me. Just another person that owes me money.

In hindsight, she must have been hiding something at her apartment that she did not want me to know about. One week it was come over and I did, she yelled, and the next week it was come back. She had lots of fluctuations with her moods, which is typical for drug users.

Chapter Fifteen
Party --- Party --- Party

Party Number I

The very first party I had was at a client's home. He had only been using my service for about six months when one day a writer phoned me about having a party to showcase my women. The writer phoning me was an editor of a local rag sheet for people in Marin County to know what was happening and where to go to be seen.

This writer, I will call Mr. Writer, had a photographer friend that he wanted to bring along to take photos. Mr. Writer and Mr. Photographer's main intention was to give my business publicity. Or that is what they told me and I believed them. The entire time that I had *Professional Escorts*, I was always open for free advertisement.

I phoned a bachelor client (Mr. Annapolis) with a showcased home in the hills of Tiburon and he was receptive to have a party. His home had recently been featured in some magazine as a home that you-should-have-one-too if you are a bachelor. The home had at least three levels and a fantastic view of the San Francisco Bay. It was part of the scenery on top of a hill in Tiburon. The lower- level of the home had a hot tub and this was a time when hot-tubing was very popular in Marin County, during the late 1970s. Peacock feathers in every home in Marin was also a must have.

The bedroom area was on the second level and the living room and kitchen were on the first floor. The client was a man that had served his country after graduating from Annapolis. He was single and free of all obligations and just wanted to have fun.

Mr. Writer found my service fascinating after enjoying one of my talented women that danced at a bachelor party in Corte Madera. He thought the way I handled the entire situation with the girl was commendable. She had to phone in and I had sent a man with her to make sure she was safe. He also wanted to meet the woman behind the voice on the phone. The deal would be that the photos were free to me and to the girls and they would sign releases to be used in a story. That is how I remember it. But I may have paid for the photos and the photos were free to the women. It has been a long time and my memory goes in and out for the details. Also, the escorts could pose nude or clothed or both. The people who decided to have themselves photographed, all of them, happened to consent to both clothed and unclothed views of their bodies.

There was only one man who posed for both photos. His body was nearly perfect, so the shots were very nice. He had been a pro football player and kept himself in shape and he was an African American and very endowed, which may have intimidated other men from undressing for the photos.

The party was to be held during the afternoon and into the early evening. This timeframe was picked by the photographer, so the lighting and the view during the day and evening could be appreciated and utilized for the photos.

Finally, the day came and I was very nervous. It was my first party for the business and I had invited the women working for me and one of the men I had on file at that time.

The details of the alcohol, etc. are missing from my memory. I think Mr. Annapolis was of average height, brown hair, and a nice body with a very cute smile and friendly eyes sported upon his face, he looked like an intellectual. He supplied the beverages, which included champagne and some cheese and crackers. There was plenty of alcohol to drink, so the inhibitions of the models for the photos would be eliminated. Not the plan on my part, just a fact.

I made the decision that I would only pose clothed. After modeling and going to modeling school, when I was in my early twenties, I had decided a long time before this business of mine, that there would never be nude photos floating around of me. I had two sons and did not want them looking at their mother in the buff. My choice in clothes this day was a long white flowing evening gown. I love and loved wearing formal attire. I had a beautiful white feathered fan that would grace my hands and give me something to fiddle with when nervous. I have always been an introvert; that had to turn into an extrovert in order to succeed in this world. But my shyness usually was hidden behind a glass of vodka.

After having a few drinks I was able to talk to a lot of people without wanting to run for the nearest closet. But as the years came and went with my business, I became much more reclusive and the parties were more strained for me. This day I was gulping down the champagne to loosen up and I was able to mingle fairly well.

The location in the home for the photos was to be on the first floor, which had the best lighting and was nearest to the door in case someone wanted to bolt out the door and run home. (I was just expressing the many cartoon thoughts circling in my head.)

The nude shots and the clothed shots were next to a bookcase close to the front door and this area was adjacent to the living room. All the photos were in black and white. To the best of my knowledge we did not do color photos that day. All the people being photographed had to sign a waiver and I had to have a copy because I asked the people if I could use the photos for advertising; the other purpose for the photos were that and they were to be used for a magazine article that Mr. Writer was penning.

People may have glanced over when the photos were being taken, but for the most part the, entire, individual photo sessions were creatively- ignored and people were milling around talking to each other and it seemed as if everyone was a reporter. People did not stare at the nakedness of one another, there was a shared comradely that the photos would reflect their passive acceptance of escorting and their bodies.

They all wanted to know information as to what jobs each and every one had, besides working as escorts. It was a noisy gossip party. This was a party that could never be captured again; the entire essence of the people was incredible and everyone was relaxed and smiling. When I think about the calm and each person with a beverage in hand, looking out the window over to the bay with all the shimmering ice cold blue water stretched out there for them to cast their hopeful eyes upon, all was a casual photo landscape that I will always remember.

It was clear to see that these people felt special for a moment, and this was just another one moment to remember, a onetime event, if you will. Ultimately, I did see the article written. It was memorable enough for me and then it is forgotten. I think I used one or two photographs for advertising. The photographs were lovely. Very descent and not pornographic and I once had the photos on my walls where I lived in my office.

The party, actually, went very well. Mr. Annapolis got a date or two out of the party and the photographer and the writer enjoyed meeting women that worked with me at the time. Maybe they got dates too. I just don't know. That is something they would not have revealed to me.

The writer, I think, had fun interviewing the women and asking the usual questions as to why they made the choice to be an escort. Everyone knew it was for the money, but some girls would say it was because they wanted to just meet people. Whatever they said, Mr. Writer hung on each woman's pearls of thoughts, as to what she was getting out of being an escort.

These first women were very opportunistic and had other jobs. Each one of them wanted money and place in escort history. The article would be their vehicle to be noticed or given a positive reflection of doing escort work. They believed me when I told them that the article would not be written sleazy.

Actually, I did not know for sure if these two men would put together an article that was not full of sensational material. I just trusted the two men and the women trusted me.

Fortunately, nothing horrible came from the party or the interviews. What did come from the party was my belief that people were interested in my escort service and those women that worked with me. That interest turned into dollars for me and the escorts. Money was the new name for our game. Thankfully, we were the best game in town at that time.

After the party there was an added influx in phone calls and this not only surprised me, but cemented my desire to have more parties to advertise my business. Parties now would be used to introduce the escorts and give the clients a little something for their loyalty. Did sex go on at the party? I did not see any sexual behavior but it may have happened and I really don't care if it did. A new promotional tool for my business was born.

Party Number 2

After the success of the first party it was time for me to think that having a party for clients would take my business further and make it a more visible force in the escorting world at that time in the San Francisco Bay Area. The first party had been held at a client's home because I was still living at my mother's home.

Plus, the location of his home helped the mystic of my business.

Interest was growing in the escort services and my service was out distancing the other services through word of mouth and customers "singing our praises". Now it was time for the second party. Due in part to the success of the first party and the overall eagerness of clients to use *Professional Escorts* above other services, the money was beginning to flow and I had moved out of my mom's home and into a leased house in Novato. The house was in a track of homes in a location called *Pleasant Valley*. This home had three bedrooms and two baths and was what I needed to 'grow' my business.

Logistically, the home added a private setting for meeting potential escorts, and not only did the move work well, the business was filled with new clients multiplying exponentially and they all wanted the pick of the litter from the escorts working at that time. I had to hire the best possible escorts, which I did, and the escort service took off like a runaway circus traveling on a railway with no brakes. There was more business and more escorts to contend with and operationally the service was going full-steam 24 hours a day, so my time was filled with answering phone calls. And it is almost impossible to explain, here, how many calls would come to my phone lines, but it was a huge amount, and daily non-stop ringing.

Plus, I was still hiring just about every person that phoned me. Some people did not make the 'cut' because they were not civilized in some area. What I mean here is that their English was very poor or their clothing was not up to what and I wanted my escorts to look like. Some people applying just did not have transportation. In rare instances I would drive a new escort to someone I knew. But it was rare and I only did it so the person could make some money and hopefully get their transportation issues resolved. This could mean that their automobile needed repairs.

One day one of the people working with me, as we gathered in my bedroom gabbing, asked me if I wanted to have a party. It sounded like a good idea. This party would be to showcase all the lovely escorts I had working for me at the time. The rules would be that everyone had to attend or be fired. No   excuses would be accepted. All those escorts in my bedroom agreed to the strict guidelines for having the party.

The same day I began planning the party. By this time, many musicians were using my service, so it was reasonable to ask them if they would play at the party, because I wanted to have a band at my party. My thoughts were music and dancing, so I asked several people if they would come and bring friends to play. No problem. Now I needed a location.

The spot chosen was a hideaway place on the way to the beach. It was a dinner house and bar with a place to dance and a stage located in Nicasio, called Rancho Nicasio. The fee to rent the place was fair. Next, I had some very plain cards made up announcing the date and time of the event. All my clients were told of the party and asked to come. The motivating factor for them was that they could meet escorts there. The food and drink were on me. I must have been insane.

Finally, the day came and I had made chili that I brought for the guests to eat and the booze was already there. There was this huge bin or something to keep the chili in and it was actually very nice; plus, I absolutely loved the place with its outdoor area and it had lots of room for parking, just a down-home feel location for any party. I was expecting a huge crowd and that is what came. Gosh, free food and booze and women. A party made in heaven for most men and many women. Some of the women dressed up in dresses but most of the people there were wearing jeans and nice blouses or shirts. I was proud of the people who worked for me and that night they all shined.

One of the guys who worked for me was a kick-boxer and he felt I needed bodyguards for the event. No problem. Well, I was taking some sleeping pills on a regular basis that were given to me by prescription and should not have been taken with alcohol. Well, I had a drink and I went on stage to sing and a friend of mine had the sense to drag me off; I was already bombed by then and wanted to sing. One drink and I was ready to jump up and dance or sing.

The musicians came and played and I guess they were great. A lot of well-known guys had shown up from Marin and they played at the party for free and I was told it were a nice jam session. You see, I was just plain out of it and my body guards watched me drive myself home. How could they allow me to drive was a question bouncing around in my soggy brain the next day. Someone should have drove me and put me to bed. What I heard later was that the party was a success.

All or most of the attendees did not know me. That is what they told people who asked them. I asked everyone that told me that stupid line....."Well, why were they there?" Of course everyone knew me or had wanted to meet me from speaking to me on the phone. But hardly anyone copped to knowing me or each other; Marin County is not that big and people with money or fame know each other.

This party was a success, even though I was home enjoying the private party there. My thoughts for future parties ... do not invite so many people, again, another thought creeping into my memory banks for future use. The count was close to 500 people. Where did they come from? All the girls showed up except for one, I believe it was and she was fired. If she did not care to put the effort into the business, then she did not deserve to work with me. Plus, my word was on the line. If I had let her continue to work, the other escorts would never believe me, again.

Next party I should not drink.....this was stenciled into my brain. I missed a great party. Some of the party people followed me home. So we had a min-party at my house. I slept well that night. The pills and booze did a number on me. The next day I was back to being 'Mother Superior'. No more drinking. It was obvious that I could not hold my alcohol. But if I had stayed at the party I would have been in a corner all night. My shyness was in full-swing when at a party of more than five people. I began to hear people asking where I was and pointing at me. It was all so embarrassing to me. Not because of my business, just because it was me that the people wanted to meet. I was too shy. What was I thinking? Have a party and meet people? An awful circumstance for a person in fear of crowds, but the advantages were that people would want to phone the service and take my escorts out; and the main disadvantage was that I had to be on display and meet people.

A strange circumstance for a person running an escort service that catered to meeting people, but those were the facts. I was too introverted; but very bold on a telephone; I could speak to anyone on a phone. In person I was okay with one or two but once the room filled up I wanted to escape.

After this party the phone was nonstop. The party did bring more business to me. But I was running my body and mind into the ground and I was totally exhausted, hardly getting enough sleep for a spider, let alone a woman. The web of calls was expanding and my lack of sleep was something a government agency could do research on and find that money drives the body and the brain follows. Mistakes were beginning to be made ... I just hoped that I was selecting the right girls for the huge amount of work coming into the service.

Party Number 3

This party was, also, held for my customers. The location was at Mr. Annapolis's home, Tiburon. Once again it was necessary for the escorts to come to the party. I had asked if it was okay with my host to have another party. He was up for another party. Must have been the sailor in him; he was such nice guy.

The party was hosted by me and all drinks were on the house and so was the food. The clients loved the food and the party. Some of my escorts made after-the-party-deals with clients. I was not happy about that and eventually fired the women.

The hot tub got a lot of action and some of my close friends were reprimanded, by me, for occupying the escorts when those escorts should have been seeing my regular clients. There were not as many people and it was fine by me. From what I remember I gave bottles of wine with the name *Professional Escorts* on them, just so the clients would know where they had been. I used a limousine to bring people up the hill, so they were able to park at another location down the hill that would not block the road leading to the house. Also, neighbors would not be upset. It made the customers feel special and added to the allure of the party.

The next day the phone was ringing off the hook with people thanking me for the party and calling to see my escorts; a successful party, once again, for me and the service.

Plus, many clients loved the wine I had given them. It was a nice party and comfortable for me. The need to drink was minimal and the cleanup found the usual condoms. So I suppose some people were making money and not telling me.

Party Number 4

A friend recommended I have a party at his comedy club, hum, which would be nice, I thought at the time. He would give me a nice deal and maybe even some well-known comedians would come by and tell a few jokes. I liked the idea of comedy to make the off-color jokes more appealing and give the clients a different location to come to that was just for them. I wanted them to feel special because if not for them, my service would not exist. To have a party at a location in San Francisco was ideal. Everyone always had a joke or two for me regarding my escort service. Some jokes I had already heard many times before and every now and then the joke would be something new. My hope was that the party would entice some of my older clients to come, which it did.

The location was very public but that night the club would be mine. The party was held at the now defunct *Holy City Zoo* on Clement Street in San Francisco. There was a small office upstairs at the back of the club and that is where I wanted to hide all evening. My shyness was, again, in full-swing that night. I drank upstairs and I let a couple of the ladies come up to drink privately or do whatever drugs they wanted to do. The office was private and the women were told, by me, to make sure they did not do drugs downstairs or in front of anyone. I was not approving of their actions, but I could not stop them, so I allowed them to just hide their actions. My friend was not in the office at the time, but he was always coming upstairs to see what we were doing, so the women were warned to hurry up.

But actually, I did see some of the comedians use drugs (Marijuana), so what I was hiding, were my escorts use. It wasn't anyone's business what they did. I still feel that way. This was an era when many people were doing drugs and just because my escorts were doing drugs, did not make them bad people. It was the constant knowledge of drug use by some escorts that had me fighting to keep the business out of trouble. That is because some of the women did have very bad habits and those habits kept them from making as much money as they should have been making. It was strictly business for me to make sure the escorts had any bad behaviors in 'check'. If they did not, well there were consequences. Some had to be fired. The firing of the women in multi-groupings was almost hysterical; but had to be done at one point, in the first two years of my running *Professional Escorts*.

The women showed up for this party because the usual commanded-performance attendance of my escorts was still in force. They would be fired if they did not show to a party, I was giving. Actually, the ladies looked lovely and mingled well with the few clients that came. I was very disappointed by the lack of interest in this party from my clients.

It seemed, since the huge party in Marin County had been held at Rancho Nicasio a very secluded location, which was perfect for a party. That clients or customers were afraid of running into their friends or business clients at one of my parties. I understood; but that did not mean I liked it. Even the comedians that were on stage did not do very well. One very well-known comedian did drop in for a look see and I was introduced to him. I won't say his name because he did not seem too thrilled to have come to the party. All I said to him was, "You look pretty tired." He responded with the affirmative. I did not expect him to go on stage and he did not. He eventually left shortly after coming. I was actually relieved to see him go. He would not have added anything to the party because of the shape he was in.

The doors were open the entire time we were at this club and I was not happy about that, because some people would try to come in and were told a private party was going on. There were bouncers at the door. I would not call this my best party, and actually thought it was the worst attempt at a party for the business that I had; but it did have the same resultant cause-and-effect by my phone going off the hook after the party. People may not have jammed the place that night, but someone was telling them about the party. Lots of business was had by my escorts for a good month after this party. Maybe the people that did not come felt bad about skipping the party, so they decided to just call for escorts. Whatever the reasons; I was happy to have such loyal clients. There was a lot of money spent by me for the party and I did not get drunk, so I was able to comprehend what was not going on, and that was, the place was devoid of a huge crowd.

Another note was jotted down in my memory "brain-book" …never have parties at a comedy club, again. Never, Never, and

Never! I loved my friend......but to have a party there was disastrous.

Party Number 5

Gosh, just thinking about the parties makes me amazed at how many parties I actually had, when running *Professional Escorts*. And that is not counting the 'get-togethers' at my place that happened many times and were spontaneous. Just like combustion, women, men, party favors and location, my place.

This party was held at another night club. It was a place called *Uncle Charlie's* in Corte Madera, California. The owner was a woman that had inherited some money from her Uncle Charlie and she decided to have a night club. Many of the local musicians would showcase their new music or albums in her place. Over the years this club had even been featured in a few music videos.

The club was the 'in' spot for a while in Marin County. It was where the people who wanted to be seen went. Really an unlikely location in the center of a strip mall, but there was plenty of parking and people love their parking in the San Francisco Bay Area. When you entered the front door ... the location for the band or entertainment was on the right side and the bar on the left side. There were two bathrooms located back center and these rooms were always filled with people. Some were doing drugs and others were vomiting in the toilets.

Yes, it was a happening spot for single people or married ones on the prowl. The owner would not be happy about me saying that people were doing drugs in the bathrooms, but they were. As before, I have to say that even if the owner wanted to stop it, she couldn't stop the flow of drugs, this was the beginning of the 1980s and drugs were still everywhere.

(I would also like to take this opportunity to thank a group for using my phone number in one of their music videos. It was very nice of them. I believe they used the entire phone number except for the last digit. I forgot which group it was but I would like to someday have a copy of that video in my collection.)

Anyway, I decided to have a party at this club and made all the arrangements. This party was to be for my birthday. My birthday is March 28th, so that is in the spring of every year and this particular year; I thought it would be a great time for a party. Have no idea how old I was that day, that year; but I would never have told you my age in those days. Now I am just happy to say I survived a very wild time in America.

Many of the musicians showed up for my party and played for

the party. They were real angels. I cannot remember if I paid some musicians to play or if I paid for entertainment of some kind. But I do believe they did this for free. The reason I don't remember anything is simple. I was only at the party for no longer than one hour and due to how I left the party, well, I just want to forget the whole thing.

I had taken a couple of pills to relax me, because my shyness was not going away. Then I drank maybe two drinks. Well, you know from other parties what happens to me. Of course I got drunk. Thank God I had invested in paying for a limo for the night.

The investigator at the DA's office came to my party with someone else and he saw the condition I was in. He obviously wanted to take advantage. I went into the limousine with him and he was grabbing all over me. I was not happy about it and got out of the car and wanted to walk back into the club. Well, I was wearing this cute little outfit for my party that had a cowgirl hat and some fake guns on either side of my hips and short skirt.

There were two police officers standing near the entrance of the club and they had their guns on and I pulled one of my fake guns out and said, "I have guns too." I was just joking around but they did not like the joke. They began to arrest me and I wailed very loud, "I am not going to jail, do you know who this is? He is the 'blank' investigator in the DA's office." They both looked at me and him and he just said, "Put her back in the limo and if she comes back then arrest her."

They wanted to arrest me for being drunk in public. Yeah, I wouldn't have been drunk in public if the investigator had not brought me out of the club. Anyway, I was thrown out of my own party. My limo driver drove me home and the party was over for me. But I did not go to jail.

Also, another reason to hate the investigator, he ruined my fun because he wanted to have fun. My birthday party went on without me. I did cry on the way home. I really wanted to have a nice birthday party. I was told that it was a great party. Well, not for me. I began throwing up at home and was very sick from the mixture of pills and booze. People thought I had ditched another one of my parties.

The end result of this party was, again, lots of calls for my escorts. Me? I, again, looked like a fool leaving my party. All that money spent and I did not enjoy my birthday party. Many people told me they had fun and that was probably because I was picking up the tab for the booze. There, of course, is no memory of clients, who may have showed up. To even speak about the party is a little odd because I don't have any recall concerning it, but I was told that I was missed. Ah, how sweet. Not!

Last Party

There were other parties before this one (not mentioned), but it was the last party that meant something to me. It was held at Mr. Annapolis's home in Tiburon. Remember his home? It was the home with three levels. Hot tub at the lowest level and still working well; and the owner was now thinking of selling his home and I wanted a party there before the for sale signs went up.

Since the home was featured in a magazine, he would be able to get his asking price. If I had been single, meaning without children, at the time; I would have purchased the home. I had the money and it would have been a lovely home to continue having parties at. The only drawback for me, which I could think of, was that it was in Tiburon. This is an area that houses an assortment of 'new rich' people and they are the worst type of neighbors. They want everything their way. Spoiled brats most of them, and after living in Ross where much of the 'old money' lived it would have been going down a step or two to live in Tiburon. I had phoned Mr. Annapolis that I wanted to have a party at his home and asked if it was okay with him. I did not really give him a chance to say no.

We ... meaning some of the girls and me, had decided to hold a party and were just informing him that it would be at his home. He agreed. But he did want me to stay after or come the next day to clean up with him. I agreed to the terms. He was very nice about me, sort of, forcing a party on him. But what sailor is not up for a party, again? This man had served his commission on a submarine. Surely a party every now and then was what the doctor ordered and then there was always the possibility he could meet Ms. Right. Up to that point he had already met a lot of the women that worked for me.

The parties were a win for him too. Maybe a client would want to purchase his home. He was not losing anything to have the parties at his home. But I believe he knew what facts would benefit him.

I was now living in Ross, California and could have had the party at my home. It was large enough but my privacy was still very important to me. This home in Ross was where my sons lived and to have a lot of clients over was not what I wanted. The police in Ross are more like a private security company. They stop any vehicle that does not live in the area. The police know who does live there and I believe they have cameras everywhere. Some very well-known people live there and demand their privacy. Just like me. This "security" was bad enough, or on top of things, that some of the women were stopped by the police and asked where they were going when coming over to wait or drop off money. But the police or the majority of them are men, and what red- blooded man does not want to stop a pretty face? Not many, so the price of having my home there was the occasional complaint from an escort that her vehicle had been stopped on her way to my home.

Well, I would tell the girls not to be drinking when they came over because there was always the possibility that a policeman would stop her before she made it to my house. The house was near the park. [They have since demolished my home and put up another house. I really think they should have kept the lovely Carriage House that sat on the property. But some people just have no taste for history].

The day was picked to have the party. I sent out invitations that showed directions to the home in Tiburon. Some clients had been there before, so it was not a big revelation as to where it was located. Many of the escorts gave out invitations to selected clients that had been using the service for a while. Again, the people would park at a specified location and wait to be picked up by the limousine. I was to have a Rolls Royce for me. The party would be catered by a French catering company from Mill Valley. I hired a bartender to pour drinks.

Everything was set.

A limousine service I had used many times from San Francisco was where my Rolls Royce was coming from and the owner decided to pick me up himself. I thought that was very nice of him. He arrived on the day and I could see in his eyes that I looked just the way I wanted to. There would be no pill taking or drinking alcohol for me this time. I wanted to have a good time. My dress was an all white evening gown. It matched the Rolls Royce that was sparkling white. The dress, because it was all white, was just like the very first party where I wore an all-white evening gown. I looked the best I had looked in a very long time. My hair was piled up on top of my head. It was as if I was going to a fairy- tale party. In looking back, I have no idea why there were no photos. But I think it is because if a photographer had been there, maybe the clients would not have been there. But a picture of me would have been appropriate.

There was an undercover police officer who had come and if he has a picture I would appreciate him giving it to me if he reads this.

He was not invited by me or anyone else, but one of my loyal clients clued me to the fact he was there. The client pointed him out to me.

At the party I was having a nervous and shy day, so I hid behind the bartender most of the time; which may have caused this one girl's attitude, because I was told later that she thought I was flirting with the bartender and she wanted to 'get' him before I 'had' him, which was ridiculous, I was just being me at a party and she ultimately ended up sneaking him into the bathroom at the end of the party.

This girl was the one who answered my phones at the time and she had come to the party in some hooker outfit and embarrassed not only herself, but the escorts. Her makeup were exaggerated and almost clown like and the black leather short skirt, with fishnet stockings, finding the top of her stockings showing, because the skirt was too short for the chubby body wearing it. She was the only person who took someone to the bathroom and had sex on the toilet.

How disgusting! I was not happy with her and fired her shortly after the party; which was less, of what I would have liked to have done to her. And to top it off she kept saying for anyone in hearing distance, that she was not a prostitute. Yeah. So what was her point? She was an idiot girl that was stealing from me and working with a couple of other girls to give them calls and take a percentage without writing the call down or giving me my cut. She actually thought she was getting away with it. To add insult to injury she wrote me some outlandish letter telling me how bad I was … after I let her go. She had been under psychiatric care for parts of her life and I really think she should have continued with the therapy. When I dropped her as an employee, she was furious. With all the information out there in the 21st century regarding bio-polar psychological conditions, she was a classic example of a person with either that condition or she fit the case study in the *All about Eve* movie where the lead role is played by a person with multiple personalities.

While working for me she married a man that was gay, because she just wanted to prove she could do it. We asked her why would anyone want to do that and her comments were that she did not like sex. She went on to say that he did have some sort of movement on top of her with his clothes on to have sex with her and she liked his friends knowing that he was married. So odd, that I cannot figure out what or why the marriage happened. Everything that came out of her mouth was a lie, except for him; she loved supporting him and worked two jobs to do it.

The food for the party was fantastic. There was salmon and some other main course that I just cannot remember how it was prepared, but I know everyone ate everything. This was not a chip and dip spread. It was costly but worth it to me. The well-known French restaurant in Mill Valley had out-done the arrangement of food. The bar was pretty well stocked and the drinks were all provided by me. I wanted everything to be very nice for my clients.

The usual bottles of wine were to be given out to the clients and those bottles always had the name of my business on them and the clients really liked the consideration I had shown them … to be able to take home an adult party favor.

There was some music played, but not live, possibly albums. I was very pleased with this party and very happy that I had attended it being sober. Drinking is just something I should never do and only did it when I was young because of my inability to socialize within large groups of people. In thinking about it, maybe that is why a lot of people drink. The alcohol leaves the inhibitions at home and people are better able to speak with intimidating people.

The results from the party were tremendous. Lots of phone calls and unfortunately for me, this was to be my last party for the business. In my next book, The Madam's Clients, I will speak to the issue of why it was the last party. But I have to say it was the best party for me.

The next day, as agreed, I returned to help the owner of the home clean up.

I had intended to just hire some people to clean but then felt that I could do the clean up. It was not too bad and I don't remember Mr. Annapolis complaining about anything specific, maybe a few condoms in the hot tub or bottles and glasses lying around where they did not belong. Overall he enjoyed the party and the food.

The party ended close to midnight or before and so his neighbors were not offended by noise. The limousine that chauffeured the people up to the party and then back down to their cars was in use all night. The chauffer did a great job with the people. All and all I was very happy. Really happy for the first time since I had begun my business; my confidence level was rising and I could see that my business was a success. My escort service was respected and the police were afraid of how much publicity I was getting.

There had been some recent interviews, done by me, for television and the increase in police calls let me know that the police were not happy with me. I suppose they wanted my business to be some quiet little nuisance that did not attract attention and would go away someday soon. For me, I just wanted free advertising. Being on television talk shows brought attention to my business and lots more clients, but it also brought the vice cops. They were very interested in my business.

Plus, the police wanted to see if drugs were part of my business. Drugs were not a part of my business. You might say this had been a quiet party but friendly and nice.

The people there were clients and felt comfortable. No mad sex going on and all the women, except for the tramp answering my phones, looked absolutely lovely. The woman felt good about coming and all in all it was a nice night. This party showed that my business was at the top of the escort ads and we all were feeling happy. I had rented some rooms at a hotel that screened X-rated movies, but they were not used. A surprise, and a good one at that; the clients preferred to see their selected escort at home.

The many phones calls for women ... continued.

Chapter Sixteen
More Case Studies

What follows is a combination of the escorts that once worked for me. I hope you enjoy their individuality. It was their individualism that kept my business surging forward into the escort history books. Many of these women had sad stories before they came to work for me. Other women worked for and with me because they wanted to have the experience of being paid for their time.

It was really not very complicated.

These women just wanted to feel as though they were worth more than a dinner and to bed, or to bed and then a dinner. I would just term that the "fuck'um and feed'um" or "feed'um and fuck'um" life cycle that most dating falls into. Men and some women have a way of turning a perfectly beautiful evening into a very shallow experience by wanting to have sex after dinner.

Why?

There is no earthly reason that a woman or a man should feel like they have to give their body for a meal. No reason at all. Ladies and gentlemen you should have the meal and say thank you. That is all you have to do if someone invites you to dinner or lunch or breakfast. You do not have to give up the most precious part of your being for a meal.

The escorts working for me were becoming more in tune with this philosophy of mine, "Do not feel compelled to give yourself to anyone". I stressed all the time, "That as an escort you do not have to sleep with the client or the boyfriend". I would go on to say, "If it is the client, you had better want to do the bed games. Otherwise, just take the money for being an escort and give him or her conversation, but not the "body" your "body"."

In some instances or escorts it did not matter what I said, because the person was going to do what they felt like. It just did not matter to them, to be respectful of themselves. Because all my escorts were over 18 years of age, it was impossible for me to stop some of their behavior. As I said during my interview for the *People Are Talking,* television program in San Francisco, "What happens between two consenting adults is between two consenting adults".

My son, Adam, informed me that many television programs and movies use my statement. These are movies or made for television movies that have people saying what I said on television in the early 1980s. But I actually used that phraseology from 1974 and into the 1990s. So they borrowed my line. Well, I am not sure if I should take the credit, but if no one said that line before that television program, then I will take the credit for saying it.

Enjoy the next few women. Some of them just made my day "peachy" and others had my blood pressure rising. Everything in escorting was logistics.

Letter L

She was from a small town called Rodeo, which was once the home of the Ohlone Indians for many years until the influx of Europeans and Spanish settlers. When L lived there and even today, it is a spot used for the shipping of oil and other large container type goods. She was small-town girl, in both mannerisms and speech. It is surprising to think of a small-town country girl so near a bustling hub such as San Francisco; there are many small towns within a 100 mile radius of one of the United States premier tourist spots.

L was 5'6" tall, with brown hair, dark eyes, and olive complexion which sparkled as a clean and sober person would. I thought at the first meeting of her, "She was not the best looking girl, but a wholesomeness that was saleable". (Maybe she was in need of her drug of choice, heroin and that is why she looked so bad when I first met her.) Another girl that I should not have wasted my time with, because she had too many issues. Next time I saw her, almost thought it was a different girl because she was, now, a very pretty girl. Perhaps she began to like herself with all the compliments the clients were known to give each girl. She was around 23 years old and possibly weighed 135 lbs. and dressed poorly. Not the high-fashion escort that I preferred. She had been a waitress and also had done escorting work before finding her way to me and I don't believe that work was for very long.

L had worked in Nevada. Her friends and family knew what she did for a living. Yes, she did have a boyfriend. L did not have children. She supported her brothers and sisters, and the all lived in Rodeo, which is near Concord. Because she did not have a car, she was only able to last with my service for a few calls. She was good at what she did, but was unable to make a lot of money due to her car situation. Her money went for her family. Transportation was her main problem for not working with me. The second problem was, she preferred working in the houses of Nevada; those counties where prostitution is legal. Working in Nevada was appealing to her, because she did not have to drive to see someone. She did have a heroin and speed, drug habit.

L had average intelligence as witnessed, by me. Because she was so pretty and young she appealed to most men. Her mental problems, no doubt, had a lot to do with her family situation. She really allowed the poverty she came from to get to her. When you met her it was evident that she did not come from money. It was all over her *being* that money had been a problem for her. No matter how pretty a girl is … there is something about poverty that shows. It may be the way she eats or how she walks and dresses herself. The cheap jewelry she wears well and is accustomed too. The teeth that have not been looked after and along with them you just knew that medical doctor's care was only in emergency situations.

Women that had natural "class" showed through just like the women who did not have any "class" and she fell into the no "class" group. A woman with natural "class" could hide her lack of money and any hard times she may have fallen on. There was a woman once, who I worked with at Macy's department store when I was young and their store detective. This woman oozed out "class" but was dead broke and had to work as a sales clerk because her husband had lost too much money on *Wallstreet.*

I knew by the time L was 30 if she continued using drugs, her face and figure would go. I hoped that if she went back to Nevada, the money she made there could be used for her own education. L could not take care of herself, due to all her money going for either her habit or her family. She was possibly bisexual from working in those dens of lust in Nevada. She felt guilty and self-conscious about being poor. This was something you could not talk her out of because she was convinced that being poor was a bad thing and no good came from poor circumstances. Therapy could have helped her think more of herself.

The work was "okay" with her because it was a means to an end. She would sell drugs or do anything for herself and her family. But given different circumstances in life, she would have been a very honest person and a church goer. I liked her and felt sorry for her. The girl was lost; I felt she was very lost. L was sinking and on a collision course with herself and there was no one to show her how to change herself or her life's circumstances, so she could live for herself. I also knew that L had lost all desire to help herself. That is what made me feel sad for her.

After trying to work with me … the transportation issue just compounded her already hopeless feeling of inadequacy and I believe she returned to the brothels in Nevada. Nevada was an escape for her and she did not have to see her family or bother about vehicles. For her, the brothel life was the best case scenario. If ever there was a person lost by circumstances that were chosen for her, this girl stood out. L came from a family or mother and father who were not able to provide for all the children. As the oldest child she was forced to work for the family and her choices in life were limited by her lack of education.

Number 96

This 96 was a quasi-groupie and "grouped" along with her boyfriend. Sometime before working with me … she had worked for a well-known rock group called the *Grateful Dead* that was living in Marin County. 96 and her boyfriend lived near the beach in San Francisco. Number 96 also had a very nice resume. She had lived overseas and went to school in Switzerland, where she studied languages. This woman was around 36 years old with longish stringy-brown hair that framed a well-scrubbed face. She was around 5'7" tall with a natural large chest. Her figure was alright, but she could have used some exercise to frame her body better. I just wanted to stuff her into a girdle because her stomach always stood out. Her general appearance with clothes was older and a hippie.

The lack of, needed, makeup did not help her appearance. She had been into office work but mostly in a managerial position with emphasis on her ability to put things in order. She had worked for political parties in Washington D.C. She could dominate a conversation and had an authoritative manner. I would have liked to have seen her do dominatrix work. In that line of business she could have made a fortune, no matter how old she was.

Her friends were not aware of what she was doing; only her boyfriend knew that she worked for me. She never wanted to have children or could not have children and that story fluctuated. Lying came easy to her.

This woman lasted many years with me in an off and on again working pattern. When working it was to meet some bill she had to pay. Do a call and that was it. She did not want to work on a regular basis. Yes, for the work she did do she was okay.

There were a couple of clients that liked her for a long time. She could have made a lot more money if she wanted to put some effort into working. She paid expenses for herself and her boyfriend. Sometimes the expenses were for Marijuana. She was not handling the work very well at first and she needed a rest. Then she would come back to work for me just when she needed money. She liked liquor too much and was now on the wagon and would use

Marijuana to stay off of alcohol. Her boyfriend was also a habit for her. Number 96 was smart and very moody. Men that liked large chests on older women were the clients she appealed too. She was seeing a mental health doctor for her problems. She always had trouble keeping up with her expenses. Her boyfriend had her paying half of everything at their home. He owned the home. He was getting the better of her but to tell her ... would not have worked because she loved him.

96 loved sex, and she had many guilt feelings about the work. She was honest if she knew that you could catch her. So she played it straight with me most of the time regarding money owed. She would do anything for money. I liked her but never trusted her because she was too smart. She always had an opinion for me on how to raise my sons. Many women that do not have children always had an opinion for me ... how to raise my children. I enjoyed the insights she had and others had but they needed to live with my sons 24 hours a day to fully enjoy the problems I had with my sons.

Those problems would have been there and were there prior to my having the business and since having the business. The business was not a cause of our personal problems. My not having a live-in father for my sons was the main problem and no one could fix that situation. My boys fought with each other all the time, so finding a live-in father was not an option. No one would marry me given those circumstances. But number 96 liked my sons and I appreciated her for that caring about them. She may have made a wonderful mother but something in her background, which surrounded her father, did not allow her to envision herself as a mother. I did trust her to take care of my business for me when I went away on trips or vacations. But I knew that any money she made during those times – well I was not going to receive all my fees.

Letter E

E was a woman that looked much younger than her years, because she was short and kept herself very fit. She came from Boston, Massachusetts and was from Jewish heritage. I featured this woman in my book, The Making of a Madam. E was 5' tall with short dark hair. She had a good figure and was around 33 years of age when she began working with me. E had been a school teacher and a photographer. Maybe, was a guess with her about the teaching of school on the East Coast. While working for me, she did not teach school but concentrated on her photography. Her family did not know about her career as an escort. One or two of her friends knew. E was a very private person about everything she did or said. A very secretive person. Yes, she had a boyfriend when she began working with me and he was black. After working with me for a few years … she went through many boyfriends and one was a client. She did not have children. I believe the reason for no children; possibly, she was unable to have children.

She lived in a lower-income area of San Francisco.

This woman lasted with me a solid year of working full-time and the second year she worked off and on again. Then she worked till she was completely off. It was hard for her to give up the money. For some men, she was very good. The other men felt she was okay and not necessarily okay to see again. She was not a beauty but she was fresh looking and appealed to men that liked small women. As E learned more about escorting she was better able to extract more money from the men. I would say her technique improved. She became a better escort rather than a dating person.

Before working for my service, she had worked for another service and with that service she was busted. One night I sent her to a client in Tiburon and she was arrested for a warrant. I was very upset thinking she had been busted working for me, because I did not hear from her after she left the client's home.

Letter E told me several Tiburon police surrounded her car and she was so small it was typical "over-kill" by the police department. She did land in jail that night. And I had a few restless thoughts concerning the entire evening. I worried like hell about her. Why hadn't she called? Where she was and who she may be with? Then jumping to the worst case scenarios, has she been killed, car accident, whatever? I was very worried.

When I spoke with her, finally, I hope that I got through to her, that phoning in was very important. Then I heard all about that night but what really bothered me was that she never told me that she had an arrest record from working with another escort service. While working for me she improved her living arrangements. She bought odds and ends at garage sales. E was not very flashy with the money she made. Her mind could not handle the facts of what she was doing. It was better for her to have a straight job and continue trying to make a career out of her photography. Her work and dating black men when she first met me and this changed after working with me. She changed to dating white men and preferably customers with money.

Yes, she had some drug issues, but I did not know what drugs she used. I only knew that she used drugs. E was very intelligent, but lacking in self- respect. Kinky customers she appealed too. Those men that liked small girls for fantasy trips and also men that liked sexual favors that included doing sex in a "Greek" fashion. That means a woman does not have sex through her vagina. It is where the waste from her body comes from and out and into the toilet. Just thought I would inform the reader who is a novice to this term. Many gay men use this area to have sex. But, I am told that some women like this area of the body to have sex, because there is a gland there that stimulates a woman to orgasm. Men like this area if the vagina is too large or worn-out. Not my cup-of-tea, so- to-speak.

This woman was seeing a psychiatrist. She was organized and was able to maintain her standard of living. She fantasized a lot over women. In her liking sex in a "Greek" way she probably liked pain. She felt it necessary to keep her inner-most desires and needs ... for only her doctor to hear. Guilt played heavily on her heart. I phoned at times and she was crying. As some women would share their inner-most feelings with me ... E preferred to be more closed mouth.

Some of the problems in her life were related to her religion. With her, if she could sneak some extra cash from a client without telling me about it, well she would. But she never made a habit of anything dishonest.

I liked her.

I had her do some photos of my sons and she did an excellent job. She was very talented and should have done well with photography if she was up to the work it took to advertise her business, etc. She went with one client to Europe and he left her there to continue the trip. She was happy going it alone without him and she told me that he was coming down from all his drug use and that is why the trip for him ended. He had to hurry back to all his drugs in San Francisco. I was told that this woman is now married and appears to be happy with her new life.

Number 18

This woman had a lovely name, which I am unable to use. It was unique. Number 18 was a woman around 33 years of age. She was 5'7" tall and had long dark brown hair. Her eyes were brown and she was pretty with a good figure.

She had been a model and was always a girl in the business of meeting men for money. She had done a lot of pornography work in films and still shots. Everyone she came in contact with knew what she did. She was trying to find a steady boyfriend. She did not have children. Number18 lived in an expensive house in Marin County. A woman who lasted for only a few calls. She made more money doing the pornography work ... she liked doing. Number 18 made money because she did not want to give me a fee. She spent it on clothes and liquor. I caught wind of her trying to steal customers.

That was a big NO for me in running my business.

Liquor and clothes and if there was anything else, I did not know about it.

She was cleaver but not very bright. You might say she was slow. She was more for the educated well- breed man who liked a bobble on his arm. She looked very good and wore expensive clothes, which would impress anyone, but if a man wanted a smart woman, this was not the woman.

Number 18 had lots of insecurities from her childhood and the fact ... not a lot of money flowed through her home. She lived too high, spending more than she should, which was very high, even for her income that was, at times, off the charts. She liked to beat men and play a dominatrix role. This person would do anything for money. She lived in a desperate mood, all the time. Number 18 liked being with other women. No guilt feelings. Surprisingly, she was fairly honest. A good person deep down inside her soul and would help you out if you needed it. I liked her. I would have liked to have been her friend for a long time. There was just something about her as a friend ... made you feel as if she liked you and was able to transmit this "I like you" attitude to just about everyone.

Number 19

This was a hard girl. Not a lot of soft qualities surrounding her, except for maybe her white skin and she stood around 5'3" tall. She had blonde hair and blue eyes and very white skin. She appeared to be around 20 lbs. overweight. That extra weight would have brought her total weight to around 140 lbs. She was close to 23 years of age. She had been a waitress and also a real life hooker, street corner type of hooker and swing the purse and hips type of street-walker. Her friends knew what she was doing. It was difficult to tell the boyfriends from the clients. She had a lot of men around her or phoning her ... all the time. She did not have children and lived in an apartment complex in San Leandro. Just about two weeks was all I could handle her ... then I had to tell her to hit the curb.

No pun intended.

Not right for my business and she did not make much money. It went for expenses and also for her drugs. I fired her for carrying a gun and just being a crude person.

Drugs occupied her time and life. She definitely had below average intelligence and she was not getting any smarter using all the drugs smothering her life. No one likes her, or at least not any of my clients, because she was too loud and vulgar and had way too many rough edges surrounding her character. This must have been due to her streetwalking days. Girls that walked the street were always rough. From the way they spoke to how they perceived clients. They always spoke about the men as "Johns". She must have thought the whole world was going to hurt her, because she was very militant. Similar to any animal that had been beaten, unexpectedly. She was overly cautious and had trouble keeping up with her household expenses.

Most housewives are not pigs. She was filthy about her home and self. She was losing touch with life or reality and needed a doctor to treat whatever condition she was suffering from and she was suffering.

This woman had no feelings. I can only wonder what horrible treatment she must have had before I met her. She was not an honest person. I did not like her. She was more animal than human. She was also one of the few Hispanic women that ever worked for me. I was happy when I fired her.

Sometimes I fired a person by just not giving out calls to the women. She was one of them fired in that manner; I just refused to hand out calls to her. End of story with her and it was over, completely final and over. Almost wish I could say that again.

Number 23

This was a very large girl. She had been very close to a very well-known rock and roll group. That is about all I can say regarding the group because it once was a popular group. She told me she worked for the group and I had no way of checking that out. I could have gotten in touch with the group, but for my purposes of having her work as an escort … it just was not feasible to phone the group. My choice was just to believe her. I would call her a fat groupie. The work she did for the group, may very well have been giving "blow jobs" to each member.

This girl was overweight and stood around 5'6" tall. She had red hair and blue eyes with her face sporting a lot of freckles. Her chest was very large. Number 23 did have a pretty face. She had been working for an escort service somewhere in the middle of America. The place had been busted and she came west for work. Her friends knew she worked for an escort service.

Her boyfriend was a musician and white. No children to impede her insanity with the, alleged, rock group. She and with her boyfriend lived in San Francisco. Number 23 just lasted a couple of days. Maybe she was okay. All of her money went for drugs. She did not want to work for me. She wanted her own escort service. I was surprised to receive even a little money for my fee. Her intent for working with me was to use my knowledge of the business. She, of course, never told me. Drugs and she liked money were her only habits. She was cleaver, but not smart. If she was smart I never would have found out what her intentions in working for me were. She appealed to most men who liked big breasted girls. But the men who wanted large chested women did not want fat women and she was fat.

I did not have enough time knowing her to make my observations about what her mental problems were and after all I was not a psychiatrist. Some of my thoughts about the girls that worked for me mental problems came from them. After time the women would confide in their lives and what brought them into the business. But you could tell by just speaking with her that self-esteem was one of her problems. She was not an honest person. She always needed money. I did not know any sexual differences, but I did know #23 liked to see and wanted to see, only black men. No, would be the answer to her making a lot of money, because of her appearance. She had a lot of trouble with her honesty. I did not like her because the girl could not tell the truth and she still owes me money.

Plus, she went out and started her own escort service and was very dishonest in not telling me she wanted to do that. I would have given her advice on how to begin and run her service if she had just asked. I did not care if people were in competition with me. But not telling me was crossing the invisible line I had with my escorts. I was pissed off then and I am sure you can tell that I am still upset with her actions. I had given her a chance and she just squatted down and urinated on me. Not in person. But when girls like her take a shit on me, after I go through lots of efforts to help them out ... well, they deserve all that comes to them.

Number 20

An unhappy Hawaiian girl with typical Hawaiian features and

black hair worn short and her eyes were black. She was 5'2" tall and had a medium build. She was an average … pretty girl. Nothing spectacular about her appearance, she was pretty but not on the verge of being beautiful.

Many of the women working for me were on the verge of being beautiful and this woman was not. She worked as a receptionist when doing escort work. Only her immediate friends and not her family knew what she was doing. Her boyfriend was a black man. She had two children not living with her in South San Francisco. About four weeks was her time with me. She was so, so. Some money was made by her. The money made went for living expenses and drugs. I really hated the girls working for me who did drugs. They never worked out and were a complete waste of my time.

A lazy person and did not want to work very hard, because she preferred to live off her boyfriend. Her boyfriend could have been called a habit of hers. She had average intelligence to below average.

Those customers who liked foreign women or should I say women that came from other areas of the world … would want to see her. No doubt some mental problems. She found it difficult to take care of herself and her personal needs and just loved sex, but did not want anyone to know what she was doing for money. She missed her children and confided in me that she was in psychological pain without them. Honesty was a tough word for her and I believe she lied more than told the truth; telling me about her two little girls may have been her way of attempting to get on my good side; because I had children. Maybe her viewpoint was that I would be more sympathetic to take her whining and shit flinging to me in order to have me give her calls … when she felt like working. I thought the girl was okay, but I did not care if she worked for me or not. What I mean to say is that she was more trouble than I needed to care about … at the time.

Number 10

This was a girl that ended up moving to the South of the United States and bought a home there. I believe the state was Georgia. She wrote and told me that she was still working as an escort and making a great deal of money in Atlanta. She would write me, every now and then and I was glad she kept in touch with me. I was unable to write her back because I was working the business and it took all my time.

If I began a letter I could not finish it when I wanted to, because of the phones ringing all the time. She had been at the first party at Mr. Annapolis's home and had her picture taken both with clothes and without. She was a very pleasant person and a very good mother.

It was a little embarrassing at that first photography shoot, because she would play with herself when she got nervous. Very unusual to have a women masturbating in front of people and I believe she hardly knew she was doing it. I had to speak with her and ease her tension. She explained to me that she had masturbated since she was a child in front of people when nervous and hardly knew she was doing it. Just a little bit of a show for the men there, and the women felt uncomfortable.

Number 10 was around 35 years old. She stood 5'5" tall and weighed 110 lbs., but did not look skinny. Well built. Small features and medium length brown hair with brown eyes. She looked much younger than her years. She had been a secretary. Some of her friends knew and some of her families knew about the escorting work. She was very particular about who knew what she was doing. She did have a boyfriend at the time. She had two boys. She lived on the peninsula in an apartment. That means she lived near San Mateo, California. She was in California about three months and then left for Georgia. She was a great escort and did make money. Her money went to support her boys.

This woman enjoyed the company of men and liked having them around her. She was smart and very nice. Most men liked her. She did have some mental problems that were deep seeded. Something in her past, which she never talked about but did allude to me. And must have been why she masturbated when nervous; an unconscious reaction to stress and very interesting, no doubt, if you were a psychiatrist.

She had a little trouble keeping up with her bills, but the point is she would work very hard to make sure her bills were paid. Only thing strange about her was that she played with her genitals when she became nervous, as I have said. I believe working for me was the first time she had ever been paid to go out with men.

This genital thing was not really funny when we were trying to photograph her. Everyone had to leave the room for her. She had some guilt feelings, but not many about doing escort work. She was an honest girl. Did not want to have any trouble and only wanted to raise her sons. I liked her and I still like her. I consider her my friend, even though we have not spoken to each other in years. I hope she is doing well and her sons are just fine. They would be grown men now. She invested in a home within the first two years of her move to Georgia; a very practical women. She was one of the friendliest women that ever worked for the agency.

Number 24a

Number 24a: This was a real working girl and a professional prostitute. She loved to work. She had begun working for the Mustang Ranch, which was a well-known brothel in Nevada. She was there at a very young age. I believe she told me she was in her teens and just barely able to work, when her life drifted into the hands of the owner of that brothel. First she hung around the ranch and then they let her work when she turned 18. It was the first time she ever had sex exchanged for money. She felt used by the owner of the ranch who, she said, had introduced her to working in a brothel. Some of the story was a little unclear but she had been with the original owner of the Mustang Ranch. He was not a nice guy after she got to know him. I am not sure who talked who into working. If she was hanging out there before she was 18 then she wanted to work there.

This is all second-hand talk by someone who was at the ranch. I asked her if she wanted to be in a photograph that was placed in an adult newspaper to advertise my business. She liked the idea and was happy to poise for the photos. She had absolutely no problem showing off her body and was an exhibitionist. One of the photos has her lying on the ground in front of all the other girls with one leg up as though she was exercising. No clothes on and acting as casual as if she were at home raising her leg.

This girl was around 25 years of age and about 5'3" tall with natural blonde hair and blue eyes. She had a flat chest and the rest of her figure was very good. At times her face looked hard and at other times she looked very young and innocent.

Number 24a had an unusual way of changing her appearance to meet the need of the client. She had done one of her "work stays" at the Mustang Ranch in Nevada just prior to coming to work for me. A "work stay" is when the women working for the ranch just lives in the place and customers see them in their various rooms.

Brothels are the easiest way to sell sex.

The men come right to the girl and all she has to do is keep herself clean and her room spotless. Having sexy outfits is part of her expense. The problem being she pays the owner for the room and each girl has to pay for the in house laundry service. Each woman has to be licensed by the county. That means she has to go to the county offices and say she is a prostitute and they fingerprint her and she has to have a medical screening to make sure she is free of disease. Then the owner has her work, but the owner also takes a fee or percentage for each client she has. The women are always giving money out for some purpose at the houses. The good part is that if she is desirable in some way, she can make a lot of money by having many men see her in one day. I believe I remember this girl also telling me that it was mandatory for each woman to take a week off from seeing people. This could be when the woman had her monthly period.

{Another girl I knew that worked in one of the houses, told me that everything depended upon who you were working for. If the owner was greedy, then you could work 24/7 as long as you kept it to yourself. She worked in the mountains of Nevada and her busiest season was when the hunters came for whatever game they wanted to kill. It could be elk or bear; I really am not totally sure what they were hunting. All that matter to her was that they had the money and saw her often while they were in town. She kept her room up and played whatever music she wanted. Her preferences for music were show tunes. She said the guy would be on top of her and she would be singing from the *Sound of Music* or *Oklahoma*. And sometimes she just read a book. We laughed at that and all the gossip that she told me went on at the house she worked in.

The place was dingy when the guy entered and the women would all come out for the guy to pick who he wanted. It was straight out of many of the movies you may have seen about brothels. There was an array of red rooms and old wallpaper with pictures of women in all sorts of dress and undress decorating the walls. The "house" was filled with dusty chandeliers from better times and dirty windows. She complained that she was paying for the laundry and cleanup for her room, but it was not a high class operation, so the lighting was kept down and the clients could not see all the dust and dirt and cum on the walls. I could not believe she worked there, but her stories were funny.}

Everyone #24a knew was aware of what she did for a living. She would find a boyfriend but did not keep any of them for long. No children. She was able to maintain having an apartment, sometimes. Otherwise, she lived with men or girlfriends that she had known from the Mustang Ranch.

Off and on she tried working about one month. She might have been good in bed, if she could keep her mouth shut long enough. She talked incessantly and her favorite topic was the Mustang Ranch and what she had done there. She was too scattered to work effectively and make a lot of money. A brothel was better suited for her personality, because the people there collected the money. Her earned money went for her living expenses and also for her habits while with my agency. I did not ever see her do any drugs or drink but she alluded to the use of drugs by saying she loved taking them. She was just inept and seemed naïve about life.

Moving from location to location was a challenge for her ... she just plain talked too much about things that should have been kept more secret. Such as her relationship with the owner of the Mustang Ranch and what went on there while she was working. She might have been intelligent if only she would have had some education in her life. She had been working in houses in Nevada since the age of 17 years old; from her standpoint and may be the truth because identification (ID's) were always easy to obtain on the street and this woman was very street wise, but that was all; her English or language skills were lacking. She really should have gone back to school. I am sure the Mustang Ranch was not the first brothel she worked for, but was the one she aspired to be a part of. I never believed her that the owner of that business "turned her out" to prostitution. Why? Because you don't hang out at a brothel unless you have been to one before.

Those customers that liked drugs and those that liked little blondes were the people able to see her without complaining. I felt the girl was border-line for going into a mental institution. She appeared at all times not to have a grip on reality. Perhaps she had a chemical imbalance from using drugs at an early age. As I got to know her better, I saw that she was getting worse about keeping her living situations together. She liked women and would do almost anything sexual. Perhaps some of her mental problems were that she felt guilty about her life choices. She was basically an honest person.

Unfortunately, her honesty was hampered by the fact that she would steal, if given half a chance and she sold those drugs she loved. I know that sounds odd, but she was honest and would not steal from people she liked and everyone else was fair game for her criminal behavior.

I liked her but felt if the girl was too close to my operation she could cause problems for me due to her indiscreet talking.   I encouraged her to go back to the brothels to work. Picture a person that had no filter when she spoke. If you asked about another person, whatever she knew about that person, she told you. She needed guidance and constant supervision. The world of normalcy did just not fit her lifestyle or her motor-mouth and at a brothel the manager there would be able to keep her under control. Or the next step, for her, would possibly be a sanitarium where she could work out her mental problems and have the drugs she needed to maintain her needs. Possibly, she needed to have other employment possibilities open for her once she was on the correct dosage of medication for whatever her conditions were at that time.

Returning to school would have helped her once she was seeing a doctor on a regular basis and not just for venereal checkups.

Number 43

This woman was from the great state of Tennessee and that state's women had the sense to throw her out or that is make sure she was on a bus or train out of town. She was so stupid she actually told me and others that she was run out of town on a rail. So perhaps it was a train she took to California, so she could start trouble for me.

This girl/bitch was a natural strawberry blonde with freckles sprinkled all over her face and body. She had hazel eyes and wore her hair to her shoulders. Number 43 was around 5'8" tall with a pretty good figure. But her stomach stood out, due to poor posture. She was around 28 years of age and had been working for another escort service and also worked as a cocktail waitress, when to my misfortune, she found me. Her friends do know but not her family what she did for a living. No boyfriend at the beginning but she did have one that I introduced her to, who was my boyfriend's best friend. She did not have children and that was God taking care of the world; great move on God's part. At first she lived in a shared apartment with another girl working for an escort service and then she lived with me for about six months. She worked for me around eight months. She was pretty good when she was working. She did make a lot of money.

Her money went for whatever standard of living expenses and drugs she had at the time. I could not handle her living with me and working for me. The only reason I got my fees, after she did a call, was because she was living at my home. If she were not under my nose, then I doubt I could ever have had any fees paid to me. I finally had to have her leave my home because she was too far gone on "speed", which is a drug that can make a person crazy. She was filthy and I had many problems with her. She had me yelling at her and I did not want to do that. Her personal hygiene in my home was a big issue. Her drugs use another issue. And she would not keep the drug use out of my home and when I caught her using drugs for the last time … I had to kick her out. She was crying and those fake tears would not work on me again. That happened too many times and she also offered Marijuana to my sons. She was not responsible enough to be around my children. At first she maintained herself … than she just went "bananas".

One time I went into my shower and she had left her used tampon at the drain in the shower and towels all over. Just a messy pig she was and there was the clothes habit and her fondness for the drug called "speed". She had average intelligence when not taking "speed", but she was just stupid when she was using the drugs and appealed to the drug clients. She had a great many insecurities and could not handle responsibility very well. She meant well, I thought, but because of the drugs, could not carry out what she needed to do or desired to do and would only pay her bills after a lot of prodding. She preferred women to men and was bisexual and very vindictive.

This vindictiveness is why she went after my boyfriend, when I threw her out of my house. I no longer wanted her around my children and I found out from my oldest son that she gave both boys Marijuana when she took them for a drive. She was a nut case and if I had known what she did with my sons, I would be writing this from a jail cell. I still hate the bitch. She felt guilty and sorry for everything but was unable to change her behavior. She was not a friend to any person, a very selfish person.

At first she was an honest girl if she liked you and this is when I first met her. But would do anything against you if she was mad at you; a very manipulative person.

I liked her a lot as a friend and human being, but could not handle her drug addiction and that 'like' was in the beginning of our working relationship. My yelling at her did not get through to her soggy brain, which was flooded from alcohol and drugs. Finally, I had to give up the friendship. She thanked me for taking her in when she needed a place to stay by going after my boyfriend and having sex with him. She was "white trash" in every sense of that word. I would not say that, usually, about people, but she really deserved the title. Just another pig in the sty that was created by her inability to be honest with people and my boyfriend deserved her. I would still love to put her on a rail and send her back to Tennessee.

Number 67

Here was a woman that was brought to me because of another

girl that was working for me and that girl recommended her; so I hired her. Many times I took recommendations because the person I was interviewing already knew how my service operated and it was easier to already have the flow of information between us and the interview was just a formality.

Number 67 was about 5'9" tall and had short dark brown hair. She had an average face and figure. She was big-boned and around 35 years of age. She had been an antique store owner and also sold drugs for a living. Her friends and family knew she worked as an escort. Her boyfriend was a white man and she did have children. She lived with her boyfriend in an apartment in Novato, California. She was with me for about a month and a half and worked regularly for that time, this was surprising because she was so large. I suppose most clients were not intimidated by her built ... and she was built.

She made some money and supplemented her other business of either selling drugs or using drugs ... with the money she made from being an escort. I found out she was lying and cheating and stealing from me.

Also, she was trying to undermine my business. She had a big mouth and was telling everyone some untruths about my business. She was giving out lies for whatever reason.

Sometimes you just never know why a person has to say they know something about you that they do not know.

Her habits were the drugs heroin and cocaine.

She was above average in intelligence for book-work (accounting), but below average for practical or common sense life experiences.

She appealed to those clients that liked big women and also fantasized about two women together. Many clients may like that action (of two women together), especially if they did drugs all night. Number 67 paraded around the client's room in all sorts of lingerie, all evening. She was seeing a psychiatrist for her problems and she spent her money too quickly and did not know how to take care of her money, or herself, or her child.

This woman liked women. Lots of guilt feelings about not taking care of her child. Not an honest person. She was a chronic or habitual liar. I liked her but did not want anything to do with her. She could not be trusted and distorted conversations to mean something else than what was being said. This was a born trouble-maker. I had no idea what she meant when she told me she was not able to take care of her children. I would think she meant that she had to do escorting work because she had no money to care for her children.

Number 49

This girl had come to Northern California from Phoenix, Arizona. Number 49 was around 5'6" tall with brown hair worn a little short and had an average face. You could say she was around 30 years old and maybe about 25 pounds overweight. She was a graphic artist. Her friends and family did not know and she did not have a boyfriend or children. She lived in Marin County in a share arrangement for an apartment. She was working with *Professional Escorts for* about two months. Not particularly good at the work and because of that she did not make any money worth telling about. The money she did make went for her living expenses. She did not really want to do escort work. Girls who were into doing escort work always made money.

There were many women over the years that came to me because of necessity not because working for an escort agency was a lifetime career goal. In my own way, I tried really hard to help their situations and be receptive to the fact that this was their last chance to pay some bills or be out on the streets. She fell into this category.

No one particular habit that stood out enough to mention. She was a smart girl and very talented in her other field … doing graphic arts. She did not appeal to many customers because of her appearance that fell short of being spectacular. She appeared to have some problems when speaking about her family. The usual problems of keeping up with her bills. Not too many sexual differences or excesses. Lots of guilt feelings about doing this type of work. She was an honest person not engaged in anything criminal. She was too afraid of the consequences of any wrong doings. I liked her but felt she was not a good candidate for escort work.

My thoughts were more to get her the work so she could pay her bills and then move on to a job she really cared about and work in an environment that best suited her and utilized those artistic talents of hers.

Number 55

This was another one of the women that had or was still working in the pornography film business when feeling the need to contact me for work as an escort. She had an interesting persona. This girl was around 5'7" tall and had a soft round figure and had a little trouble keeping her weight down. She had long blonde hair and fair skin with blue eyes. This woman was around 34 years old at the time and she was pretty. She was a licensed masseuse and also did pornography film work. She wanted to be an actress. Her family and friends knew what she was doing because she had been in the sex trade in many forms, for a long time. No boyfriend, she had a girlfriend. No children. She lived in Sonoma County, California. She lasted a few calls but she did return a couple of times to make a little fast money. She was great and she could have made a lot more. Her money went for living expenses and drugs and her friends.

The preference for this woman was doing the pornography film work and also having her own clients for massage. Her desire was to be in a great pornography film and be a huge star and this would mean that she had a lot of lines to say. By now, as you read this, to say that she had a drug habit would not be a surprise; well, that is exactly what she had and she really liked women and appeared to be of average intelligence. She drew those clients that liked seeing two women together and clients that did drugs all night.

Lots of mental problems and some of those problems were obvious to any observer. She had problems keeping her money straight and that was about it for the word 'straight'; her preference was to be with only women, a true and very real lesbian. No guilt feelings about anything. She would sell drugs, steal, and do anything to further her ambitions and those of her girlfriends. I felt her to be one of the truly evil persons I had met in my life.

This girl looked innocent but smelled of evil. My meaning here is that if she could find a way to do harm and get money from someone, she would do anything. I would not put it past her to murder for hire, especially if the 'hit' were to hurt a man.

Number 75

This number and her sister began their own business after working for me. They used one of my clients to help them purchase their home. This girl was around 22 years of age and had long brown hair and blue eyes. She looked about 16 years old and acted that age, but she could act as old as she wished. She was pretty but not beautiful. She had almost a flat chest but was not overweight. She was around 5'5" tall. She worked for retail stores as a sales clerk. Her friends and family knew of her escapades.

Yes, she had many boyfriends, or they were possibly clients on a leash. No children when she worked for me but I heard she now has children. She lived in a situation with her sister and a friend in a house in Marin County, California. She worked my business to obtain clients for her own business and I put up with her for about three months. I would not say she was any good. Not for my business, but yes for her own purposes. If and when she wanted to make money for my business she would work. Her money went for drugs and her high-living antics. She was always high on something.

I fired her for cheating, stealing, and lying to me regarding clients. She liked drugs and alcohol. This was a stupid woman, so her sister or family must have had the brains to not only motivate her but invest her money. She appealed to those clients that liked young dumb girls and who faked everything from movements to sounds coming from her mouth when having sexual contact. She should have been seeing a psychiatrist. I saw problems keeping her money together. She and her sister liked women, and many times together went on calls, whether I allowed them or not and they did not pay my fees for such behavior. Taking her sister and the client having two girls and I was only being paid for the time for one girl had me furious.

She did not have enough intelligence to have guilt feelings. In fact there were no perceived feelings at all or about anything worth speaking about. Her, every now and then opinions were not earth shattering and may have been based on someone telling her how that person felt and she liked the comment so made it her own. She was a person who could commit any crime imaginable. She was working her way to prison for life. At the writing of this I know that she and her sister eventually did get arrested for their business.

They had clients over to their home for years. Surprising that the neighbors did not report them, but they may have been having sex with the entire neighborhood. I would not have put it past her or her sister. I actually immensely disliked her. She irritated me and few people are able to achieve immense irritation in me at just the sound of their voice or mention of their name. Some possible escorts would see my face distort if they mentioned them during an interview. The interview would go downhill from that point if I knew the person had worked for those girls to mention this girl or her sister would not be a selling line to have me hire the person, who was bringing them up to me.

Yes, they got over on me. That is not the reason I hated them. I thought then and now that people in the business should have respect for themselves, but these women just wanted to be tramps and get paid.

Number 74

This was a two-sister basement level just barely above trash women. They had office jobs but insisted on being sleazy for this work. No matter how much I tried to explain to them to project their persons as ladies; both women wanted to act out and you might think they were auditioning for a prostitution part in some low-cost movie. It was a losing battle to ask them to refrain from a "swing-the-hips" attitude. I think when sisters are doing escort work they take the work to levels that should not be gone too. Just like Number 75 and her sister. Real waste of womanhood.

The colors of their clothes were mixed in offensive distortions of body parts that found the clothes hung way too tight or too short and glittery.

This girl was about 28 years old and stood 5'7" and she wore glasses. She was much prettier without her glasses and should have invested in some contact lenses. She had brown hair and blue eyes and her figure was carrying about 18 lbs. more than it should, but when fixed up she gave a pretty good appearance, except for the way too-sexy outfits that she had to wear. I mean she refused to wear nice clothes. This clothes thing must have been part of some bi-polar exchange with scripted part to be an escort. She was a computer programmer. Her friends and family knew and she probably told them for the shock value it gave. Yes, she had many boyfriends.

What guy in his right mind would not want to be going out with a good-looking computer programmer? No to children but she would have liked to have them. She lived with her sister and another girl that worked for me at the time. I had to put up with her for about three months give or take a month. Sometimes the girls would stay available for work even though they did not want to be available full-time. She was fair to good as an escort. I mean put up with them, was because I needed the extra women at the time.

When she was working she made good money. No different as many others before her by blew the money on drugs and personal needs. I fired her for lying. But I did allow her to work occasionally when I desperately needed someone. I had and still have a 'thing' about people lying. Just can see not one reason for a lie, the truth is the best voice a person can put forward in most situations.

Unfortunately, she was into drugs, liquor, lots of clothes, and anything that made her happy. She was not saving for the emergencies that may turn up in life. Number 74 was a smart girl from the South that was in need of some guidance for the future.

There was only one girl that worked for me from the South that had her life on track. This was not the girl nor her sister or friend.

She went with and appealed to the drug dealers of the time. She liked playing a slut role with men. Yes. She had a problem keeping her expenses paid. She was always calling in when a bill had to be paid. She liked women and was with her sister sexually. No guilt feelings. Not an honest person. I liked her outgoing personality, but I never trusted her. I never liked her sister.

Number 62

She came to me through another girl that was working with me at the time.

This girl was busty, pretty, and around 23 years of age. She stood about 5'6" tall with brown hair and brown eyes. She had a lovely smile. She had been a waitress and also a masseuse. Only her friends knew she worked for me. She did not have children but she had a close boyfriend who was white. She lived with her boyfriend. She worked a couple of months ... working on and off again. Yes, she made money when she cared to work because she was pretty good at what she did. She blew the money on drugs and clothes.

Number 62 was afraid her boyfriend would find out that she worked as an escort, or that was her story to me when she decided to stop working. She liked cocaine and buying clothes and was a smart girl and appealed to just about every client phoning. Yes, she had mental problems. They were obvious.

Yes, she had problems living, she could not save money, and she also did not really know what she wanted out of life and was a little lost. She liked women and had lots of guilt feelings, especially regarding her boyfriend finding out and about liking women sexually. She really must have had him thinking she was a virgin, which was funny under the circumstances. I even presented her with that scenario and she did not say it was wrong. Way to go girl if you are able to do it. Not an honest girl, but not really a crooked person.

I liked her and wished she would have gotten her act together enough to care about doing escort work because this girl was a natural for the work and really did like meeting clients. She loved the work. I was surprised when she decided to quit. Maybe she began her own thing or stole enough clients to work on the side. I could never trust a girl with a virgin mind-set.

Number 71

This was a white girl from Mexico. She had been born in

Mexico and was now in The United States. I do not know what her citizenship was at the time. This girl was around 5'4" tall with medium length strawberry blonde hair and it was complimented by pale white skin and blue eyes. She was around 23 years of age and had been on Welfare and married. Some of her friends knew. She did have a boyfriend and she did have children where they all lived in an apartment with another girl and that girl was also working for me.

They lived in San Francisco, California and worked about two months. Not really very good. Not enough money was made for her or me. She took care of her child and her living expenses. I fired her and the other girl for not coming to a party that they were told was a requirement for employment or that is for receiving any more calls. I stopped giving them calls. Parties had to be attended and their lack of interest in going to the party was an insult to my business. I made sure I told every person who worked for me at the time that they were fired. If I did not fire people when they ignored coming to an event, then the other escorts would think that they did not need to show up and the possibility of no escort coming to an event, well, it boggles the mind as to what an effect the entire possibility of no escorts showing would have on the eventual continuation of the business; so this was a business decision.

This girl was stupid. Maybe liquor or I should say drinking was her habit of choice. She appealed to most men. She was totally not together, from her finances to her personal needs and taking care of her children.

I believe Welfare was investigating her and also how she took care of her children. Money was always an issue for her. Nothing particularly different in sexual appetite than most women who may be a housewife and fairly normal when it came to sex with clients, she was not very inventive.

Lots of guilt feelings about what she was doing, must have been a Catholic girl. She should have gone back to her husband. She was not an honest person and would lie, cheat, and steal for herself and her children. I liked her but felt the girl was on all the wrong roads in life. She really needed direction or just a husband to take care of her. She was not equipped for life on her own. I would be very surprised if her husband had not ended up with the children. I could see her going from man to man with a marriage certificate for each living situation and ending up with no person to take care of her. Every woman like this I tried to tell them that going back to school would benefit them.

Chapter Seventeen
The Holidays

The holidays were a time when many girls wanted to be with their families.

There were, of course, those women that had no family life or family to go home to for the holidays. These women were without a place to share the holiday spirit. There was an open invitation to my home for people that I knew did not have a place to go to for the holiday season. It was fun cooking up turkeys and roasts that everyone would enjoy.

In order to be prepared for the Thanksgiving and Christmas seasons; I had a distributor from a vineyard make sure that a case or two of wine would come to my home so the girls could had them out to the clients.

One year, I believe, the purchase also included champagne. The bottles would have *Professional Escorts* written on the labels and some holiday saying.

They looked very professional and businesses around the Bay Area did the same for their valued clients. When a phone call came in I made sure that if this person was a regular client the escort would come to my home and pick up a bottle for the client. Of course I gave some of the escorts a bottle of wine. But not all of them … those escorts making a lot of money deserved the extra gift.

The escorts that were lazy or I had difficulty with … did not receive any gifts from me.

Back at my house I was busy baking cheesecakes and making sure I had all the ingredients on hand for my little feasts. If someone was working during the holiday season that person was always invited over for something to eat, if they wanted to have some home-cooked food.

The cheesecakes were distributed to my family and friends and some business people. My mother was usually upset with me for inviting people over and she did not want to come to my home. That was okay with me. Mom felt it was strictly a family time and I disagreed. My families were my clients and people working with me. The clients paid my bills by using my service and the escorts paid my bills by making sure I had my fee from them and they worked the holiday. It was a non-traditional family but a family just the same.

Sometimes I would join her (mom) and other times I was way too busy to leave my phone. I was tired of hearing her criticism of my business and there wasn't any words she could come up with that would make me quit or give up my business. I was all grown up and this was how I wanted to live my life.

The holidays were very relaxing for me and I felt very close to my clients at this time. Some of the escorts that had been working with me for a while, also, liked the holidays. They enjoyed the closeness of people who really wanted to see them during such a special time.

The holidays worked out well for everyone. It should not be surprising to know that many clients would phone during the holidays. A person may have a big family gathering and was in too much "family shock" or should I say "family overload" and needed to relax.

The client would phone and I would ask how the day went and some wanted to talk about it and others just wanted to forget the entire day.

The person phoning wanted to have a woman over that was not going to criticize him or insult him as the day may have gone with his relatives.

The ladies were ready to hear the woes of the clients and happily went over to the home to hear what transpired during the day. Some of the women had their own experiences to talk about. So holidays were the times when therapy sessions were in full-force.

The women made more money during the holidays. I encouraged everyone to work during those times, just for the added income. "Go do the family thing and as soon as you get home…..phone me". I repeated that sentence over and over again. Many escorts would phone to work. Others had strong family connections and did not care to work. Back at my house the table was set and the people that had popped in for food were all seated or uncomfortably walking around waiting for my signal that they could dine.

Ready set eat.

I was in the kitchen shuttling food to the table.

A few Christmas holidays I gave unique gifts to my escorts. I thought that money was too shallow to give and I wanted them to have something that they were able to hold onto long after Christmas and be able to say, "Hey, Dian gave this to me for Christmas."

One Christmas I gave music boxes to the girls.

The boxes were beautiful and reflected music that I liked and hoped that they would like. Another year I gave six crystal glasses in their boxes. They were lovely goblets that the girls enjoyed receiving. Another year I gave out lingerie.

Did the women give me anything?

Not usually. Anything given to me by a girl was actually like the old saying, "Beware of Greeks bearing gifts." I would say that line in my head over and over again. But what did upset me at the time and why I gave up giving at the holidays was because they were unable to even give me a thank you note. It was as though they expected the gifts. A quick thank you as I handed them the gift, but no note for me so I could remember them. All I thought was how rude of them. Lots of takers and no givers worked for me. But I was still old fashioned enough to want a written thank you note, and none ever came. But happily the escorts that were working for me at the time enjoyed the benefit of an extra holiday gift from me.

The holiday was my vacation. After returning from one of my vacations to a foreign country, which this time was Egypt … I gave souvenirs to the girls. They came in the form of papyrus that had beautiful colorful scenes on them. I had picked the hand-painted papyrus that was very well done.

The manufactured and assembly-line production type papyrus I did not purchase. Or if I did purchase the assembly-line papyrus it was given to women that did not work very well and gave me a hard time.

One Easter my sister and her family had come over to have Easter dinner and the mother and sister and baby nephew of Bill's family; my live-in boyfriend of many years.

His family had flown in from Chicago to see us and have a tour of the area. I was so very happy to see them. Bill and I were fighting off and on, as usual. No drop-ins this Easter. I kept the employees away and friends. But there may have been a close friend or two. We were living in Ross at the time.

Well, the food was hot and we had just begun to eat, after warming up with some alcoholic beverages. Bill would never miss a beat or occasion to drink. He usually began in the morning and was pretty drunk by evening.

This fine Easter day there was a knock at the door.

Well, it was the police.

I mean it was the police.

Not one car but a fleet of cars looking for Bill.

Bill was 6'4 ½" tall and very Polish and German. He usually had a beard that was red and his hair was reddish blonde. He looked like a Viking. He went up to our bedroom (on the third level) and had taken the screen off of the window, after opening the window and then slid into the closet.

The police were serving a warrant because he had failed to

appear for a court hearing about hitting me. I had a drink in my hand and just sat on the end of my circular couch. My sister gathered up her young son and her husband and defiantly headed for the door mouthing the words, "This is the last time I will ever come to your house for Easter or any holiday". Gosh. Was it really my fault? I sat there trying to yell back at her to stay and she just vanished with her family. His family was perplexed. They looked at me and I just did not know what to say. His sister was angrier than his mother. They went upstairs.

One of my sons went into my bedroom and there was Bill.

He came down after the coast was clear and we chuckled a little about how he had fooled the police. I thought it was rude for the police to come in on a holiday with guns drawn. The children were in the home and the police looked like idiots pretending that Bill was some hardened criminal. As it turned out, this was the last Easter Bill and I shared. Our relationship was ending and it was a slow death. The last time he hit me was it. I had put a restraining order out on him and I just did not really want him in my life.

The restraining order was gotten through the help of one of the women that worked for me. She drove me to Marin County Civic Center to place the order on him. If not for her strength, I may never have done it.

After a little research into spousal abuse or abuse by a boyfriend, it was clear that I was an abused girlfriend. I fit all the symptoms of a woman that had been threatened or hit for years. The "why" I put up with it was simple, my son. My middle son, Thomas loved Bill. I know that seems lame but it is the truth. Very few women have any other reasons stronger than mine. But this killing of what could have been and should have been a beautiful holiday was the end for me with Bill. By the next Christmas we were history.

Bill and I broke up.

Chapter Eighteen
The Lady Escorts

Yes, I did have some very prim and proper ladies that worked for me.

The following women were special in a way that was different than the other women mentioned. Why? Because they thought they were special. All of them worked for me for a long time and knew how to get along with not only me but the variety of customers that phoned. I would call them my *Professional Escorts*. Not all are mentioned but here are a few.

Number 15

This girl was a cool unique. A person who had idiosyncrasies too many to count, but when you looked at her eyes and the total package before you, well, she was beautiful. Kinky, but lovely, and this work was just another fling in her life. She was willing to try anything and probably did. Did she eventually cheat me out of my fees? Yes. Did I put up with it? Yes. Number 15 had a simply lovely personality and could have been anything or anyone she wanted to be.

One day a client wanted her to model for him with some new cars that would show in some pricey and upscale magazine. She was very excited about the shoot and when the photos came out she brought them over to me to see. Number 15 was every bit the model. Were the photographs used for the magazine? I really don't remember. But the look on her face as to what she could be was worth a million dollars. I always wished her well. She needed someone to encourage her dreams and number 15 dreamed big. Or maybe it was the drugs talking as I listened to her.

Whatever it was, I still wish her well.

This girl was around 19 years old when she came to work for me.

Actually, she could have been 18 years old. Number 15 was 5'8" tall and looked very slender weighing in at about 110 lbs. with her clothes on; she complimented that figure with short dark brown hair and dark eyes. Her makeup was impeccable when she put it on. Her skin was pale and she occasionally would tan; and in retrospect reminds me of Angelina Jolie when Jolie had short hair. She was a dog groomer and part-time student at the junior college.

Everyone knew that she worked for an escort service. She had many admirers while she worked with me and most of them were close to her age. She never wanted children. She went through the process to have herself 'fixed', so there would never be a possibility that she would become pregnant. The doctors found her to be mature enough to make the decision to never be able to have children; and after seeing a psychologist to determine, by law, that her wishes were her own. Her fallopian tubes were tied by a gynecologist. This happened while she was working with my escort service. She had lived in Marin County her entire life and at first she shared an apartment with other girls working with me. Then she preferred to have her own apartment or they just found other living arrangements and she had the place to herself. She lasted about a year and a half or maybe two years. Yes, she was very good. She made lots of money for herself and me. The money she made went for her living expenses and her eventual drug habit. No longer worked with me because she wanted to have her own price list and her own private customers; I ended up firing her with some of her friends. I had put up with her disregard of my rules for a long time, mostly, because she was well liked by the clients and many asked to see her.

This was a time, when I fired her ... after I had surgery and I was not too happy about their cheating on me. So I began firing some of the escorts in fours.

That means four women at a time. They would make the mistake of phoning me and I said, "You are fired." Some were very angry at me. She was upset but understood that she was taking my clients. She loved cocaine and clothes and loved to have men admire her. In the intelligence factor I want to call her stupid, she was just plain stupid and not in touch with reality.

Okay, that is not fair. She was bright and maybe a genius, but losing brain cells daily from all the drug use. She did everything in excess. If she had brains, she was not using them to benefit herself and her future. She was doing nothing with her life. She frustrated me because she could have gone anywhere with her beauty. She appealed to the kinky clients and the drug dealers. There were lots of mental problems for her and in her family tree. She needed the help of a professional and, thankfully, she saw a psychiatrist quite regularly. She came from a family of "shrinks" (Psychiatrists) and they really hurt her mentally. This girl was very lost. She had trouble keeping up with her habits. She loved women and animals and all perversions, such as urination on clients, etc.

Perhaps she did have guilt feelings and that was a part of her mental problems. But in no way was it the complete reason for her behavior. She was seeing a psychiatrist long before working with me. At first she was an honest girl. But from seeing drug dealers and other influences around her, she was changing into a dishonest and lying girl. I liked her at first until I found it difficult to believe anything she said or trust her. She was becoming more and more unreliable. I had to let her go and unfortunately it was by firing her. Just one tidbit about her was that she had a snake and was very cozy with that snake. Just imagine sleeping with a snake. She was very unusual. The snake would go looking for her bed and the warmth there when the snake got out of the cage. Some real live issues between her and the snake.

One of my friends at the time began a quasi-relationship with her and he told me the snake was a little too freaky for him. He told me she urinated on him in the shower and wanted him to do the same to her. I felt that to be some special ritual of hers for boyfriends. Instead of boyfriends "turning her out", she was "turning boyfriends out". This "turning out" refers to a person showing another person about sex. It may be used for other things, but I only heard it used for sexual games. A little similar to "christening" a location by having sex in the back or front seats of a car or boat or anywhere that is new to someone. Even a person's office desk or chair.

Number 16

This was a very nice girl. I liked her from the moment I met her. She had never worked for an escort service before and I was not sure if this was the type of work she should be doing. But after just a few calls I knew it was something she enjoyed exploring, even though she preferred the company of women. She needed and wanted the very high amount of money that went along with many of the clients she was sent out to see.

Number 16 was around 21 years old with short brown hair and brown eyes. She had what I would call a medium to slender figure. She weighed around 115 lbs. and was 5'6" tall. Number 16 sported a very average face. She was a dog groomer and a junior college student. Her friends knew but not her family. But she did have a girlfriend or two. No little tykes running around her home. She lived in Marin County sharing a house with another girl that worked for me at the time. Around eight months give or take a month that had her on my employment rolls. She was pretty good. Yes, she made a great deal of money with me. Her money went for her living expenses and old bills and also, unfortunately, went for her increasing dependency upon drugs. But in complete fairness to her and the other women finding themselves lost in drug use, the clients had huge amounts of the drugs and just kept feeding the willing women.

Not every client, but those that kept the women overnight and/or for hours. The clients wanted the escorts to join them in their dependencies for drugs.

There had been an argument with her roommate that had also worked for me and I ended up firing them both. She liked drugs and alcohol and women.

Number 16 had above average intelligence.

The clients she appealed to ... liked drugs and seeing two women engaged in a sexual position. She felt she had inadequacies. Possibly because her friends where more flamboyant than she was; I would not say they were prettier, just more outgoing. She was too trusting and was always being taken advantage of in regard to her living situations. I think it was because she was more lesbian than bisexual. This person ended up paying more of the bills than she should have had to pay. A nice girl who had trouble keeping up with all the bills and the requirements of living with women she had a sexual relationship with. She liked women and lots of sex with men. Hum. I guess she was really more bi-sexual and felt no guilt about her work with me or her relationships with women. This was an honest person. She only sold drugs, usually, to help others out, because she was a very nice and helpful friend for too many people.

My feelings about the girl while she was working for me, I liked her a lot. I thought of her as one of the nicest girls that ever worked for me. She was caring and had a lot of heart. One time when I had surgery on my nose to correct it from a car accident, I was home and taking too much medication. She saw what everyone was doing to me. The girls would prop me up in bed to answer the phone for them, so they could have calls and they kept giving me my pain killers or anything else I asked for at the time. She took some pills away from me and said,

"No Dian. You have had enough."

I looked at her and said, "Enough?" (This was in a very childlike voice due to my being so looped on drugs.)

She said, "Yes. Enough! Now go to sleep." She tucked me in and made the other women go out of the room, so I could rest and get some needed sleep. She also took the pills from me and probably saved my life that day.

The other women stopped giving me pills (they were pills from my doctor) and I suspect she was the reason. I did not know any better because I really was drugged up and in a great deal of pain from the surgery. But everyone was afraid to say no to me and she was the only person who said to me that enough was enough with my taking pills.

When I got better, I tried to train her on the phones. But I was a perfectionist at the time and just brow-beat her until she just wanted to do calls.

Plus, the calls gave her more money than working as a phone operator for me. I did feel bad about my behavior when trying to teach her the phones. But it was because of my intenseness on the phone that kept the escorts safe and out of trouble. I have always wished her a happy life and I hope that she is well. She was one person that I really believed would do well, if she went back to school or owned her own business. She was a very nice and good person. It would have been a crime if she ever changed. I hoped that she found better friends to have than the ones I knew.

Number 17

This was a friend of number 16 and she had grown up in Hawaii but was not Hawaiian. Both of the girls had been friends in Hawaii. She was a white girl with lots of energy and ego. A girl around 24 years of age with short natural red hair and very white skin; she was also slender and 5'4" tall weighing in at about 105 lbs. She was cute but not pretty. Number 17 had a young looking face, but was not young. She was a dog groomer. Her family knew and most of her friends that she was working as an escort. She had a husband when she started, and later, a boyfriend when she was eventually fired. No children at that time that they lived in Marin County with roommates while working for me. Stayed just around eight months give or take a month. Yes, she was a super worker. Yes, she made a great deal of money.

The money went for drugs and clothes for her and I found her to be a very selfish person. It was all about her. She went out with a very good customer of mine behind my back and thought she could get away with it. I found out. She had the habit of taking boyfriends from other girls and she loved drugs and lots of sex; possibly a nymphomaniac. Not too bright.

Her appeal was to the drug dealer or drug addicts and these were the men that loved to be with her. She did not like herself or anyone else. She had a real chip on her shoulder and should have seen a psychiatrist. Yes, she had trouble keeping her money situation together. She liked women and would do anything sexual with a man. Anything, the man wanted sexual, she was up for it.

None, absolutely no guilt feelings, very guilt free and loved what she was doing. She was not honest and I really wish she could have had better character. But there was the ever thought that she would lie if she thought she could get away with it and with any person.

I liked her a lot at first, until I caught wind of her actions to people and her cheating by going out with clients behind my back.

This woman had come over to California with two other women ... I have already spoken of from Hawaii. They had all been born in Hawaii and liked the mainland. She was a person that had a great smile and was very friendly but behind your back she was the typical two-faced person. I was revolted by her meanness to the other girls that she called her friends. This high school mentality of hers was childish. If one of the other girls had her eyes on a guy, this person would purposely seek the man out to make him hers. A very shallow woman. If someone told me she was in prison for the rest of her life, well, I would believe it.

Letter H

This was a well-dressed woman that looked a lot younger than she really was. A special person that just wanted to support her family and I enjoyed the fact that she kept her day job. 1. She was one of my older women working and was about 36 years of age and she stood 5'8" tall and had medium length brown hair. Very light skin and she did look over thirty years old, but not too much over. She had the appearance of being straight, because she dressed nicely but not too flashy, nothing that would stand her out in a crowd. She was a secretary and remained one even while she worked for me. Some friends knew and I am sure some of her family knew.

H did not want her co-workers to know. She was afraid of a scandal or any scandal that she might get caught up in. I understood her fears. At times she had a boyfriend; it was very off and on. She had older children and lived in South San Francisco. She was with me about three months give or takes a month. If the client wanted an older escort, she was perfect. She supplemented her income with what she made working for me to pay living expenses and some past due bills. She made money if she liked the person. She was very picky about clients. She definitely would not sleep with someone just because he might ask her too.

She was no longer working with me because she did not like

giving up a percentage to anyone. Paying my fee was something that bothered her and I think this was idiotic. Someone had to pay the advertising costs and answering the phone for clients. Was she going to be on the phone 24/7? No. She needed me but all she wanted to do was use my service the same way she used other services she had worked for, by getting clients to be regulars of hers and call her at home. She just did not take my warnings of having men phone her home very seriously. I tried to impress upon her that her children should not be picking up the phone calls.

The clients may call her a couple of times but they would always come back to my service. The men wanted variety and she probably wanted a lot more money from them, and men do not want to go to a home where children are living. It takes the mystic all out of the game they are playing.

I suppose her habits were her children and clothes for herself. She was a smart woman and she appealed to the more intelligent customer, the client who wanted to have a steady affair. She was afraid and insecure doing this type of work. It made her progressively paranoid to be working with and for a service.
Not necessarily my service, but just any service. I knew she had to be juggling more than one escort service for calls.

That type of working person did not fit with my service. I wanted loyalty. If the other service had police problems it might roll-over to my service; so all my escorts knew that working for some other service was a no, no with me. She liked nice things and was having trouble keeping up with her wants. That is why she did this work part-time. Her day job did not meet her needs. She liked doing things or having sexual relations with other women and clients because she was definitely bisexual. Her guilt feelings encompassed everything. She felt guilty she had to do this type of work, but she needed to it for her other sexual outlet, which was having sex with women and not being open about it. A life of openly having sex with women in her private life was never going to happen. Because her desires for women sexual had to be in the 'closet', so her family was none- the-wiser.

There was not room in her private life for women coming to her home to have a relationship with her. She was only dishonest about the money and the "why" she wanted to work with me. But I already knew her reasons and was many years ahead of her in how she presented her truths and half-truths to me. I had heard it all before. I liked her but wanted out of my service. She smelled of trouble. I just knew that if she remained with me there would be police trouble because she would not listen. If she had been busted they could have extracted any information out of her. There would not be any loyalty with her. I ended the working relationship we had and was content to do it quickly.

Letter V

This person was a black woman that looked very statuesque and did model from time to time. She wanted to go out on her own because she thought she was smarter than me. All the women at some point thought they were better than me or had more street smarts than me. I laughed about it a lot. They were funny, especially when leaving me and then getting themselves busted for some infraction of the law that I tried to explain to them "don't do that". No one listened for long.

She stood 5'8" tall and had saline breasts which she loved to show off. She was pretty but aging and had a good figure for her age. Her figure was enhanced by stylish clothes and had a very well-groomed appearance. She had been a model and was a nurse while working for me. I don't believe she was a registered nurse. She also freelanced at the bars picking up what men she could.

Her friends knew and so did her family. She had a boyfriend. He was black and she also would have customers as boyfriends, so she could use them and get all she could from them. Three of her children lived in Hayward with her. She lasted working for me around nine months give or take a month. I thought she was good. She felt she had to try extra hard because she was a black woman. I believe it was because she was older and it had nothing to do with her ethnic background. But for the sake of argument ... I did not explain that it was more her aging that was a problem. I was unable to softly touch on the real reasons, so
I just let her talk about the race issues that were her main concerns about why she did not make the money she thought she should be making; ultimately she did make money.

V still owes me money because she was another escort who did not want to give up the fee to me. I think these women thought I was their personal slave, who they needed to answer their phone calls and never pay me for the work I did. Her money went for her living expenses and her children. She did live high. Spent her money on whatever she wanted. I caught onto her ripping me off from one my customers. The clients always would tell me when an escort saw them behind my back and this was with few exceptions. Usually, the clients would phone me when they were angry at a girl and that was the best source I had for finding out if a girl was seeing customers.

Also, the girl had the misconception that I was holding calls from her. Which was not the truth; if people don't want a girl, I never forced one on them. Of course there was the occasional coaxing. Her habits were everything that made her happy. A perfect narcissistic personality.

She liked cocaine and liquor but I would say her clothes habit and hair grooming were the most expensive habits she had. She loved to look nice. That was good for business but not all clients wanted an older black woman.

The clients were few that liked older women. She was smart but thought herself to be clever and much cleverer than me. That was a mistake in my business to think you could outsmart all people. She appealed to the customer that liked a classy black lady; one who was, also, well under the covers.

V had a lot of problems in regard to relationships with white women. She envied them way too much. She really hated white people and it began to show while working with me. That was very sad. V had problems keeping her living situation together due to her expensive buying habits. She loved sex and liked women. She did not know the word truth or how to spell it. But she could dish out the best lies around and would steal if given the opportunity.

I liked her, but felt disappointment in the woman after giving her my trust. She ultimately was fired and opened her own escort service near San Jose and was busted by the vice cops in that town. I believe this vice cop arrest happened after her service was only open for around six months. She thought I had done something to her. She was very accusatory for no reason.

I was too busy to care about what she was doing. I think her mind was her own worst enemy. She went completely out of business after her arrest.

Those vice cops were some of the best in the Bay Area at the time. If she had consulted with me I would have told her the facts of working in San Jose. She, also, was one of two black women at the first party and is in a photo with me and had some photos done herself at that party. A complete opportunist.

Number 9

Number 9, I termed her a drug addict. She did not seem to be on drugs when I first put her to work as an escort but then she changed. This girl was around 5'1" tall and had a large chest. She weighed around 105 lbs which gave her a near perfect figure. She had very white skin and short black hair with dark eyes. Her face was cute and she had small features.

Number 9 had been an escort in San Diego and with another girl had owned their own escort service in San Diego. She was at one time a college student. Her friends knew but not her family. No boyfriend in the picture, but she had a girlfriend. And she was another women saying no to have children.

First she shared an apartment in Berkeley with another girl and then she moved to another share situation in the *San Francisco Mission District*. Lasted just about a year and then after a year it was off and on. She was very good and she made money. She lived high on her money and spent it on drugs and very expensive clothes. She could not handle having a boss. I felt that she was just another escort who thought she was smarter than me and wanted only a few customers that were meant to be her regular clients. She was on heroin. She was smart, but not a strong of character and conviction person. She appealed to almost everyone. She had too many head problems and those problems compounded in regard to her living life; as her drug problem increased in magnitude. She was a lesbian and married her girlfriend.

I am not sure where they were married, but this was before some counties and states had said people of same-sex partnerships could marry. She was not honest and sold drugs and would steal if necessary ... probably to support her habit. She was feeling guilty about her lesbian affair, marriage, or whatever she was doing in her private life.

I liked her but saw her increase her self-destruction tendencies to the point I did not want anything to do with her. She was almost past help and she needed professional psychiatric help that I could not give her. It was surprising, to me, that she lasted almost a year with my escort service and this was probably because of the various drugs use; she was too lazy to handle opening her own service.

Number 24

Number 24 was a very nice person. She just wanted to get ahead with her finances. This girl was around 27 years of age and stood 5'2" tall and had a very athletic look. She had brown hair and blue eyes. Number 24 was blessed with healthy looking skin and was usually sun-tanned. She was a school teacher. A select few knew what she was doing. No children or boyfriend in her home.

Home was in Fresno which is a farming community about 100 miles from the Bay Area. It must have been around six months give or take a month that she worked. Many times the women such as her would still stay onboard for an occasional call and would not be on call every day. She made money and she was very good at what she did. She paid off bills and traveled a little. She got married. Any habits she may have had were all connected with the out-of-door lifestyle. She loved sports and athletic events. An intelligent woman and I would have to say she had her "act" together.

The clients she appealed to were those who liked the fresh look or athletic body and a person that was able to converse on many levels. There were no noticeable problems mentally and she did not confide in me if she had any problems. She just had some issues in keeping up with her bills. Many of the women did feel the need to tell me all their problems and that is how I knew about all the women, I have wrote about, who were dealing with their own demons, perceived or imaginary.

This girl was very hungry for sex. But so are many housewives. Maybe she liked sex because of her athletic prowess.

Possibly guilt feelings, although, not expressed to me. On the whole, to any observer, she was mentally sound and could deal with going out for money. She was an honest woman. I liked her. There was just nothing not to like. She did the work and did not give me any problems. She paid me my fee and was honest when she wanted to work and when she did not want to work. I wish all the women had been as together as she was.

When the communication lines were up and running smoothly between the escorts and myself it was a beautiful experience and with this woman life was great answering the phone and being able to send her out on calls.

Number 300

Number 300 was a woman that came to me at the end of her school career and she needed to finish paying for her law school. She did not want me to send her to any judges because she clerked for them. I will not reveal, even now, the county she lived and worked in. I respected this girl and was able to send her to my affluent clients. She was my ideal of an escort, because she was sexy, smart, articulate, and honest. Another one of my favorite escorts because she did not play games with me or the clients, just did her job and did it well.

This was a very pretty brunette about 5'7" tall and had a firm and fit body from working out every day after her day job. She had longish brown hair and wore suits well and sometimes on calls with a sexy teddy underneath. She looked professional and would be able to go to any hotel and enter without being stopped by security. She fit the business like a glove. She may have worked for another governmental agency, because there was a little mystery to her personality. She was not the type of person to tell anyone, ever, what the work was or that she ever did it. She could keep a secret. Not at the time did she have a boyfriend or child.

One of my more affluent clients wanted to date her and may have without ever telling me. She would not have told me if it happened because of who he was she felt okay to keep things secret. I do know he liked her a lot. It was about six months but it may have been longer that she worked.

Yes, very good with affluent clients. I would not send her to any person that I thought was sleazy or not in her class. Yes, she made money and paid many of her bills off. She may have made some regular clients for her to have on the side. She is one person and probably one of a handful of women that worked for me that I would not have cared if she saw someone without giving me a fee.

The reason is because she always paid me my fee from other calls and was not negligent or rude to me as some of the other women could be. You have no idea how rude a person can be when they are unable to use you, anymore.

God, it made me unhappy to have to deal with people that, I know, never respected my helping them out when they needed it most. She knew I provided a service for her and she was very clear that she wanted her privacy, which I respected.

The reason she was no longer working with me was that she said her law school was paid. She had paid for her schooling and did not need me anymore. A very honest approach to business because she just used it for what she needed it for. No habits in regard to drugs or drinking, but I do believe she liked expensive suits and shoes and handbags. She, also, appeared to see a cosmetologist on a regular basis. Her hair was very well-done and healthy looking. Intelligent and probably up there with the smartest women I ever had work for me. Wealthy clients, the clients without lots of cash would have been intimidated by her presence. No noticeable mental health issues. I must say that after all the years I had my business it was very easy to pick the women that did have problems. She was not one of them. She was a straight woman who did not have a preference to be with women and she just liked wealthy successful men.

No guilt feelings.

She knew what she was doing and why she was doing it. Not in her case was there any criminal behavior or did it appear apparent that she would comment any crime. I liked her. So did a major director of motion pictures that phoned and saw her. When she was no longer working I actually missed her, because I wanted the other women to get to know her and maybe her presence would have rubbed off on a few of them.

Number 84

Many women would think of going to France to work, but in this case the girl was from France. Lovely lady that had chosen the work through a man she fall in love with, in America, she should have gone back home to live and left the creep behind.

This girl was from France and had an adorable accent and stood around 5'3" tall. She had a medium built frame but looked slender and her figure was good. Her face was pretty and was about 24 years of age and dressed well. She was a babysitter and a nurse in France.

Only her friends knew.

Yes, she had a boyfriend and he was black and there were no children. She lived in a shared apartment with two other girls that worked for me at the time.

Altogether, she was with me about four months.

Yes, to being good or excellent in the escort business. She made money when working. She kept up with her living expenses and clothes, along with drugs for her boyfriend.

The boyfriend took her to Los Angeles, so she could work there. He wanted to have her make more money for him. He was a wretched person and no doubt a pimp. Her only habit was giving money to her boyfriend. In Los Angeles there was this entire pimp culture going on at the time. He would have wanted to be with other pimps. I have no idea what they would talk about, except to say what their "bitches" were able to make. Lots of bragging in those circles. I could not see her happy there.

Smart but very dumb when it came to American black men. She appealed to most men and those that loved women from other countries. A few mental problems but they were not huge problems.

Yes, she had trouble keeping her expenses manageable. She spent too much on her boyfriend and clothes and his needs. She liked women. No guilt feelings. But was concerned about her family finding out what she was doing.

A fairly honest girl and I liked her but could not convince her to stay away from the trouble that would eventually come her way by staying with her boyfriend. She was gone and I was actually happy to be rid of her. I knew that the boyfriend could be trouble for me. It was best to have a possible nuisance go down the road. The laws are such that a foreign national can be deported for various crimes and one of them is prostitution. So if she was ever caught working with this 'pimp' of hers, it would have been back to France for her.

I never heard from her again.

Chapter Nineteen
Songs

Some of the women inspired me to write songs for them and number 84 moved me and I wrote this song for her. It was a song about her love for her boyfriend.

Song Number I - Can't Get Out of Loving You

I Can't Get Out of Loving You
I can't get out of love n you
I can't get out of love n you
The years we've wasted have been so few
The only feeling I have of you
Is the one and only fact
I can't get out of love n you
I can't get out of love n you
There were times before
I tried too hard
There were times I needed loneliness
And still it comes to me
This feeling deep inside of me that
I can't get out of love n you
I can't get out of love n you
Would take your bills and pills
And cars
Could you go so far I'd never see you?
Would you please?
So I can stop begging myself to forget that
I can't get out of love n you
I can't get out of love n you
Not you

Many of the women motivated me to write the following song for them. This song reflected how the escorts felt toward some of their clients. Especially, due to the fact, the clients that may see one woman one day, and possibly a roommate of hers, or a friend of hers … depended upon what day it was.

The clients were never really loyal to any one escort and I tried to convince the various escorts, who would fall into the traps laid out by some very experienced clients; that these clients were just lying to them. But, a song was the best way to tell them.

Song Number II - Learning to Be Loved

I find myself in your arms
Around your life
And
In the life of love
Still it is hard for me
Learning to be loved
Learning to be loved
This fondness for you
Understanding you too
Trusting and lusting for you
Has me
Learning to be loved
Learning to be loved
Deep, so deep inside of me
Difficulties lay and help from you
Is all I need on my quest of
Learning to be loved
Learning to be loved
By you
My man of many loves
I will ever be
Learning to be loved
Learning to be loved by you

The following song was written for the women to inspire them to be more self-confident in what they were now doing. I hoped that they would someday know that I understood that many of them came to me from bad relationships.
That many had family problems to work out. They all wanted money to ease their individual pain in their hearts. This song is for them.

Song Number III - No Matter What You Do

No matter what you do
You can't change you
No matter what you do
You can't change you
The color of your hair
Or the clothes you wear

The way you walk
Or the way you talk
No matter what you do
I'm telling you
You can't change you
I'm telling you
There just is no way
To have it your way
You just can't go changing you
No matter what you do
You can't change you
No matter what you do
You can't change you
I've seen the stops all along the way
I even took you a bit of the way
And you should see by now
What I've been telling you
No matter what you do
You can't change you
No matter what you do
You can't change you
The help was there
The life did change
But in the long end
It came to be
There just was no way
No matter what we did
To have the things you wanted
Most important to you
It all was a change for you
Baby
My baby
No matter what you do
You can't change you
No matter what you do
You can't change you

This song was written for the escorts both male and female to emphasize the socio-economic problems that were mounting during the time I managed and owned *Professional Escorts*. Many of the people that came to work for me had lost their jobs and still had bills to pay and children to feed. This was a theme song for them and all people that turn to selling their time and bodies to others because of the economic times they live and lived in. The poor and under paid and lost and lonely, this song is for you. It is my favorite song.

Song: Number IV - What can't they take?

What can't they take?
Our love
What can't they take?
Our love
Packaged an sealed beyond belief
Our love
Now we know what they can take
But we have what few can believe
Today is our day
Tonight is our night
And I'll say it again
And I say it again
What can't they take?
Our love
What can't they take?
Our love
Now they've taken our jobs and pride
Pensions and Benefits undone
Stolen our money
Possessions and lives
They made us cry but now we've arrived
And I'll say it again
What can't they take?
Our love
What can't they take?
Our love
They have taken financial dreams
Taken the toll and pay away from our shores
Packaged an sealed, beyond belief
And I'll say it again
What can't they take?
Our love
What can't they take?
Our love
They've ripped our children from our hearts

Thrown them aside
Learning and food aside
And I'll say it again
What can't they take?
Our love
What can't they take?
Our love
Bringing dreams and promises fulfilled
We know inside we're complete
Packaged an sealed, beyond belief
And I'll say it again
What can't they take?
Our love
What can't they take?
Our love
Now we know what they can take
But we have what few can believe
Today is our day
My love
They can't take our love
Because I told you before
And I'll say it again
What can't they take?
Our Love
What can't they take?
Our Love
My love
Our Love

Chapter Twenty
The Short-Timers

It was inevitable that many people would waste my time and theirs by trying to work as an escort. I was very frustrated with these people and knew down deep inside my very soul that the person was going to be some rip-off or a short-starter.

A person that would go to a call and cry or just not be very professional as an escort; this was someone that should not have ever phoned me to work at my agency. I disliked these people for wasting my time. It took a lot of time to explain my rules and to meet with the people.

So if I sound harsh about them well it is understandable. Any business owner would have been unhappy with their individual lack of performance. I list some of the escorts here to show a bit of what I had to put up with.

Many of these women had me going to their homes to retrieve my fee. Sometimes I had to meet them in restaurants or libraries or just in a car for my fee. They really were not worth the trouble they gave me. I had to insist on cash from them. Occasionally one would want to give me a check and swear that it was good. Believe it or not; still, many of them owe me money. Even some of the previous escorts owe me money. They just did not understand the concept that I had to pay for advertising, telephone costs, electric, rent, and answering the phone for them was really a paid position.

That it was me they were paying to make sure they were safe. Answering the phones for *Professional Escorts* was a huge task and took a great deal of energy from me.

Please enjoy reading about these women and you just might see yourself in some of them. Or perhaps you may have already identified some of your actions with previous escorts, named.

Number 12

This woman was a friend of letter V and they both must have been working together behind my back the entire time. I liked the fact she was distinctive in her style because that appealed to some clients. But her personality was a very 'me-first' attitude. It did nothing for her at the age she was now. By now she should have been softer and full of knowledge that age brings. But for her the aging process was a cruel and close enemy for her. She did not enjoy aging. I did not pity her because she had years of people admiring her beauty. The woman was around 5'9" tall. She was slender and had dark hair; dark eyes, and was of Pilipino descent.

This woman had a statuesque appearance and was about 40 years old and looked it. She must have been very pretty when she was young because you could envision her past beauty if you looked at her face long enough. She worked for the County of Alameda. It was my understanding that she kept that job while working with me. She also free lanced at bars in San Francisco. Only one friend knew and that was letter V. Maybe others from her past knew what she was doing. Yes, she had a boyfriend who lived in San Diego. I suspect he may have been in the military. Many Pilipino women date military men with the intention of marrying them and coming to the United States. She had children. She lived in an apartment in Berkeley, California. She lasted with me around two months but that could have been a shorter time. She was all right. Not great.

She was greedy. Maybe she made some money for herself, but not for me, I saw very little money from my efforts with her. The money she did make went for extra clothes and past due bills. She was a trouble- maker and I fired her. She told lies all the time and she was far too much trouble than she was worth. Lying and her vanity were some problems hanging onto her character … at that time. She was her own worst enemy. Very unfortunate, because she could have been so much more if she would have looked upon herself in a more realistic manner … she just felt she was 'now' something that she was not. Average intelligence and she could have been better educated, but the motivation was not there to advance her mind. Going back to school was suggested by me, but she was not going for that. Quick money was all she wanted.

To listen to her … you did not think she was very smart because her language skills were rough. She appealed to those clients that liked foreign women and were tall and thin. She did not know how to tell the truth and was a habitual liar. She could not keep up with her living expense. She over-spent all the time, and there was a constant need for money. She liked women. No guilt feelings and a very dishonest person. Would lie and steal from anyone. I never liked her and just put up with her for a while, then I had to fire her and it was difficult for me because I really tried hard to help give her calls.

As I have aged, I realize that she must have been over 40 and maybe closer to 50 years old at the time she was working for me. I say, "When I have aged". Because in those days I was not very good at guessing women's ages, I am much better now.

Number 56

This woman had come to the first party and was a friend to another woman that had been at the first party. Number 56 was around 27 years of age and had a prominent jaw-line. She was pretty in a masculine sort of way, with brown longish hair and blue eyes.

Number 56 also had large hands and feet and an average body. She was 5'8" tall and sported a fresh look about herself. She was a waitress and also acted or paraded herself in pornography films. At the time she worked for me, I was sending women out with projectors to client's homes with graphic films. This was before the time of renting videos. So sending a woman that was in the film over to a clients' home was very exciting to the clients. This was a fantastic marketing tool and helped to advance my service above all other services. Some of these calls only lasted long enough to begin the film. The escort was onto another call. Lots of money was made by all.

Her family and friends knew what she was doing. No boyfriend in the picture, she did have a girlfriend and no children. She lived in Sonoma County, California with her girlfriend. Sadly she only lasted a few calls, because she preferred doing porno movies. There was more money in the making of those films and she did not have to drive all over the Bay Area to make money. Yes, she was very good at what she did with the clients. Such a question for this escort, of course she was great….. Dah did porno films. Yes, she made money. But she could have made a great deal more money working for me. She just was not really up to driving all over the area. She spent her money earned on her friends and living expenses and drugs. The drugs were so she could get in the mood for her movie career.

This was a person that needed the drugs to perform, or so she said to me. She was one of the many women that had been with a well-known male porno star that died (John Holmes). And her eyes lit up when she spoke of him. She wanted to do porno films and would do anything her female lover wanted her to do. The female lover, she had, did not want her driving all over to make money.

Women and those relationships she had with a few of them and drugs were her habits; I suspect her female-lover did not know about all the other women. Average to slightly above average intelligence, schooling would have been very beneficial for her. She appealed to those clients that liked seeing two women making love together in front of him. Bad self-worth and a clear identity problem, she just was lost in sex. The day rose and set with sex for her.

Could not keep her money together, she was doing possibly too many drugs. She only wanted to be with women after a while. Lots of guilt feelings. A very suicidal potential was in her or part of her personality.

Not honest with herself or any other person. I thought she was all right, but totally caught up in some very evil things, she had a strong dark side to her character. Similar to another escort that was in porno films and I found it very interesting these women also liked black magic and areas of criminal behavior that I have forgotten, what those behaviors were; but she was up for anything that was against the law and that, in-itself, covers a huge territory.

They were totally free in their minds as to how they would use black magic and there was a look in their eyes, which I once saw when I was at the hot springs on the outskirts of Palms Springs. There I was with some male friends of mine splashing and jumping from one pool to another and just having fun in three pools of natural spring hot water. Each spring was a different temperature and we went from cooler, to medium heat, to very warm. None of the pools were too hot to enter and the local Native American tribes may have been the only people to have used the pools before civilization came to the area.

This was the nineteen seventies and many Hippies were finding the well-hidden trail to this location. The Charlie Manson women were swimming this one time, we are relaxing and, the pool was not large enough to avoid them ... I saw they had the same look in the depth of their eyes that these pornography women had in their eyes. That is the only time I have seen that look. It would make a person wonder what similar situations those women had been exposed too. A deep connection with evil and I was almost intrigued by the look.

When they were done working for me ... I never saw them again.

Letter U

This girl was a young girl ... still attending school at a college in the Bay Area. She was 5'8" tall with thick long brown hair. Lovely looking girl, sweet looking and she had dark eyes and a nice figure. Not really in the best of shape, she could have used some exercise. Her friends knew but not her family. Somehow, she managed to have lots of boyfriends, but no children. She shared an apartment with other single girls. She lasted only about a month and during that time was good and made money when she wanted too. "Good" for me was the person worked and I could rely upon her. But she was more interested in herself ... rather than working for an escort service. She wanted to be able to rip off the service for the best customers and then have them as her own regular clients. (Many women did this and as you have read in previous case studies, I always needed to weed these women out of my service.) She bought and used drugs with the money she made. She partied a lot and bought a lot of clothes and a redeeming factor was she paid for her schooling.

She decided that working with escort services in San Francisco was best for her, because she could rip them off easier than me. Many times she alluded to that behavior with me, which gave her a few points for being more upfront than other women that had done the same to me, which was to take clients and have them as your own. U was too young to have too many habits, bad or good. She did have trouble sticking to anything or completing projects. She was a little scattered. A smart girl, but not too bright or she just lacked a lot of common sense. She appealed to most men but had problems just standing still, let alone running her life. Maybe she had some attention issues. She liked having sex with women. No guilt feelings about her sexual needs and I would never call this person an honest girl. Except for the time when she was no longer going to be with me and confessed that she had given her number out to clients. I thought she was nice, in spite of her divulging to me how she wanted clients to phone her directly.

Although, she had wasted my time phoning her for calls. Constantly refusing them or would take them without me knowing about it. But eventually the clients would tell me; just like with the other escorts who thought they could keep their cheating behind my back a secret. Maybe that is why she volunteered the information that she had crossed the line and given her number out. For her honesty I give her a few more points.

Number 8

This was a person that was a professional person and I had not the foggiest idea as to why she wanted to work. All I knew was what she told me and that may not have been the truth. Maybe she was writing her own book on this type of work and analyzed my business because she was a licensed psychologist.

She was around 45 years of age and stood 5'4" tall. She had gray hair mixed with brown hair and her hair was never neat. She wore the same clothes all the time and had lines in her face, which was an average looking face. She was working at a bar in the city (San Francisco) as a cocktail waitress and was a psychologist, who was not working full-time. Really a mixed up life.

She did answer my phones for maybe a week or two, but she was unable to do the job well. Those close to her did not know about her attempting to do escort work. A couple of her associates in the psychologist world knew. That is why I think she may have been trying to do some research and did not have a clue how to research this type of business. No boyfriend, although she did have a couple of men she said liked her. She had two children but they were not living with her. She lived in a small cottage in Berkeley, California. She remained with me about a month of working full-time. She was not good. She really did not make any money working with me; there were a few dollars, but it was slim and could not have been much. Whatever came her way went for living expenses. The money was from me for answering my phones. I made it increasingly hard for her and had her answer the phone, which she was terrible at doing. The reason I made it difficult for her was to show her that escort work was not for her. I really should have checked her out to see that she did have a degree in psychology.

My escort phones were a way for her to learn; so she had some idea as to what the clients said on the phone and the type of female escorts those clients were calling and wanted. It was an attempt to let her down easy that she should not be doing calls. Appearance in escorting is and was everything. Men don't want a woman who is not fashionable or put together well. Men pay for the total package and I had to let all the women know that their appearances matter. Especially if they wanted to make some money.

Absolutely no personality on the phones; she was very dry when speaking with potential clients. She was a boozer and that may have been the real reason she had resorted to escort work, because she could not keep a job working in the profession she had a degree in. She was intelligent and on the borderline of being termed insane or crazy. She did not appeal to anyone, at all. Lots of mental problems and they were all obvious. Any person could say and would say that she was mixed up. She thought she could do calls and she displayed herself as a person losing contact with reality. If anyone that worked for me needed therapy, she was the one and could have competed with the craziest of the craziest that I ever met. Little wonder she had trouble paying her rent. She did not want to have sex. Not with anyone. Maybe there are a lot of women that do not want to have sex, and that is why my service existed for so long. But for her to want to be an escort without any "touchy feels" on the table for a client was just absurd. What else did this woman have to offer? Her conversation was boring.

This person had lots of guilt and she fantasized herself to be a hooker. She was demeaning to the other women. She chose to believe that everyone was a hooker and that was not true. I was disgusted by the way her ideas of right and wrong were skewed to favor all that she thought was right with the world. Many women working did not wish to be called 'hookers' and especially by an older and unattractive woman such as her. She was half-way honest and she felt or saw herself to be a revolutionary by even wanting to be an escort. But for my purposes she was rude and insulting, which did not go over well with me or the other people actively involved in my business. I call her a lady and that is because she thought of herself as a lady. A lady unable to communicate well with men or women.

She would also sell drugs if she had the opportunity. I liked her but felt her to be a danger to my business because she was not careful. She drank too much and had too many fantasies for me to deal with. I had barely begun my business and was not able to reach out to her to counsel her. The time was not there to give her any mentoring. To think she was a psychologist … I felt this had to be a lie. The woman was not living in the real world. I felt she had allergies and was allergic to alcohol. Code for she was an alcoholic.

My mother thought she was insane. And then the next moment mom liked talking to her. Very unusual, these two women connected on some level and it must have begun with the woman calling all the escorts 'hookers'. My mom expressed those same feelings … the women were garbage and because those two were not doing the work … well … they were perfect.

I was very happy when she was no longer around. There were enough negative statements coming from my mother in those days and I did not need her having a partner in conversation about what was wrong and right; when they both had really no idea what was happening.

The business was at my mom's house then and this woman was over there and mom seemed to like her company or entertainment, not sure what was the attraction.

Letter S

Letter S lived in the Canal area of San Rafael, California. She worked her own "book" (client list) with her sister. She was 5'9" tall and had brown hair and blue eyes. She was large boned and weighed around 145 lbs. and was pretty and 22 years of age. Waitress jobs had preceded this line of work. Her friends and family knew; including the whole town and/or County of Marin. She had lots of boyfriends. She should have charged them all. No children.

The apartment she lived in with her sister in the Canal area of San Rafael was a vacation spot for half the single men in Marin. She lasted about three weeks; due to the fact she and her sister were working on their own ... out of their apartment. I found out through the same phone service person that my mother knew and I knew. He had put their phone in for them. In those days I had spies everywhere. People would phone me just to get on my good side and tell me things that were going on with the people that worked for me or with other services. She was okay. She could have made more money with me if she was not so hell bent on having her own service with her sister. Her money went for drugs and living expenses, such as booze and food for all the "action" she had coming to her apartment.

After finding out about their working from their apartment; I wanted nothing more to do with her. Drugs were her habits and clothes, plus, she just liked goofing around. Not doing anything. She liked men too much to attend school or do something creative or technical which could open career opportunities for herself. Below average intelligence and a seedy person, this helped her be guided by her sister. The sister being the "brains" of the duo.

She could have appealed to most customers and if she had lost some weight, that would have helped her appeal, because she was young. She was just not a bright person. All her watts in her brain were not sparking. She could not live on her own. She needed guidance from her sister all of the time. She must have used drugs for way too long or very early in life. She and her sister would have sex in front of clients. She had an abnormal sexual appetite; possibly a nymphomaniac. She did not feel guilt. This was a very dishonest person. She could not tell the truth and was very depended upon her sister for truth or what to say to people. I thought she was okay but I did not want to get too close to her. She could mess up a wet dream. I felt she and her sister were a threat to the security with my business.

They were way too vocal and outspoken ... telling too many people what they were doing. No sense of loyalty. Even the phone installer told me to get rid of them. No telling what they had told him. I got rid of them.

Number 14

Number 14 did not have the appearance or personality to sustain working as an escort, but I did not have the meanness in me to tell her that she was too plain looking and her conversational abilities displayed an unsure person. No confidence, at all. She needed self-assurance and I could not give or extend myself to help her poise enough to survive in the business, my business. The effort would have been more than the reward or benefits to my service. This woman was around 28 years old. She was not attractive but had a nice figure … and was basically her only redeeming asset for escort work. She stood around 5'6" tall with reddish-brown hair. She had some facial and body freckles and was a plain looking girl and was a secretary. None of her family knew about the escort work but her boyfriend knew what she was doing. They did not have children. Her home, with the boyfriend, was on the Peninsula, this is on the way to San Jose from San Francisco, California.

Number 14 was with me for around two weeks. This is a big no, to being good at the work and no to making money. I do not know what she did with the few dollars she made with my service. I did not know why she stopped phoning for calls. Perhaps the girl knew she was not the type of person for escort work. I do not know if she had any habits, she was not with me long enough to find out. But I considered her a lady by the way she dressed. Not a flashy dresser and not a person who liked tight fitting clothes.

Some of the women it was easy to know what their habits are or were at the time but with her … she lived a long way from me and I just did not have a lot of contact with her. She was of average intelligence. She did not have any appeal for many of the clients. Paranoia was a constant with her, because she was afraid of everything and every person that phoned into the service. I would call this a mental problem. She was not able to meet her living expenses is what she had told me. I knew of only one habit she had and that was she loved sex. She once voiced that to me. Lots of guilt feelings about liking sex; and I could never have sent her on a date going to dinner or the movies, because she would have been paranoid or delusional all evening with the client.

She was unable to express her feelings to me in an honest way about what she was doing with her life and especially about escort work. I had not known her long enough to have feelings good or bad about her. I allowed her to stay or leave; it was up to her. It did not matter to me.

Not long after beginning she just stopped phoning into work for calls and I never pursued phoning her for work. I presumed her boyfriend talked her out of working by telling her about all the problems that could happen.

Number 3

This girl was a pleasant person and a redhead around 5'6" tall with a good figure. She was about 23 years of age and had blue eyes and a pretty face. She was an aspiring actress. No one knew about the escort work and her involvement. She had many boyfriends and should have been charging them. No children. She lived in an apartment in San Francisco near the Marina District. One big week with my service and then she refused all calls, except one call. She might have been very good if she gave herself or the escort business a chance. Only one call was done, so she did not make a fortune with me. She paid a bill with that one call. Escort work went against the 'grain' with her. She did not feel comfortable charging for her time. She preferred to give of herself for free to all her boyfriends. I did not know whether her habits were men or drugs or liquor or clothes.

But perhaps her 'drug' was her acting. She was a very sincere actress and that is all she wanted to do with her life. And I found her to be smart and she would have appealed to many clients if she had remained working.

Paranoia was a problem for her; she was afraid of getting caught working for an escort service. She was having trouble meeting her bills. She was frigid. She was feeling guilty that she had ever picked up the phone to call me. She appeared to be an honest woman. I liked her and had wanted her to stay on working with me. I felt she would be a natural for this type of work if she were able to settle down and not be so judgmental of the work. Is she now a well-known actress?

That is my secret.

Letter R

A blunt girl and had no problem speaking her mind. A very pretty black girl that stood around 5'8" tall with a very good figure and she appeared to be more Caucasian than African-American. A nice dresser and who had a lovely personality. Welfare money preceded this endeavor and she had also worked for pimps. Her friends and family knew what she was doing. Mainly she had worked the "streets" prior to working for me. She had too many black men and as she called them, 'big-dick niggers' around her. Her family consisted of one set of twins that were home and she needed to support. She lived in the Fillmore District of San Francisco. She lasted about a month of working and that was off and on. She was good. She did not make a lot of money with me. Transportation was her problem, if she had a vehicle things may have turned out better working for me.

Her money went for her living expenses and drugs. R was no longer working with me because she was lazy and would rather sell drugs. I call her "lazy", because if she had worked hard to get a car then all her "needs" would have been met. Her habits were as she called them, 'big-dick' men and drugs, liquor and clothes. She loved all the excesses of life. She was of average intelligence. She appealed to men who liked black girls or men who just liked beautiful women.

The men that liked good looking women … did not care what the ethnic background was of the woman coming over, because most clients were having sex with the face or body not the ethnicity. The person did not count.

R had problems dealing with her twins. They were too much for her to handle. R could not juggle her money well enough to pay her rent. She just loved sex. No guilt feelings about what she was doing. Her only guilt was how she was going to handle raising her children. The Welfare department was on the verge of taking her children away from her. I was never in her home and possibly it was not clean or something like that; I did not understand why the Welfare department wanted to take her children.

She sold drugs and 'honesty' was a little and foreign word to her and did not fit in her life style. She lived by the 'hustle'. In 'hustle' everything is fair. I liked her. I felt her 'game' was justified. The girl had no way out of the ghetto. She was not higher-education material and did not feel a trade was for her. Hopefully, she was able to finally go back to school and do something more positive with her life and for her children, but it would have taken a huge amount of encouragement to get her to return to school.

R gave me a huge insight into the ghetto life in San Francisco. She let me know that sex was her only way to raise the kids she had. There were no other options for her. Her life to her was hopeless. And with that thinking … she could not raise herself out of the poverty she found herself in at the time.

I often wonder if she ever tried some other way to make a living. But after me … she was probably on the streets and most likely lost her children and worst … her life.

Letter M

This person is not worth talking about except to say that the following describes her best. She was a 5'6" brunette and was foreign looking. She appeared to come from the islands. She had dark hair; dark eyes, and was very slender and had dark circles under her eyes. She was a smoker. She was on welfare. Her friends and family did not know about escorting and she had no boyfriend. She did have a baby girl that was a sickly child and she lived in San Francisco on the avenues. She lasted about two weeks. M was the worst girl at the time that I had who worked for me. M made a little money in that period of time. She drank up her money. I could smell the booze on her breath when I came to her place to pick up my fee. With the unstable women, such as her, I would go to their home to pick up the fee, either the night or day they worked or the first thing the next day. If I let it go too long, there would not be a fee to retrieve.

M was no longer working for me because I fired her for trying to rip me off and out of my fees. M was an alcoholic and possibly a drug user and abuser and had turned just stupid from all the pollutants she put into her body. She did not appeal to any client and had many mental problems. Used her child to get anything she needed.

The poor child was in danger with her at that time. The woman should have been locked up because she appeared to be a schizophrenic or have that type of personality. She could not take care of her person or that of her baby. The child was no doubt sick due to her mother's neglect. I know I am stressing that opinion of her, but it is what I saw and I almost called authorities on her. I did not phone and I wished I could have done more for her child. I doubt if she even liked sex. She had no guilt feelings. She would use anyone if she could. She was and appeared to be crazy. Not honest and would lie cheat and steal. I disliked her. I would prefer to say I hated her and regretted allowing her into my business and life … long enough to know how truly twisted she was and could have been a disaster for my business.

Number 36

This woman was a nice girl to have working with or for me. She was how I wanted all the escorts to be. It was too bad she did not stay working with me for very long.

Number 36 was a most conservative executive looking woman around 35 years of age. She had short dark hair and a very pretty face, but definitely had a stiff look, also, about her person. You would never think in a million years she would want to be paid for going out with men. She looked like a politician's assistant and in reality her day job was as a public relations assistant.

None of her friends or family knew she was escorting.
Boyfriend was White and she did not have children. But I should say, no to mental problems, because I am not sure with her. She was not the type to speak about her personal life and very-well may have had lots of mental problems.

She lived in a share situation in San Francisco. Around one month she had lasted working for me and was all right. Not enough flash about her for the type of work as an escort. She only appealed to a small amount of clients and their fantasies. No, to making money with my escort service and yes, to, she should have made some money.

Great story that she was trying to bring a relative over from one of the European communist countries. She had a foreign name and accent. She just faded away. Perhaps clothes were her habits and she liked nice clothing for the day that went along with her office work, such as suits, etc. A very bright and vibrant woman with a lot of potential to do, well, any job she wanted to aspire too. She appealed to executives ... who fancied themselves to be going out with their secretaries. She had trouble keeping up with her expenses. She did feel guilty. She was most afraid someone would find out what she was doing to pay her bills, because women "hooking" are sent back to their country of origin if arrested for any prostitution. She just liked sex and was an honest woman. I liked her and would have liked her to be a friend for a long time. That did not happen, because very few of the women really ever wanted to be a close friend of mine.

They wanted calls and would speak to me about the calls and many times they would tell their most intimate secrets to me ... yet friendship was not there. In a special way, I was their psychologist (without a license) to turn to, when they needed to talk; but not a real friend to hang out with and have fun with; I was just there to be used and it was okay with me, as long as they paid my fee and were honest with me.

Number 11

This particular woman I have notes on her that I did not hire her. But in reality there was a point and time later on that year that I did give her a couple of calls. Only because I knew the clients would be okay with my sending her. Number 11 just was too obese to hire on the spot, as I did with everyone else. She was around 5'8" tall with very long blonde hair and blue eyes. She had pale skin and weighed in around 250-325 lbs. She looked like a full-back with the Ram's football team. She did have a pretty face and was around 24 years of age. Had, at one time, been a dancer and that was in Alaska. She did not shed her winter coat and just was not someone that men, unless they like the chunk, would want to see and pay for her to visit them. She really needed to return to dancing and lay off of the drugs. Not too surprising, had, also, worked in Alaska as a prostitute. Her friends knew and so did her make-believe boyfriend. She fantasized her driver to be her boyfriend. He was married but drove her around for extra money. (Eventually he became an escort for me.)

I knew she was working with other escort services. That is another reason I did not want her to work with me. She did not have children. Sometimes she lived with her parents and she also lived in share situations with people that were escorts, but escorts not working for me.

Only for the interview did I consider her; I would not hire her because she worked for other services and because of her extreme weight. It was difficult for me to tell her that her weight was a major problem. In fact, she may have been closer to 350 lbs. because she was so tall … the weight may have been that high. But as I said before, I stayed in contact with her and sent her to a couple of calls several months later. I heard she was good. But for my purposes she was not. Her appearance as a gothic or witch dressed … all in black and this did nothing for her appeal to clients. She made money with other services and for the two calls I sent her too. Her money went for her expenses and for her driver, quasi-boyfriend. She enjoyed buying him presents. The redeeming factor with her was that she had a nice personality and that was her saving grace. She only worked with me the two calls, but she did not work after the first time I met her. It was months later. Whether her habits were men or drugs or liquor or clothes; her main habit was her driver and the 'want' she had for him. Her intelligence was average.

Guys that were into big 'mammas' or heavy women for their enjoyment would have liked her, and she had a big identity problem; she actually thought she was not that large, and that she could still get any man she wanted. She took pretty good care of her living situation and her needs. She enjoyed going out with another girl on calls. She had no guilt feelings and was a fairly honest girl.

I liked the girl but was unable to have her work for me on a steady basis, due to not only her weight problem, but the fact she worked with other escort services.

Repeating this working for other escort services is why I never gave calls to some women. It was a dangerous game for me. I had a great escort service and other escort services, at the time, were in the business to make all the money they could and would send women to police or nuts, just because they could make some money. Those services did not care for the women and their lives when I found out a woman was working for another service I fired her. I could not say this enough; if something happened at the other escort service it could rain down on my service and I know that I have repeated this a lot, but there was a losing proposition to having a person work elsewhere. I could see the girl bartering to get out of jail by giving my service up to the police.

Number 95

This girl lived in Marin County and should never have picked up the phone to call me. She was never cut out for escort work. This girl was tall and stood around 5'10" and was very large boned. She had short brown hair. She was average looking and her look was fresh. Number 95 was around 23 years of age. She was a student. Her friends and family did not know that she wanted to work for an escort service. She had a white boyfriend and no children. She lived with her parents. Just one call was all she did. Maybe she could have been okay, if she had lasted longer than one call. With only one call she did not make the kind of money she hoped for, if some effort were put into the work. This was proven to her by the one call. She had horse expenses that were getting out of hand. So she thought she would try this line of work. She just faded out of the picture. She never called in again for calls.

This was really not to her liking. Her horses were her habit. She was of average intelligence. She appealed to those clients that liked big women. Not really did she have mental problems, but I did not know her long enough to find out if she had any noticeable and obvious delusions.

Very normal sexual drive and when she spoke I felt as if this was just a quick fling to pay a horse bill. Lots of guilt feelings and worried about people finding out what she was doing. She was an honest person. I liked her but felt she was not really cut out for this kind of work and I was more than happy that she did not push me for more work. Some women could do the work and never look back; this girl would have looked back and cried.

Number 61

This woman wanted to work or perhaps she wanted information on what was going on with my service or any escort service. The girl wanted to be considered, but also had trouble deciding if she wanted to do escort work. She was unattractive and overweight and the only thing going for her was her personality. She was 5'2" tall with mousey brown hair and blue eyes. She should have been and would have made a great public relations person. She had been a legal secretary and was, also, an artist. No boyfriend or children and her friends and family were unaware that she wanted to be an escort. She lived in Mill Valley, California.

She was never hired. But she always wanted to begin working with me. No good at the work, because she never began working, so it follows that she did not make any money. She never started, but money she did have from whatever sources she spent foolishly. I could never hire her in good conscience. She would have been unhappy after the first call. I preferred to have her as a friend. God, this person phoned me a lot for work and that is how I got to know her well. She liked drinking and socializing and was always hunting for a man. She had above average intelligence.

Those men that liked girls with sacks over their heads she may have appealed too and I know that is cruel, but appearance was everything as an escort. (Except for the school teacher I spoke about in my book, The Making of a Madam, a 20th Century Woman.) Maybe I was wrong, because the school teacher had lots of requests, but by the time she had come to my service, the escort service was pretty well known and people expected a good looking woman to knock on the door.

This woman had a problem centering her being, which was so hyper she could not concentrate on what was appropriate for her to do with her life. She could not keep her money or handle her money, well. She appeared to be a normal woman about feelings toward sex and her desires were not 'out there'. She just could not find enough warmth and sex from the men she was attracted too. If she had started working for me, I am sure she would have had a lot of guilt feelings, because she felt guilty just thinking about starting as an escort. If she could get away with it she would try to cheat you. I knew this after being her friend for a while. I liked her, but felt she was a fair-weather friend. But as a public relations person, due to her strong personality, she would have done very well in life if she had chosen that path. This was a very chatty person and you felt as if you had known her all your life. I liked speaking to her on the telephone but work was always out of the question.

Number 53

This girl came to me as a friend of another girl that worked for me for a long time. She was not the best person to have as an employee. Number 53 was around 5'7" tall and very slender, in fact slender to the point of unattractiveness. She had brown hair and an average face. Her manner of dress was not the best. She was a waitress and had a variety of other jobs. Some of her friends knew and family. She had a husband and he was white and there were no children. She lived with her husband in Marin County, California. She was with me on and off for about a month and was all right. She could have made more, but she did make some money. It went for extras in life that she felt necessary to have.

Her husband did not want her to really do this type of work. Drug....she liked cocaine. She was of average intelligence. She appealed to the customers that liked skinny girls ... into drugs. Lots of issues going on in her head and she was very unhappy. She had trouble keeping everyone happy; mainly because she wanted to keep everyone happy, which as any person knows is impossible to do. She liked being with other women.

Lots of guilt feelings.

Not a very honest person with herself or anyone else.

I did not like her.

I had only hired her because she was a friend of a woman that was currently working for me. I think because of her husband not wanting her to work as an escort caused her to lie to him and me and absolutely any other person. I could see her sitting down in her living room chatting with her friend that did work for me and then convinced herself that being an escort was the way to get the money she wanted for drugs.

Then, after working a few calls, realizing this was not the work for her.

Number 52

This girl had worked for a beauty school and loved doing nails. The woman was around 5'4" tall with a cute figure and a cute face. She had a very nice smile, but was not a beautiful girl. She was around 23 years old at the time she first began working with me. She, concurrently, worked on nails in a beauty salon and then at night as an escort for me. No family knew about the escort work and only a few friends knew she worked with me. Yes, to a boyfriend and he was a white man, and a big yes, to children. She lived in Marin County with her boyfriend and children. She only did a couple of calls and was acceptable as an escort.

Not as much money made that she could have made. She spent the money on extra things she wanted. She preferred to be a cheap tramp and give "it" (sex) away, so that is why she was no longer working with me. A prissily woman, who was caught up in a film of her making, that she wanted to do it all and was worthy enough to do it all. This was because she liked herself and she did like to drink. Totally, and I do mean totally, a self-centered person. I would call her a stupid woman and feel that was an accurate description of whatever you might find inside her skull. Just about all men she appealed too. Poor identity and thought process. She and her boyfriend were not getting along at the time and she was worried about possibly living without him and how her finances would be. She liked sex and was a latent bi-sexual. She pretended to have guilt feelings, but in fact, felt no guilt about anything, she wanted, all, for herself and would prefer to weasel things out of men than to be honest. A gift from a man was telling her that she was special. Not honest with herself, but not smart enough to do anything crooked. Although she could be talked into anything, when given enough time necessary to convince her.

I liked her, although I did not think she was very bright. Her eyes were open but no one was home, most of the time.

Actually the perfect escort, the type some men wanted. When I got rid of her I was not worried, at all, that she could find some guy to take care of her.

Number 57

This girl was a friend of another girl working with me at the time. That is the only reason I gave her a chance. Number 57 was around 25 years old and 5'4" tall with brown hair and a round face and a chubby little body that it was a wonder that she thought anyone would pay for her. I know that sounds brutal but she just was not attractive or had the personality to wow someone as an escort. She was sort of pretty but not really. Some of the other women I hired who were heavy, actually, had personalities that could get them in the door and they could make money. Not her.

I had met someone working the streets in Hollywood, California and she was overweight and had a face that was very average, but the men loved her and she made money due to her personality. If a woman is without a personality and lacks appearance she is not meant for the escort business. This was that type of woman. She was a student and did some sort of office work. Some of her friends knew but probably not her family. Sometimes she was with this man; their relationship was not always a constant in her life. Thankfully, she did not have children. I say, thankfully, because she was a mess and could not take care of herself. She lived in San Francisco in an apartment with other girls attending school. With me, she did just about a couple of calls; I did not want to send her out to people because I felt the girl was not attractive enough or into the work enough to benefit herself or my business. She was not good for the business and did not make any money with me and the money she did make was minimal and paid her bills barely. My business came from ads and a great deal of word of mouth. She would have spoiled the word of mouth clients calling.

I did not want her lack of services with my escort service any longer, so I did not give her anymore calls. She liked drugs and liquor. She was or had above average intelligence. There was a lack of not only physical appeal, but personality was lacking. My clients would see someone, even if the person was not great looking, as long as the person could keep a conversation going.

This person failed to have any assets worth promoting to a client. A complete dud in speaking to people she first met. I tested her out by just having her over the house when other escorts were in the room. She failed miserably to speak to them. She was caught up with the moral majority and that was a mental problem or dilemma if she wanted to do escort type work. This was something I could not understand; if you hate the thought of escort work, why waste the time trying to work? She could not keep up with her living expenses, so that is an excuse to hound me for work? I do not think so, and wished she would have just gone to some political organization to work.

Number 57 liked women and that is probably why she wanted to do escort work ... to work out her sexual desires, but there were not woman phoning or not a lot, who wanted an overweight and horrible personality person to come over and take their money, while the person worked out her lesbian uptight problems. And continually spouted her political beliefs.

Lots of guilt feelings. Not a particularly honest person. I sort of liked her but did not really want to have anything to do with her. I felt that if I encouraged her to do this type of work it would go against the girl, because the girl was just not suited for escort work. Against, meaning she would not flourish in the business and would have great disappointment doing calls. Even greater disillusionment than she thought she would have.

This was a judgment call for me and there were times when it was necessary to dissuade the willing. If you call her being "willing".

Number 46

This woman picked up the phone and called me to ask about being an escort. Another time, later down the road; I wish the phone had burned her hand and she dropped it and thought about street-walking or something else other than phoning my service.

Number 46 was around 38 years old and looked it. She had a flat flabby chest left over from having children and really needed a breast augmentation. Her face looked to be 38 years of age and she was average in appearance. She was the Queen of Polyester. Her clothes looked like they came direct from any stores bargain basement, sale. She was around 5'4" tall with short brown hair. Surprisingly, worked for a well-known clothes company in San Francisco as a secretary, which was very surprising because the clothes she wore just sucked. Perhaps only a couple of people that she knew, did she tell, what she was doing. She was lucky enough to have a boyfriend and children. Her boyfriend may have been her husband. She lived in Marin County, California. She was with me about two weeks. She was well liked. I can't understand totally the "why". Other than she gave great conversation. I thought she was another "school teacher" type that had worked for me before and was accepted by the clients.

Not particularly a money maker, but I suspect she could have made money working with me. The money earned went for her many living expenses and bills. She was too afraid people would find out what she was doing. Also, she had caught up with her bills, but she did call me back and, wanted to come back to work for me. After those bills were paid. I would not have her back, because she was inconsiderate when she left and did not tell me. She just avoided my phone calls, which I thought was rude behavior. No noticeable habits.

Perhaps her family could be considered her habit, their wants and needs. Average intelligence and a very typical housewife with few goals in life; all her goals were immediate needs. No long term aspirations.

Those clients that wanted a girlfriend and companion who made them feel at ease is where her appeal ... lay. She had been an abused child and was fearful of being in a violent situation. She was having problems trying to keep her from abusing her own children. I knew this because she confided in me.

I knew many things about the women because they felt that they could tell me all their secrets, which was the truth; I still will not reveal whom these women are. She had problems to discipline her children and keeping up with paying her many bills. She was a latent sadist. She had lots of guilt feelings in regard to this work and also in her handling of her own children.

Those children were uppermost in her mind and I do hope that the day came when she sought professional help. She was a fairly honest person, but she was sneaky. I thought she was an okay person, but I did not feel she could make lots of money at this work, unless she went for the kinky calls, which wanted whips and chains.

My service did not cater to men that wanted kinky sex. There were a few men that filtered in occasionally, but there were other services that could have fulfilled their needs of malicious intent on a women's body. She would have had to work elsewhere, in order to be the 'acting out' sadist; she had hanging out inside her mind and soul.

Number 73

This was a southern woman who should have returned to the South for some training in manners.

Also, she needed some Bible knowledge, concentrating on the Ten Commandments, because she was not keeping up with the language, and desires of God. This girl was in the cute classification, but she was not beautiful. She was around 25 years old and from the South and she came complete with a southern accent in her speaking voice. She was around 5'4" tall and slender with almost a flat chest. Her hair was brown and her eyes were blue. She was referred to me by a couple of male friends of mine and each one had been with her and called her a pet name as Ms. 'tuna fish'. At the time I wondered what that meant. She is the one that said tuna fish to me and I had to chuckle because that was not a nice statement and all I could think of was that it had to mean smell.

Maybe it meant something else, but I do believe it meant she was smelly.

She was some sort of waitress, I am not sure if it was food or alcoholic beverages. She was also a hustler and a thief from the South. Her friends and some of her family knew what she was doing. She had a white boyfriend. Maybe there were children in her life, but she had trouble with the truth, and she never said she had children. She lived in a share situation with two other girls that were working for me.

Possibly three months, give or take a week, I had her on the list of women to phone and give work too. She was good, but not a clean person. Yes, to her making money and no for me, because she did not give me my fee. She spent the money on drugs and clothes and living high on the hog.

I fired her for lying, cheating, and stealing from me and customers. Drugs and lots of men, she could not have enough men, so they became her addiction and increasing habit. She was sharp. Most men liked her. She did not know friends from enemies and right from wrong. Keeping her expenses paid was her issue. She liked women. Not a guilty bone in her body. Although, she did dress well and that deceived a person into thinking she was clean.

This person never saw an honest day in her life. She would use anyone she found in her path. Men were the first victims and than people such as me that were nice to her. I liked her as a person until I found out how two-faced the girl was and had been to me.

Every mean cliché can be attached to this person. But I do believe my two friends summed it up best, she was Ms. Tuna Fish.

Number 47

This girl was not the sharpest tack in the home improvement box. Slender blonde with blue eyes and she was around 21 years of age. She was 'sort' of pretty, but I felt she wouldn't look very good at thirty because she was aging fast. She was a student and worked as a waitress. Not her family knew about the escort work, but some of her friends knew. She had more than one boyfriend and thankfully no children. She lived in a share situation, in an apartment. She lasted off and on around two months. She was 'sort' of bad, if anyone can be bad at trying to be nice. She was not a star performer and spent her money on anything she felt like spending money on. She was lazy and did not want to put a lot of effort into working.

Her 'me first' attitude and drugs were what she found important to spend money on. Her first, just she, and no one else counted in her book … all other humans were to be used and in some cases abused. She was of average to below average intelligence.

Those customers that liked skinny young dumb blondes to listen to them would want to see her. Lots of mental problems and would have benefited from professional counseling, she may have or would have listened to a professional. She would not listen to anyone else. She couldn't keep her money together long enough to pay bills. She liked women. No guilt feelings.

Not a particularly honest person, in fact, not particularly anything; a very nondescript person; one who could rob a bank and everyone say or give different descriptions about her. I felt she was just about close to being stupid, if she was just not just plain stupid.

A hard-headed person and this was due to her not being very bright.

Chapter Twenty-One
Male Escorts

Speaking about the male escorts is different. I did not have the same thoughts about them. The women had to be protected at all costs, but the men were not usually going to a home or a location that was intimidating and possibly dangerous for them. I wish that there had been more work for the men.

The interviews were always interesting. Some of the men actually thought that they had to 'hit' on me in order to get the job. I found that to be funny. I drew the line in dating men that worked with me or signed up to work with me. But there were a few men that I knew and they did not answer any advertising I may have put in the newspaper; I may have had relationships with them at times. For the most part I would have the men on a list and there was a description of them that I was able to draw upon when the need arose. As the years of my service increased, so did the list. Looking back, if computers were as abundant as they are now, I would have had all the men's photos on the web site and could have had many more calls for those guys.

With a few hundred men phoning to be escorts I just asked them to send their resumes to my P.O. Box in San Rafael and I would look the resume over and put the man in a 'to see' list or a 'see if he phones back' list. I just did not have the time to meet all the men and explain to them that the calls were not that abundant for them.

Many of the men were very persistent and wanted to be only seeing men. I tried sending men to other men about two or three times. I never received my fee. So I was not going to give anymore effort to have men meeting men through me. It was an easy decision for me because when I did not receive my money there was not any other motive for me to be handling men for men meetings.

There was a rise in the escort services for men that just wanted to see men, so I do not believe that my limiting my business to heterosexual couples was any big deal for men, who wanted to be male escorts for other males.

I made the decision to just have a heterosexual business. Some men tried to talk me into sending them to men but I refused those phone calls. If men wanted to see women I would put them on my books or the list of men available for that purpose. There were also transvestites, transsexuals, bisexuals, and a few gender-blenders that do not know which way they are going. I had one drag performer come to me and he was very nice, but another scammer, because he did not pay me for the call I sent him on. There were a couple of men that I did have sexual relations with and that is because I knew them before I ever had *Professional Escorts*.

Those men just wanted to make some extra money and thought that their individual prowess was spectacular in the bedroom. I never paid a man but I did have some fun with the two I knew. In the two cases the men were fantastic and a joy to have sex with. The other men, I have no idea if they were good or not.

It is important to note: that the men were not to accept money directly from the women. When the man arrived at the hotel room or home of a female client the woman had been told to have the fee in an envelope and the expenses for the evening.

The male escort was to pay for everything out of the envelope and then return the envelope with any change for the evening back to the woman. Of course this would be minus his fee for the evening. Both parties liked this way of handling the money because the women that phoned me wanted to parade the man as their companion and that accompanying person was paying for the evening to be with her. In my speaking about the men, there will not be a long list of questions answered, just eight questions.

Questions: Male Escorts

1. A brief physical description
2. What other employment did he have?
3. was he able to woo women or did he have sex appeal?
4. Did he make money and have call backs?
5. Was he the bedroom type or the strictly dating type?
6. How long he was on the books to work?
7. Was he a homosexual man or a heterosexual man?
8. What did I think of this man?

Letter A

This man came to me with his girlfriend. She wanted to work and he wanted her to work. They were students at the time in Berkeley. Or maybe it was just he that was a student at the University of California at Berkeley. Anyway, I do not list her as one of my escorts, because even though she was pretty good as an escort, it was letter A that was more interesting.

In the time I knew them both, he stood out as a friend to me and she and he eventually married and with time divorced and she went back to Connecticut where that they had come from or lived before coming to California. She told me her father had been killed and may have been in organized crime in the East.

Letter A was around 5'4" tall with black hair and pale skin and no facial hair. When he briefly worked for me he was just a student. He had his girlfriend working so they could meet their expenses. They virtually had nothing extra in their budget to live on before meeting and working for me. Their apartment in Berkeley looked barren and their automobile was falling apart. The car was a working wreck. He thought he was attractive to all women and he belonged to some group where he would hit on many or most of the women in the group. But to say that he was some man that women would just run to and want to meet. I would say no. He was not what I would call a 'hot' guy.

He was cute and loveable when he was young and at this time in running my service. As he aged, he became an alcoholic and a grumpy person.

Well, in his working day, he only saw this one man. Yes, a man. He thought that he could go to the call and not do anything. He was always harping on his girlfriend about how to do a call and what not to do. But when it came to sending him on his first call with a man, well he was a complete failure. I do not know what he and the client did, but I do know that the client wrote him a bad check and never made the check good. I gave him a rather bad time of it … letting him know that he had broken the cardinal rule of not accepting checks and on top of that … he did not get paid the correct amount for the time he spent with the client. No checks to a person calling the escort service for the first time.

All and all it was a failure for him and he never wanted to see a client again. But the client did phone back for him, which was pretty funny because I guess he must have been able to woo this guy. In actuality, the guy probably just wanted another 'freebee' from A. He was mortified that the guy wrote the bouncing check. If a client wanted wonderful hours of intelligent conversation … this man was the dating type. He did not have overwhelming sexual appeal that could classify him as a bedroom type. He did not look like a sexy guy or some guy that women would want to jump all over him and write lover letters too. But he did have some charm. He was on my call list of men for about a month. But after the check bounced with that initial guy, he did not want any more calls to do. He was just going to leave the work up to his girlfriend and when he gave her some lip for not doing this or that correctly we were able to put him in his place after reminding him of the mess he made of his only call.

He and his girlfriend would sit at my mother's home for hours waiting for calls. He would wait there, while his girlfriend took the car and went on a call. My mother wanted to charge them for the amount of use from watching her television. That was pretty funny and we all laughed over it. But in reality, mom was probably very serious about charging. Mom would have put a meter on the bathroom if she could figure out how to install it. He was bisexual and not too happy about it. I think as he grew older he may have come to grips with his attraction to other men. But he did drink a lot as he grew older and would do heroin and other drugs after meeting men in bars in San Francisco. I liked him for many years. But he did something to me that made me very angry. He accused me of stealing some gun he had at his home. I never did steal the stupid thing and it was probably a girlfriend of his. But he eventually became a lawyer and told me to burn my papers on clients and escorts. Well, I just did not take his advice. That is why I am able to remember so many of my escorts. I have notes going back 25 years. I also hope he found out who did take his gun.

For him … I would be considered a 'skeleton' in his closet. In this revision of the book … I found out he is now deceased.

Letter W

This was a British man that had gone to school at Cambridge and wanted to be an escort. He also was paid, by me, to initially help me write my book when I lived on Graceland Avenue in San Rafael, California. My son, Adam, says he was just another con man and wanted to take money from me. If truth be known, the book he helped me on went absolutely nowhere. But he did write some agent or director in Hollywood to find out if the man was interested in my book. The man showed some interest, but Letter W and I just stopped working together on it. I was tired of paying him. He was around 6'1" tall and a white man with very white skin. Nice looking. He was married and lived in San Francisco in a small apartment.

He really needed extra income.

At the time I was impressed with him, because he had gone to Cambridge University in the country of the United Kingdom. He had a degree and knew Mr. Rice who had a few well-known musicals out at the time. He told me he wanted to tell Mr. Rice about me and see if he wanted to do anything with my book. Nice con and it worked for awhile. I paid him well for a lot of notes from my talking to him about the business. He tried working at various jobs but was not doing well. He did not last at anything long and wanted to own his own business, which he eventually did. He owned a winery with a partner in the Sonoma County area.

I am not sure what he did with the winery, but I do know he was an excellent sales person. I think he was very charming and intelligent. He could woo women and was not faithful to his wife. I did not find him attractive enough for me to have sex with him. I am sure he had sex appeal for women that liked foreign men or men with British accents.

The only money he made was, from me for helping me put some notes on paper for my book. It was the early 1980s and he was having trouble finding his niche in life. I never sent him out on a call, so there would not be any call backs.

There just was not any work for him. I would say, from my point of view, that he was strictly the dating type of man. He had manners and if there had been calls for him … I would have sent him to a client.

He was not overly attractive or a sexy man. But that was my opinion. He may very well have been sexy to some women. I do remember a few of my escorts liking him when they came over to my home and he was there. But I would discourage their thinking about hitting on him by telling them that he was married and it seemed to work and because he did not have money worked even better to keep them away from him. He was on the books for a couple of years. But he never did a call that I can remember.

Although, he may have had one call, I am just not sure. He was a heterosexual man and I liked him. He was a great companion and gave me many ideas and kept me thinking about writing. I was happy to have him around because he was a pleasant person.

I wish him no ill will.

Number 5

This was a man that had been at my first party and we photographed him both with clothes on and naked. He had a beautiful body and was not afraid to show it off. He had been a football player long enough to have a pension coming in. Number 5 stood about 6'4" tall and was a very beautiful African-American. He had strong features and dark skin. His eyes were black and so was his hair and he kept his hair cut close to the scalp. Sometimes he would shave his head. His face was more pretty or feminine and he was very muscular from working out at gyms.

Before I met him he had been a guard at San Quentin and was also an ex-pro-football player. He smiled a lot and he wore white clothing a great deal to show off his blackness. He had a lot of pride in being an African-American. At the time of working for me or being on my books ... he worked as a chef and then as a personal trainer. He also modeled for someone. I am not sure who, but he did want to be a male model. Unfortunately, he got into drugs and began selling them.

He could woo any woman and had enough sex appeal to woo many women and he did just that. He had lots of girlfriends and wanted lots more. I really think he would have done very well making pornography films. He had such a great body and especially where women like a body to be great. If he wanted to make fast money that would have been the best way for him to go. He was great in bed, but I know that his brother was even better. His brother did not have the pretty face but he was beautiful to me. I loved his brother. We were friends for many years. His brother was and is one of the top three in bed for me.

Number 5 is in the top 20 for me. As a sex expert from experience, not from holding a degree in that field, (If I were holding a degree in the field it would be a PhD.) I feel more than able to inform people of how he was in bed and how he had magnetism. He had plenty of sex appeal; and this is a man that would not be happy being old. He was just too great as a young man and as a ladies' man. He did do, I believe, one or two calls for a couple situation. From what I remember it was for him to be with the woman in front of her husband. I think it was another female escort that I sent to that couple along with him; I could be wrong. But he did not make the money he should have being on my list of men to call.

There just were not the calls for him. I believe the couple phoned back for him. But again, I am not sure if this was the escort for that couple. He was the dating type and the bedroom man around town. If a woman went out with him she would have wanted to see him in her bedroom. He was one hell of a pleaser in bed. Many women would want to go out with a man that was so attractive and it did not matter that he was not white. Beautiful people can have a lot of interracial dating. He was one of these people. He was on the books, to work, for years. I knew that I could phone him at anytime for a call.

He was always open for work. No matter if he was in a relationship or not. I believe he was bisexual. But he preferred women. I liked him. His personality did not waver much, always friendly. This was a person that should not be old. If there was ever a magic wand for making people young, it should be used or have been used on him.

I would find it difficult to see him as an older person.

Number 11

This person was a character. I met him when he was 19 years of age and he went downhill and kept going downhill all the while I knew him. When I began my escort service he wanted to work. I put him down for work, but only used him a couple of times as a body guard. He was one of the men I brought with me when I had a problem over a man writing a bad check. I spoke about this incident in my prior book, which is called The Making of a Madam. This man and I do use the term lightly. Was about 6'tall and had black hair with dark eyes and always seemed to be trying to recover from a lisp he had in childhood. He did not graduate high school or if he did, he never told me. The usual story was that he had dropped out and he had the character of the guy you find as a carnival worker. Always smiling and looking at the underage girls. Trying to con anyone that will give him the time of day and this is another person that aging would be a bother to him. His antics and lack of education would never play well in the adult world and especially in the 21st century. He belonged more in the 1950s.

You could picture him with his hair slicked back and wearing tight jeans and driving a shinny sports car, so he could pick up girls and impress his other worthless friends as they cruised down the main street in any town. He worked at little jobs when he could find work and usually he was trying to get a girl to support his way of life. I can't remember any specific job, other than selling drugs.

When he was young he had some sex appeal, but as he aged, he was on the wrong end of a bad line to meet people. He was constantly trying to woo women and then he turned to wooing men or coning them out of something valuable. I would never send him out on a call. He was just not educated enough to have an intelligent conversation with a woman of means. According to him … he was the bedroom type. I believe he was not the bedroom type or the dating type because I had slept with him when we first met and he was young. After he got older he was obnoxious. A major "turn down" if you were a woman.

Many times I saw him as a drunken slob in an obnoxious drinking stupor. He was sort of on the books for years, but I would never trust him to go to a client's home. He did talk his way into doing something for a client for me and then he brought a lot of his friends over to the man's home and they tried to hustle this man. He just could not be trusted.

At first he was heterosexual and then he just turned into a homosexual man and then sometimes into being a bisexual man. He had many psychological problems and much that was wrong with him was due to his intelligence just being very low. When he was young I liked him … as he grew older I began to hate him. I totally went past dislike and right into hate.

That is where I am today.

I only mention him because he kept coming into my life while I was running the service. At first he was fun having him around, and, then as the years past he was worthless and I wanted not one thing to do with him or his friends. He turned into a quasi-con-man and creep. Again, very uneducated and had no ambition to improve his lot in life. That about sums him up.

Number 3

This man was very nice looking and was 6'4" tall and had blue eyes. He was always getting into trouble for fighting. That means going before judges in Marin County, California. He was very into martial arts and was a black belt. He was also a friend to Number 11. That friendship was brutal for both of them. They eventually tried having their own escort service and making trouble for me. Then they wanted to have a service devoted to just seeing men. How they made out with that business venture, I have no idea. Between them they may have had two brain cells to rub together and get a spark.

They felt that they could answer a phone as I had and do as well as me. Yeah. Not on their best day could they have done as well as me. Many people had a poor opinion of me answering the phone and felt they could do it too. My business was much more than just answering a telephone. I was required to know each client's preferences and each escorts likes and dislikes. Then there was the attention to all the business matters that comes with owning your own business. People only saw me pick up a telephone and had no idea all the other intricate details I had to attend too, and on a daily basis.

The brother of Number 5 went out to the bars one time and began rousting people telling them to never mess with my service. Because; it happened one time that these two 'want-to-be' escort service owners had a girl of mine come to their place for a bachelor party.

They tried to hold her there and then phoned me. I was furious with them. She had danced and they did not want to pay her. Well, the brother of Number 5 made sure that never happened again. Word was all over town not to mess with me or they would have to deal with the brother. He was very large and had done more than one tour in Viet Nam and other things for our government. He was just plain mean if you got him mad. He was a very good friend and did not like what these two clowns did. He, also, had a martial arts black belt and there were a lot of people that wanted to see these two men fight. In fact it would have been a great fight if they ever came to blows. But my money would have been on the brother of number 5.

Number 3 was 6'4" tall with blue eyes and blonde hair. He was a lean muscular body type and had a cute face. He was probably 25 years of age when I met him. If I remember correctly he was a bartender at first and then tired to have an escort service. He was able to woo women and he had a lot of sex appeal. At one point I liked him but did not want to have any problems with his girlfriend. Theirs was a very violent relationship. It would be, no, on both counts about making money. I went out with him one time to take me to a ball in San Francisco. He was very well-dressed and I enjoyed his company and dancing with him. I did not pay him. But I believe I paid for the tickets to the ball.

He was appealing sexually and I was very sad when I found out that he had also turned to liking sex with men. Sad because if he had better male friends he may never have given up women, but he did not have too many great experiences with women. He was adopted and possibly his DNA was messed up. You just never know what DNA a person inherits from their parents. I want to say that there are the body structures of a human, but the mind and all that DNA has to be measured. I am sure, someday, we will know how to measure the DNA that our minds are given from both our natural parents.

His on again, off again, girlfriend was verbally abusive and I was told she would lash out at him and belittled him in public. He used the whips and chains with her and sometimes she turned him in to the police. She was nuts because her actions found her going over to his house for the games he liked to play. He was available to me for a year or two. But I did not want to send him on a call because he could not be trusted and he was into this dominate personality. That means whipping or hitting women and letting his temper get the better of him. He had a spot in the basement of his parent's home that he turned into a location for sadistic ritual beatings. Mostly, on his girlfriend but he did beat other women. He was changing as he got older and I do not know if this sadistic side of him ever just went too far and he killed someone. I would not have put it past him to kill someone and then bury the body. He would have been the type to bury the body under the house. He was bisexual. At first I liked him and as he grew older I learned to dislike him. I did not want to be alone with him. He tried to hit me once when we were having sex and that was enough for me. He must have liked rough sex to a point that he could not have just friendly sex or casual sex.

Foreplay with him was light spanking and then he got a strange look in his eyes and the animal in you … just knew he was going to hurt your body. This was really sad because he was a nice looking guy and I did not want to dislike him but I do know that he had a killer personality. His family had adopted him when he was very young and maybe his DNA had some violent tendencies.

No telling, I just know what I observed in him. I could not understand his family allowing a den of whips and chains. Strange.

Number 50

This was a nice friendly guy and he had a wife or a girlfriend that was living as his wife. Not too sure about the story. She made all the money and they had a home in San Francisco. He was or had been a professional dancer and I believe the both of them had gone on tour together dancing. I just don't remember all the details. They had gone to someplace in the orient. She may have still been dancing. He came on *The People Are Talking* show with me. His clothes on the show were not what he usually wore and I think it had something to do with his wife that day. She did not want him to go on the show or to allow his face to be seen.

The show accommodated his wish not to be seen, but I was not happy about his clothes. He usually dressed nicely and had a positive demeanor about himself. But that day his pants were too short for him and the rest of the wardrobe did not look like a person I would have sent to women of means. I trusted him because he was not a violent person. Not like number 3.

He was about 5'9" tall and had blonde hair and I believe his eyes were blue but they could have been hazel. He was not a heavy person and not a muscular person. He normally dressed very nice and liked clothes that were in style.

All I remember is he danced. He may have gone into real estate or perhaps his girlfriend did, or maybe not, but they did own their own home. He also drove around another girl that worked for me and she worked at other services. I allowed it because the girl was very overweight and I just did not have that many calls for her. So he was a part-time driver for my service. He was able to woo women and he did have a certain amount of sex appeal. He made a little money. One of the people I sent him to, did phone back. I liked sending him to clients. I knew they would be safe with him.

Again, there just was not a great deal of straight calls to send him or anyone else. I think he thought of himself as the bedroom type and that is important. I thought of him as the dating type. I think it was about two years we knew each other. During that time, I only knew him to be a heterosexual man. I liked him and thought he was a perfect man to send on dating calls. He was not intimidating and could hold a conversation. Plus, he loved to dance and most or many women liked to dance. I felt that I could trust him to take a woman out and not be harsh or neglectful with her.

No, I never had an affair with him. He would come over to my place and we talked a lot. I enjoyed his company.

Number 60

This was a man that thought he looked like *Magnum PI* a television series, or should I say Tom Selleck, the actor, who was the star of the *Magnum PI* series, except this man was shorter. Many people thought he looked like the actor and I was rather blasé about it; for me he was too short and the real Tom Selleck was taller and more my type. He was about 5'7" tall or possibly 5'8" tall. His hair was the same color as Sellecks' hair and that was dark, which he may have colored in order to resemble Selleck. He wore a mustache and had a nice built. He was a person that entered contest as a Tom Selleck look-a-like. He may have done some parties as a look-a-like. Other than that I am not sure if he worked. He used the notion that he looked like a movie star in order to get women. I think the 'real deal' is always the best. But I suppose he was cute. I think I sent him to someone but I just cannot remember, so I cannot say if he made money.

He preferred to think of himself as the bedroom type. Only about a month or two was he available to work for me. He ended up meeting a woman that he married from one of my parties. A director was there who did documentaries for India and Germany and he fell for his niece. I had nothing to do with introducing them but the director blamed their relationship on me. He was from India and wanted the girl to marry a person from that culture.

He held a grudge against me for absolutely nothing. I heard that the guy ended up working in construction or something like that and they had a child.

The director was furious. As far as I knew he was a heterosexual man. I liked him but thought his ego was a little too big for his skull. He was another male escort that I knew at a distance. We did not really become good friends and he was not one of the people that would hang around my house.

Chapter Twenty-Two
How Much for Escorts?

No matter where I am or when a person speaks to me about this business and how it was they never fail to ask how much money the escorts were making. What did the escorts make, while they worked for me, has been an ongoing question in interviews and between friends and family. Well, I could tell you but then I would have to burn this book. So what I will tell you is that the men and women that worked very steadily made money. You can get your own calculator out and touch the subject between your fingers for awhile.

The best I will do for you, the reader, is tell you what the fees were.

Massage
- In the beginning it was $30 for an hour when I had *Fingers Outcall Massage*, plus tip.
- Then the fee went up to $50 per hour when I had *Professional Escorts*, plus tip.
- Then the fee went up to $100 and $150 respectively for an hour when I *had Professional Escorts*, plus tip.
- Plus tip and gas money if possible ----for both services.

Escorting
- . One to three hours was $100 for touring the Bay Area and the price went up to $150 for three to four hours for touring the Bay Area as I was in business longer. Plus tip
- We could arrange a limousine service
- Escorting at home $100 an hour when I first started *Professional Escorts*
- $500 per night when I first started *Professional Escorts*
- $150 per hour after being in business awhile with *Professional Escorts*
- $1,000 per night after a few years with *Professional Escorts*
- If the client took an escort out for a half hour and brought the escort back to his or her home it was still anywhere from $100 to $150 per hour and the client still had to pay the charge for going out, which was from $100 to $150 for three to four hours. It did not matter if they were only out a few minutes or a total of four hours out in public.

- Client's paid $150 for the three to four hours of what should have been going out and then as soon as he or she is in an enclosed area the price begins at $100 to $150 per hour.
NO EXCEPTIONS
- All the above was plus tip

Films
- If the escort brought films to a client's home the fee was more and in the beginning it was $50 to bring films and that was if it were only $30 for a massage or escort.
- Then it was $50 to see someone and it climbed to $75 for the films.
- Always having a plus tip added for films … this lasted about eight months then discontinued. Too cumbersome for the escorts or masseuses to bring films and machines to the client's homes.

21st Century Escorting
- The escorts make anywhere from $100 per half hour to $500 per hour depending upon what area of the country the escort works
- To spend the night the sky is the limit.

Escorting Trips
If a client wanted a companion to accompany him or her on a trip it depended upon the location. A trip to Mexico may cost more than a trip to Santa Barbara or Los Angeles. It always depended upon where the location was and if the escort found the location more appealing.
Plus expenses.
Always, the average trip was $500 and that was usually around two to four days. Plus expenses. A trip to Europe was more and could cost $1,000 for the entire trip, plus expenses. Some trips were $1,000 per day depending upon who the escort was. I charged $1,000 a day to take me anywhere because it took me away from my business, plus expenses. Many escorts just charged $100 per day for trips to any destination.
Plus expenses.
The entire trip had to be paid for in advance. I would keep the money for the escort and give it to the escort when they came back, so they did not spend the money on expenses that were to be paid for by the client. The expenses were souvenirs and most definitely food and beverages.
This up-front collection process, also, helped the escort if the trip did not go well and the client did not wish to pay the entire fee.

We were not in the refund business.

The escort had to give me a driver's license number or some photo identification before going on any trips with a client. I did not care if the client had used the service for years. Any person could flip out and hurt someone. I did not want that to happen, so we made sure the escort and the client felt comfortable that someone knew who everyone was and that "someone" was me.

For the regular escort calls, the escort had to phone me as soon as he or she was not out any longer. They could be in a hotel room or a private home and it was necessary to phone me, so the client knew that the new price had just kicked in and he or she was now on a different clock.

A lot of escorts now use the Internet to acquire clients by posting their faces and/or figures online with their own web sites. They charge a fee for their clients to see complete nudity or partial nudity. Some charge by the minute.

Many male and female escorts believe they are safer doing this type of work. Not true. Anyone can find out where they live. Some of them combine talking online with the clients for a fee. The old way was to just have an 800 number so clients may speak to a sexy voice. In some areas of the country the 800 numbers are still active for people that prefer being paid or paying by the minute charges to speak dirty to a man or woman.

There have been numerous stories in the courts that are on television and in the newspapers where clients have paid enormous phone bills to the phone companies that in turn give the revenue collected to the person that has the 800 number. For the control of disease these numbers are a god send but in the practical world they are a nightmare for the phone companies accounting departments to collect.

The many introduction services have some of those businesses using computers to mix and match people. But this does not keep people from lying on the forms they fill out. If human nature was completely honest, than the introduction services would be a great big success. But, except for the occasional marriage these services produce ... they are just a way to spend some extra cash you may have.

There are so many services, now, that all you have to think for yourself is the "why" are they around? Are they in business to make you happy? No. Of course not, they are in the business of making money. Your happiness is not important to them, but if you are happy they may want to use your face and testimonial reactions, so they can increase their coffers.

Their systems are far less controlled than how and when I ran my *Professional Escort* service. *Professional Escorts* was not operated on doing business by fractions and numbers that kept going on and on. Some services also wanted the drivers to be paid by the client; who just added more tension between the escort and client. When a girl had a driver she was compelled to ask for more money from the client, just so she could pay her driver.

Those services also wanted the girl to charge the client for having to use a credit card. But what I wish everyone to know is that I made the math very simple. This was not to be long math. It was short math and quick and easy. When an escort went to a clients' home and he was perhaps drinking, I did not want him to have to get out a calculator to add up the night's fee. No change would need to be given.

Tips were always welcome and in many cases those tips were expected. But if an escort was at the home all night she had her fee up front. No waiting until the next day. Of course there were times when the clients made the girl wait for her money. But those instances were far and few between. The above figures may have varied a little from time to time because the client may have been very difficult or just plain rude. Sometimes we would charge more for a difficult client.

Introduction Services

- The many dating services that introduce people to other people charge fees in excess of $1,000 usually to join.
- Some religious introduction services are free but for the most part they all charge some fee.
- Usually this is to cover costs associated with maintaining the web site.
- To join a person has to pay to go online just to meet the person or send them an email to meet online or over the phone.
- The services want to know whom are the clients wanting to meet people, so there is an online form to fill out. (This does not dissuade the psychopaths from calling and joining. The nuts just have to give false information and many people have died because of the online antics of some less than formal or caring service providers.)

Chapter Twenty-Three
Stories

There were many things to laugh about in those days and many an instance where the escort came to find him or her in a funny situation. Herein I will document a few of those.

If it were a slow night a couple of girls may be sitting around with me, talking. This was something we did just about every night just waiting for the phone to ring and some client wishing to see a person. To keep the girls from falling asleep we would talk. The "we" could be my boyfriend, Bill, or after he was out of the picture the "we" may be a current admirer, or just a person that liked to hang out with us. It was an entire picture of people that got along.

Even former escorts would come by and maybe they just wanted to visit for awhile. Sometimes these escorts wanted to return to work and just came by to see how the phones were going. Another added benefit to the escorts being at my place was that they could use the bathroom and primp. Those escorts not telling their roommates at home or boyfriends or husbands were able to bring their clothes over to my house and get ready.

Many of the escorts did not want to be home and the possibility of their drifting off to sleep was also pretty high. The result was that I allowed them to come over and be dispatched from my place.

My boys were usually in bed, so the stories would fly and many of our conversations should have been recorded. The stories about clients or just driving to clients locations were enormously funny.

I would say this is also how I learned so much about their lives and expectations along with hopes and dreams. As word got around with my male friends sometimes they would stop by to join in the talking. Musicians may bring an instrument or two and play. These were not parties" just get- to-getters.

Then the phone would ring and off a person went into the night. During the day people may gather and these gab fests may last for days with people coming and going.

After all, I was running a 24 hour business and the nonstop bustle was how I made my living.

Japan

There comes a time when the excitement of sending people to clients has become dull. Not because the clients are dull but the thought of a little traveling and making money sounds a lot better. One day there was a person that I met and he told me about a person in Japan that already had an escort service over there and now wanted a new connection for women to be sent over as escorts. I was approached and thought it was an interesting proposition.

As interesting as the deal sounded it was going to take an enormous amount of sweet talking to entice woman to go over there. No one wanted to be the first person sent. Safety was uppermost in my mind.

Even though I was guaranteed that the woman or women going over would be okay; it is on foreign soil and a little bit too complicated if there were problems. I was assured that the person going would be taken care of and would make at least $10,000 a month. That was like saying the girl had won the lottery. She may have to go to hotels but primarily she would be in one location.

They were telling me that her safety was assured. The first girl was the bravest person to go over. She was given all sorts of instructions on what to do if there was something wrong with the situation. Greed played a factor for every woman going over there. The trip was paid for and that was the biggest enticement. The arrangements were made and the round trip tickets came by courier.

The woman was excited to be going and I was having adrenaline rushes as if I was falling out of an airplane with a parachute caught up and I needed to use the emergency chute and switch.

Many times I said, "What was I thinking", to myself and finally she arrived in Tokyo. She was met at the airport and everything worked out well. She made at least the $10,000.00 and came back with some great stories.

Next I was to send at least one woman a month and I would receive my fee from the person over there and from the woman. It was a great second income for everyone involved. I eventually went over with one of my escorts to see for myself what it was all about.

The entire time I was concerned.

We were picked up by this small Japanese man that was the owner of the escort service over there. He was thin and did not have any special features that were remarkable. He drove us to a very nice hotel in downtown Tokyo. I believe it was a 5 star hotel. The hotel rooms were paid for by him and we decided to see some clients. I saw someone that was in government over there and he did not speak English. His hotel was very nice and I could tell that he had a lot of money.

The escort that went with me had some good experiences too.

Then on my third day in Japan, the escort owner phoned me that a man was coming to my room. This surprised me. We would go out from there.

When the man arrived he was a lot older than me and gave me a few World War II stories and how he took care of the GI's that had come to Japan after we dropped the two atomic bombs and the war ended. Even though his language skills were rough I knew he hated Americans. That is something which a person does not have to say, but his mannerisms were all to pretend he liked Americans and American women.

I tried to be nice to him and offered him something to drink. After he drank a few sips he became very obnoxious and wanted to have sex. Well, that was not going to happen with me. Because of his slight built I began sizing him up for a few Karate chops. After saying no to him a few times he then threatens me. He tells me that he will tell the hotel and call the police and say what we are doing. I asked him, "What are we were doing?"

He told me and I said, "fine, go ahead and phone them, by the time I get through screaming that you have tried to rape me, it will be you going off to prison". He calmed down a little as I threw him out of my room. The owner of the service called me and told me he was upset. I explained to him everything that had happened and I did not want to have any trouble. He did not want a problem either. I am not sure what he did to calm him down, but he did it. No money was exchanged to me directly. Everything was taken care of at his end, so any trouble was ridiculous. I don't care what country you are in … the elements of any crime have to be there. If it is sex for money … well, there has to be some money and sex involved. Nothing like that was going on.

The escort I had brought with me was going to stay for the complete month and ultimately ended up going back a month or so more. She really liked Japan and took language courses. She met a man there who took her to Europe and also paid her living expenses in California for awhile, that is until his wife pulled the plug on his little love affair in America. He was sending my friend over $1,200 a month. She really benefitted from the traveling to Japan and I was able to see Japan and felt the deal was a safe one for more women to go there to work.

The owner, in Japan, eventually, came to see me in America and brought a lovely Jade gift for me. He and I drifted apart because I was not running the business at full-steam anymore and there were not enough women available to leave for a month. He had women coming from all parts of the world to work with him in Japan. Very interesting as to how the entire operation was set up and I know that my women were given extra special treatment.

The women coming from other areas that were Asian or European were not paid as much. I liked this man in Japan and wished I had met him when I first began the business. When I was introduced to him ... I was at the tail end of my business.

Hong Kong

After or before the last adventure in Japan came about there was another person I met, that turned out to be a CIA operative, who told me about someone, a billionaire, in Hong Kong that wanted women to come over and work for his girlfriend. The billionaire son had met this girl when she was working in Hawaii and then brought her home to Hong Kong. He was young and so was she, but his parents were not very accepting of her, because she was a Caucasian and uneducated, and I have to say without a lot of special training on how to be part of the higher society of Hong Kong. With good reason, his parents wanted him to marry a woman from their social circles and have children that were not mixed. The father was a shipping magnate and in all the proper social categories.

Plus, the girl was thought of as just a prostitute and the family rejected her for that reason too. He was going to set her up with her own bar and women to be there for the clients, which is something that is part of the social fabric in bars catering to predominantly foreign clients and many coming from the USA to "party" in Hong Kong.

This whole deal smelled like government from the very beginning to me. I felt that I was being setup and handcuffs would be at the international area within the airport if I sent or went over there to work.

But I was still beyond help in wanting to have a little excitement and travel. For years I was locked up in the house answering phones and I was past bored. My dilemma was that I had to convince women, at least five that it was safe to go over to Hong Kong and work without being sold into slavery.

That was going to be a hard sell if I did not know what to expect over there. Not one younger girl I had working for me that was closer to 21 years of age would go to Hong Kong.

They had heard all the stories of being sold and each one I asked was just not going to do it. I could not convince anyone that it was safe without me having been there to see the people at the other end. So I had to go to the B team. I asked four women that were older if they wanted to go and all the tickets would be paid for and they could make some money over there. We would be at a home being built for this reason and it was a million dollar home.

Everyone would have their own bedroom and there would be drivers to carry them from client to client. To say this was a difficult sell would be minimizing the truth; the sell was almost impossible. The people in Hong Kong wanted young and beautiful. I had old and marginal for America, let alone for Hong Kong. I had never traveled there before and did not have any idea what to expect.

Finally, the women decided to go there, because there would be five of us going and the tickets were paid for ... if anything was wrong, then just do a turnaround and back to the airport. I was going to make sure the deal was sound and that the women would be okay. In reality I was just as concerned as they were. I had no idea what to expect and I was putting a lot of faith in a man that use to be a priest and was now working as a government person.

The day arrived and we had now received the tickets and everyone had their passports and off to Hong Kong. The plane ride was fine and we had some fun on it. When we arrived in Hong Kong it was obvious that the girl and her boyfriend were not happy with the women I had brought with me. I was considered "okay" (pretty and marginal for their standards, I was not in my teens and that is what they really wanted) but still older than what they wanted.

They (the couple) came in a very expensive sports car and we were driven in a limousine to the home in Kowloon. This is an area out of the downtown metropolis of Hong Kong. It looked very much like Marin County, California but with fewer lights and lots of hillside pit fires at night. Quiet and beautiful and the home had just been built and there was still some more to do to it.

The home cost a million dollars and I was not impressed with it but I suppose the costs there were different and the location may have had something to do with the high price. It was within walking distance to a major motion picture studio. Many films are made on the Chinese mainland and other locations worldwide. It was a nice home but the price surprised me. Another man came over that was the CIA contact for the other man in San Francisco.

I do not know what these men had up their sleeves but I do know it was something. He told me that the women, I brought, would not be working there because they just were not up to the standards that the very rich men over there were use too. Young, dumb, and beautiful, almost pubescent would have sufficed for them.

I explained to him that it was difficult to talk anyone into going over there. He understood but told me that he would like me to find women to come there and I could also work the women over there, etc. I was not up to that scenario because it would mean me living in Hong Kong and working for some people that could make me disappears and that would mean my family and friends and anyone close to me and all records that ever existed. So, I had my reservations about the entire fiasco and was looking forward to leaving after doing some tourist shopping and then went for a massage in Hong Kong.

My brain was killing me, along with my back. He (a steadfast drunk) and the couple took us by the bar she was remodeling to be her spot and then we went to a few bars or night spots in Hong Kong.

They were hell-bent on me knowing that the competition was stiff in Hong Kong and I had not brought competitors with me. They were right and I was shocked to see how well dressed the women were and how many women, of all ages, were behind closed doors and would be brought to the table to entertain or be privately with the various men with us.

These girls over there were wearing designer evening gowns. I mean clothes that few women in America wear unless it is to some gala event. We were very poorly dressed in comparison and the entire evening woke my eyes up to what international fun houses were like for the men in Hong Kong.

The mamma, whatever you call her, she was very attentive to any man she saw and kept bringing a woman out for each man until the men were happy with one. She was relentless with her pursuit to please the potential clients. I noticed behind the door she was going to and bringing women out from; there must have been fifty women behind this swinging door. The door led into a brightly lit room and women could be seen just waiting in all their fine clothing.

Where we went was very upscale and there was usually entertainment such as a band or singer/s. The women with me wanted to stay and work and I had to break the news to them that they were not young enough and the couple was interested in a different type of woman. They wanted as young as possible and I let them know that there was some disappointment going on. I would not be thinking of sending anyone that was not at least 21 years of age because it was out of the country. I would not think of an 18 year old to be sent there. She would just be way too young and I am sure these people wanted as young as possible. That whole … you have to be young thing … was not going to happen from my end and all in all it was a nice few days and we came back on the airplane a little more knowledgeable and some souvenirs richer.

My women were happy they got to go on a trip to Hong Kong and all of them were deeply disappointed they were not well-received. This was after they saw for themselves that it was a "for real deal".

Both sides of the Pacific Ocean were unhappy with this event, or I should say, un-event. It was good that I went there to see for myself but in reality these people, or the man with the girl, were so very wealthy that this little fun escapade they wanted to do … did not make sense, unless with the CIA involvement that there was some other agenda in motion. No matter what, I was glad that I would not be sending people over there. It just smelled of some international incident that I did not want to be a central figure in for my government or their government. This fiasco would be called what it was, a lesson in life for me and those around me at that time.

Chapter Twenty-Four
More Stories

Story #1
Well, this particular night a call came in from a regular client. He had used the service many times before and we all knew him well. He had a wife at the time and maybe one child. He phones in and wanted to see someone new.

It was not unusual for a client to say that a new person was wanted. It was what I heard daily from most regular clients. My thoughts on this were the better the variety, the better the money. I would allow the new escorts to sit with me at night, so I could answer their questions and dispel fears, etc. It was a great way for all of us to get to know each other. Then after a while the escort had no problem sitting at home or at a friend's house for calls. The escort was always welcome over my home to wait.

The girl I was sending him had never been on a call before and I gave her the phone. She made arrangements to go to his home and the time was not set as to how long she would be there. They hung up and I begin to give her directions. The whole time, also, explaining what type person he is and if she does not like him to say so with the little message we used to get escorts out of a difficult situation. No problem on her part, she was anxious for the opportunity to see someone and make a little money for the night. I continued to explain to her that this client, if he liked you, may keep the clock running for a few hours and that way she could make two to three hundred dollars. She was ecstatic at the possibility of making more money than she had ever made in a day. She liked the idea that he was a lead singer in a band. I walked her to my front door and she is gone; knowing full-well that she has to phone me as soon as she gets there. This is all part of her new beginning as an escort. I attend to my business at home and settle down to talk with the remaining escorts.

We are giggling about some story when the phone rings and it is her and she calls in to say she will be staying. I give a thumb up to the other girls and we all smile. Most girls when they phoned in had already gotten their money. She had not received the fee up front, but did not tell me that fact.

Well, a little time goes by and I receive another phone call and it is the girl. She is at a payphone. This was before cell phones. She is half laughing and half crying. I asked her what was wrong. The story was that they had taken their clothes off in the living room and were just sitting around not doing anything else, when the front door knob was being turned and a key was in the door to open it. He almost turned white, he was a black man, she grabbed her clothes and was headed for the back door and all she could hear was his Caucasian wife yelling at him that he had a prostitute in her home and the wife just went on and on screaming.

Not wanting the wife to begin yelling at her. She was out that back door and in record time as she flew over a fence and received a hurt leg when she went to hurdle the fence. She was standing at the phone booth still putting her shoes on. The entire scene was very funny. The girl came back to my home and filled us in on any details she had left out. One major detail was that she did not receive her money. The client phoned the next day and I informed him that he owed her money. He was okay with that and wanted to see her again. He had not learned his lesson.

I, in turn, phoned the girl and let her know she would be paid and that he wanted to see her again. She said that was okay but it had to be a motel. I agreed. They met at a hotel and he paid for the last time he saw her for only a few minutes, plus the current time.

Story #2

The next incident is worth telling. This work order was supposed to be a bachelor party in San Francisco. I phoned one of my escorts that were willing to dance with just a negligee on and the date was set.

The party goers' representative had agreed to the price.

The escort I was sending was in her thirties and had dark hair and was very busty. She had long legs and generally was built very well. She was about 5'8" tall and had an attitude. She had been born in Germany and was a strong-willed German. I will not be featuring her as one of my escorts because she was a great escort and I just do not want to add her or lump her with all the others. It is my choice to just give this story about her, instead of some complete description with the other escorts.

The day comes for the party and I believe it is a Saturday night or at least a weekend night. She phones in at the party and tells me that everything is okay. She has taken her clothes off down to her "teddy" and is ready to begin. But then the clients want more. She said that they want her to take off all her clothes and perform a sex act on one or more of them. She was not going to do that and was leaving.

The exact details I don't remember but that is about how it went. Anyway, one of the guys won't give her the belt that went with her jumpsuit. She is furious and stomps out into the street with just her negligee on and goes for her car with lots of police cars circling her. She is really pissed.

Well, you see it was not a bachelor party. It was a party for some new recruits for the police department. The following Monday I phone the Police Chief, and tell his office what had gone on and that the woman wants her belt or the money for it. The next thing I receive is a call from one of the guys and he asks how he can return the belt and I tell him to send it to the P.O. Box or the money for it. He also, most humbly, asks that I don't call the Chief, again. The belt or the money was sent back and she was happy.

Gosh, are police men too?

Yep.

Story #3

This story is funny and I debated upon putting it with the client's book but because the person really never was a client, I decided it should go here. One night a call came in just like most calls. The girl sitting in front of me was a short blonde and in her mid forties. She did not look her age. She had a very nice shape and worked out religiously every day for over an hour. Many sit ups and crunches. She was in shape. This woman had been a dealer at some casino in Lake Tahoe. The person phoning wanted a blonde. I looked at her and she gave me a smile that she was able to do it. She had also been on a call or two with another escort that worked for me and they were about the same ages or the other woman was younger.

The call she would be going to is in Novato, California and he just wants someone for an hour. After making all the arrangements and getting directions, she gets in her car and will phone me when she arrives. I have about every distance timed. It would take her not long to reach this persons' home. Well, no phone call. I am waiting and waiting. What has happened to her? I was very worried and thinking all sorts of thoughts that were not good. She came back to tell me, but she could have phoned from a payphone. I am just not sure. But I think she did both and then came back to give me the details.

This other woman that she knew and had been on a call with before had two cars. She had begun to walk up the driveway when she realized that she knew the car. Yes, it was the son of the other woman whose son now was phoning for an escort. He was in high school and phoning for an escort.

We laughed for hours about it.

When I saw his mother to tell her what had happened, she was not laughing. As we both stood there telling her, I loved the expression on her face. Her first comment was funny.

"Where did he get the money for it?" She was furious.

What ever happened was between her and her son. But I do not believe she told him that she knew what he wanted to do when mom was not home. In telling the story, it loses a little of the charm and falls short of being there and that moment of truth for mom and the escort service. There were a lot of, "no, you've got to be kidding" and "are you sure?" conversations that evening before we ever notified his mom when she came to my home for another call and the expression on her face made a rather otherwise boring night, a lot of fun.

Story #4

This next story is about the same blonde that use to be a card dealer in Lake Tahoe for one of the casinos. We were just talking at my home on Graceland Avenue in San Rafael when she asked me about a client. I had known this person from way back when I had first began as a masseuse at the Alter Ego in Terra Linda, California. This client was a person that went all over the country looking for antiques. His favorite "haunt" for antiques was the mid-west and up the eastern seaboard. He would be gone for weeks and then bring back a huge load of merchandise to sell at his shop in Marin County, California.

Well, on this particular night she keeps asking me if I ever ran into a blank, blank, blank? I look at her and for the first time realizes that she and I are very similar in outer appearance. She is a blonde and short and so am I. She likes nice clothes and so do I. She even wears her hair in a style I once wore my hair in. I am younger than her. I ask her more about the man. She describes his body and age, etc. Then I look at her and tell her he was once a regular client of mine when I worked at the massage studio. She stares at me and restrains herself from flying into a rage. She actually does this far better than I would have at the moment. We also compare notes as to the timetable that I was working at that location. It all matched up. I frantically try to remember some of the conversations he gave me at the time. My memory goes blank. She looks at me and confesses that he was her husband.

I die.

The first thought out of my mouth is, "You have got to be joking." She is not joking. He was her husband and they still see each other every now and then. To top it off he is still paying her alimony. We have an uncomfortable silence for awhile and I am really not sure how to address this or what she is going to say to me. The ice is broken by her telling me that she did not mind that I saw him, in fact she was glad it was me.

Glad? Yeah.

That was a great comeback for a woman that had a cheating husband. I told her that she should let him know that she is doing escort work and working with me. That would carve a dandy hole in his back. About then we both sat back laughing and thinking of more ways to make his feeble life miserable. I also reflected on the entire situation and came back with the statement,

"I should have charged him more."

Story #5

One time in the beginning of running my outcall massage business, Dee and I were in San Francisco. It was at night and I had driven there to hang out and play pool at a local bar on Market Street, where I could wait for calls.

The bar was only a small part of this pool hall, the pool hall itself had been at its location since way before I was ever born. It must have been there in the 1920s and was a hangout for people that considered their pool play to be what pool sharks are made of and they would hang out looking for people to hustle.

I enjoyed there were at least fifteen tables and the place was full of lights to see the bums coming up to you. The hanging wires above every table would tell you if you were winning or losing as the winner pushed a wooden bobble to the next side for every win. The place had seen better days and needed a new paint job with new flooring … the walls had a line of chairs along at least two walls where people could watch the action, if there was any either by night or day. A bum or two may be sleeping in the chairs. The price of beer and to play pool was the most reasonable in the city. In the old days there must have been tournaments there. I envisioned the old timers to have played there and went onto their respective fame and fortune for being the best in their game. You would walk up these narrow steps to get to the place and the entire time Dee is giving me a headache asking me if the place were safe. She is astounded that I would even go there.

We enter and I march over to the guy behind the long glass case to have him give me a rack of balls so I am able to play. He asks me what table I like and I show him the table. No problem. It was free, meaning ready to use, and we begin to play pool. My skill was pretty good and I would run hot and cold winning or running the balls. Some days were better than other days. Dee and I had our pagers on for a call.

There was a phone booth there to use and call a client, if we were paged. Sometime after being in this place for an hour we decide it is time to leave. I had received a page and there was a call for a massage close by. We both had a couple of beers and felt a good. I get to the client's apartment and give him a half hour massage and he gives me another beer.

Now it is time to leave and I have my massage money and tip in my hand and put it in a small coin purse. When I get into the car I put the coin purse under my seat so the money is safe. But the alcohol is setting in with me. I really don't need much alcohol to be tipsy. We are driving down Market Street and decided to cut over to another street and some guy flags us down.

We think he is cute and he motions us to pull into this alley where he wanted to ask us something. I dumbly pull over. The alcohol has hit my brain and I am not thinking well. He comes up to my side of the car and begins talking about some place to party or whatever. Dee is all ears and then with a flash of his hands he reaches into the car and grabs my purse.

I scream at him and he moves quickly into a waiting car and then the chase is on. Without thinking I flag a paddy wagon that seems to pop up from nowhere and on the same side of the street as our car. Frantically, I tell them that my purse was stolen and we are chasing the car.

(Okay, I am really stupid here and I know it. I am racing up and down San Francisco hills barely touching the pavement.)

My Thunderbird is moving fast and I am closing in on the car. We are bouncing all over the place and the car is flying into the air and down with the paddy wagon trying to keep up. You have to understand here that Dee and I are dressed very well and look very nice. Our nails are done and the clothes we are wearing just look like we are going to some nightclub. The car is headed for Van Ness when a patrol car flashes us with his red lights.

I pull over and stop. The driver of the police car is furious with me and yells at me to put my hands up and get out of the car. I do and the entire time I am telling him that we will lose the guys that stole my purse. He does not care and just about then the paddy wagon comes up with the guys inside laughing. The patrol guys are not amused. I am sizing up the patrol car as my next location sitting situation with handcuffs and asking Dee to make sure she bails me out.

The paddy wagon guys save my ass. They tell the patrol car men that I was chasing the bad guys. All is not well but it is not bad. The patrol car puts us both in it and we proceed to look for my purse and the guys that stole it. I mean the cops in the patrol car are men. We looked too good to pass up the chance to be with us for awhile. We are now going up and down hills in a patrol car and I think there is nothing wrong with what I had done or what we are now doing.

Then the report comes over the patrol car's phone that my purse was found. The guys who stole it threw it out on Market Street and I was thrilled. They were not caught but Dee and I had one hell of a ride. It was just like in the movies and I was driving just like Steve McQueen in the movie *Bullet*. What a rush I think to myself.

The patrol car guys brought me to my purse and then back to my car and I did not even get a ticket. All in all it was a fun night. Dee and I laughed all the way home. My more mature self now … believes I was an idiot to go chasing after thieves and driving like my car was on steroids up and down the hills of S.F. without caring if I hit another car. Fun then … now dumb.

Story #6

Once upon a time one of the male escorts went to see a woman at her home. To his amazement there was another woman there.

Well, many people say that men cannot be raped or made to do something that entails an erecting member of their body to perform. May I happily say that is not true; and the man was not paid up front and he was very upset that he was not going to receive his fee. The two women were attractive and began throwing their bodies all over him.

Was this fun for him?

Well to hear him tell the story he was upset from the moment he got there. He did receive his fee after he had satisfied both women. He told the story to me and a couple of other people and we laughed at him. The part I left out was that they wanted him to entertain them in one of their cars. He went out to the car and they had a wild time. He was trying to say that he had been raped. I did not believe him then or later when he went back to see the same two women.

Why they wanted to have an encounter with a strange man in a car just eludes me. But the laughs we had from this episode were many.

Story #7

Another female escort was sitting with us one night when the telephone rang. I answered it and took the message and the type escort the client wanted. As I was repeating the address the female escort listening asked me to repeat the address. She looked at me and asked me if I was sending someone there? Of course I would be sending someone. She said that she preferred I phone him back and tell him that no one is available and I asked her, "why" I should do such a thing. It was simple, he was her father. I did not send the man any escort that night and we did laugh a little about this man phoning. The girl was shocked her father could phone for an escort but she was not equally shocked that she was an escort. Hum. This was the double-standard with a new twist.

Story #8

When my first escort returned from a month in Japan she was chock-full of stories. Many of the people she had met were in politics and some were very wealthy business men. We were all intrigued to hear about the culture that most Americans do not hear about. Many of the women, living in Japan, still wore the traditional dress.

This was something I had observed, also.

Nowadays that dress is no doubt only for special occasions. But what had us laughing the most were her stories about the prophylactics. It was the size. She said that the first time she had to buy a 'rubber' (condom) it was a lot smaller than the brands she was use to purchasing in the United States. We asked her if it were really necessary and she said if not the 'rubber' (Prophylactic-condom) would fall off. Did we laugh? Of course we had a few laughs over the visual representation of a prophylactic in Japan. We were not laughing at the people of Japan, just the fact that there was such a distinct difference in Japanese men and American men.

In the future, sending people to the orient, I told my escorts not to purchase any prophylactics that were made in America. They were told to purchase them only in Japan. Information not inside any tourist guide.

Story #9

Another time I sent a female escort to a man in Sonoma County. She was not happy with the man and had left. She came directly over to my house and I wanted to know what the problem was and if I should send someone else to him. She sat me down and began to tell me about the call. I excused myself to get her something to drink in the form of a soda. I got myself a diet coke. I thought that it was going to be a long session and I may have to help her out with whatever she had encountered that night.

There were at least two other escorts in the room and I felt that whatever had happened needed to be shared by all because the guy had phoned back and wanted another escort. I did not want to send him anyone, unless I understood what the problem was and if it were too dangerous to send someone else. I immediately made myself comfortable on the couch and she was sitting in one of my chairs. Then she began. "He was so nice looking. I really liked his looks."

"That's nice, but what was wrong with him?" She was now laughing.

"He, um, he."

Her laughter got louder.

"He took me into his bedroom and sat me down on the bed."

"Yes."

"Well, that is when he left the room and came back with this dog that was huge. He must have been as big as a small pony."

"Okay. Did he want him to watch?" She said laughing,

"No, he wanted me to have sex with his dog."

I was shocked and said to her,

"What did you do?"

She said that she told the guy, "He wasn't my type."

Her......she meant the dog. We both began to laugh and the other two escorts were also laughing. Her type, I just kept saying those words over and over. It was so very funny. She had declined to be with the dog and she explained that the dog actually looked sad.

The more she spoke the more we rolled over and over again laughing. The guy had a camera and everything. No other girl wanted to take the call and I let him know that we did not see dogs.

Gosh that is still funny.

Chapter Twenty-Five
Where They Came From

In the beginning of my time operating the escort service ... many of the women coming to work were recently divorced or separated from a bad relationship. Most needed money. But there were a few women that had other jobs and just wanted to supplement their income.

AAA

Terry was a woman with bleached blonde hair and beautiful blue eyes surrounded by heavy makeup. She had tattoos covering a great deal of her body and most of these tattoos were in color. Because this was not an accepted way to decorate a woman's body, her look was very cheap.

The tattoos were actually very intricate and she must have had a strong love for decorating her body. This was in the late 1970s and tattoos were not as common as they have grown to be in the 21st Century. She stood about 5'8" tall and her figure was good but I would not say great. The tattoos could not hide her belly. Not a big belly, but more than she should have for the work she was doing.

Terry was dancing at one of the strip clubs in San Francisco and decided she wanted to make more money and had heard about me and decided to work for *Professional Escorts.* There were plenty of grapevines about my service. One of the grapevines, where many of the women came from, after they heard I had an escort service, where they did not have to sleep with the owner to have a job. Good news always travels fast in the escort world.

I liked her because she was a thinker.

Her mind was always analyzing and if she had gone back to school her future would have been full. She was a latent academic searching for a reason why she was on the planet. This woman could think and her thoughts were all well thought out. She would bring beautiful poems to me that she felt were songs. They had a great deal of depth to them and I have kept a couple of them all these years. We instantly liked each other and she was someone that I would have trusted my life with and that of my children.

Her heart was in the right place.

If she had not been dancing ... I believe that she could have made a lot more money working as an escort but the dancing was a love of hers. I never saw her dance but I am sure she was coordinated enough to make the patrons of those clubs come back for more.

We had some disagreement over something that is not remembered by me and I always worried about her. I was concerned that she might get hurt because she was too trusting. She loved the musicians that would come over my house and possibly the writing she did was to get noticed. With all her tattoos it was not a stretch to think she liked being noticed. She was a flower and at the clubs I envisioned her among a lot of weeds.

In sending her to clients the response I always received was that she had tattoos and seemed a little hard. I, on the other hand, did not see that side of her. The gentleness and disposition was strong with her and she seemed to pick her friends ... rather than people pick her.

The reason I have brought her up is because she existed and gave of herself to all she met. Very few people are as spiritually beautiful as she was and the fact she liked other women or may have done drugs is secondary to the side of her that was kind, caring, and giving.

When I landed in the hospital one time for allergies ... she and another escort snuck up the back stairs of the hospital to see me. She and the other girl brought me money (their fees to me) and some food to eat. We took some pictures of our little party and it made me happy to know that these two women worked for me. The other woman was working her way through college and is now a pharmacist. I am happy for her. Each woman made my life a better place in those days.

BBB

Some people in reading this portrayal of escorts have indicated that there is not enough excitement. There was excitement and everyday held adventure but many of those adventures are really no one's business.

The escorts gave me a great deal of adventure through their eyes as to how the world was away from the phones I was answering. Some had been raped long before they ever came to me and wanted to be escorts.

Being an escort worked out all the aggression inside of them from the rape/s. In telling stories, to me, about being raped the women were encountering support from other victims. Receiving payment for being with a man helped empower every woman who worked. Whether the prior rape victim had sex with the clients or

COMPILATION OF ESCORTS AND CLIENTS   True Crime

not; just receiving something of value from a man made up for the ravaging of each one of their bodies by sick men.

Somehow the taking from a man helped. The power was there which had been absent from the girl's reach when a rape had happened years before ever working as an escort. Many had been molested as children. A huge amount of them were in conflict with their families and were estranged from relatives and husbands.

The male escorts were not as damaged but they all had a history that brought them to my door. After returning to higher education, myself, I have since realized that if I had put in for a grant to help the people coming to me, that I might have received one. A grant to study the underlying causes for women and men to want to sell their time and their bodies.

When I left my business there were still hordes of women and men that needed direction. Miss BBB was one of them and this escort almost died just because she was too close to me at the time.

One day I received a call from BBB. I am not sure what month it was now but I spoke to BBB and she seemed a little disoriented while trying to maintain a conversation with me on the phone. I wished her well and left it at that; in the past I knew she had occasion to do a lot of drugs, but I never saw her in a state of "high". She had been one of the women I sent to Japan and she loved it there and had a great time. Let me say it could have been a Friday when I spoke to her and then by Saturday she phoned me back and was upset. She did not speak to me for long but told me someone had burned her clothes on her bed. I thought it was strange and she said that she was now at some hotel. I told her to call me back if she needed anything.

That call never came.

Someone else phoned me and told me to look at the newspaper and another person from the hospital called me. The first person told me that she had threatened some drug dealers and used my name; no doubt believing that would hold more weight because the service was used by many of them.

The threat was taken seriously and she was drugged and put in a car and down she went off a cliff and she just about died. I have no idea who the people were but I assume they believed she would tell of their activities. She did live and doesn't remember very much about the entire event.

This was told because it shows how risky telling about client's activities was at the time and still is. Clients engaged in illegal activities want their privacy and the last thing they need is a woman yelling at them that she will tell the cops what he is up too. And it should be told that she never worked as an escort again.

This woman has since died.

And now I can reveal how she got even with some of them.

While she was in the hospital I brought someone over to her that worked for a government agency and she gave up many of the people she knew who were dealing drugs. I was not in the room but I hoped that her life and healing mind could be helped by having some retribution on the people who tried to kill her. She did and told me it felt good, very good.

CONCLUSION

Professional Escorts was an amusing, amazing, and enjoyable business.

The escorts, I have put on paper, were representative of many people who worked for and with me over the years. The names may have changed, but the character of the people and their habits were not so varied.

Not as varied as many people would like to believe.

It seems that there are similar factors which have been taken into account as I have tried to mirror the escorts well. All of these people just wanted to make some money for their habits, living expenses, children, boyfriends, husbands, and relatives. They were, basically, good people, who had found their way to me and were in need.

This escort service provided a service to both clients and escorts. I tried never to judge and it is my wish you do not judge them. These were some wonderful people who were part of *Professional Escorts* of Marin County, California.

This was a time that was matchless.

##